Natural Liberation

Natural Liberation

Padmasambhava's Teachings on the Six Bardos

Padmasambhava

Commentary by

Gyatrul Rinpoche

Translated by

B. Alan Wallace

WISDOM PUBLICATIONS • BOSTON

WISDOM PUBLICATIONS
199 ELM STREET
SOMERVILLE, MASSACHUSETTS 02144-3195 USA

Library of Congress Cataloging-in-Publication Data

Karma-gliṅ-pa, 14th cent.
   [Zab chos zhi khro dgoṅs pa raṅ grol las rdzogs rim bar do drug gi khrid
yig. English]
   Natural liberation: Padmasambhava's teachings on the six bardos /
Padmasambhava ; commentary by Gyatrul Rinpoche : translated by B. Alan
Wallace. Karma-gliṅ-pa, 14th cent.
      p.   cm.
   Discovered by Karma Lingpa.
   Includes bibliographical references and index.
   ISBN 0-86171-131-9 (alk. paper)
      1. Spiritual life—Buddhism.   2. Padma Sambhava, ca. 717–ca. 762.
3. Buddhism—China—Tibet.   I. Gyatrul, Rinpoche.   II. Wallace, B. Alan.
III. Padma Sambhava, ca. 717–ca. 762.
BQ7800.K37513   1997
294.3'444—dc21   97–2608

ISBN 0-86171-131-9

02   01   00   99
 6   5   4   3

Cover Art: Padma Sambhava, 14c., thangka, gouache on cotton.
Cover Photo: courtesy of John Bigelow Taylor, NYC.

Book Design: L·J·Sawlit

Wisdom Publications' books are printed on acid-free paper and meet the guidelines for the
permanence and durability of the Committee on Production Guidelines for
Book Longevity of the Council on Library Resources.

Printed in the United States of America.

Contents

PART THREE:
SUPPLEMENTAL PRAYERS

Publisher's Acknowledgment

THE PUBLISHER GRATEFULLY ACKNOWLEDGES the generous help of the Hershey Family Foundation in sponsoring the printing of this book.

Translator's Preface

THIS BOOK CONTAINS A TRANSLATION and commentary on the great Indian Buddhist tantric master Padmasambhava's text, entitled *The Profound Dharma of the Natural Liberation through Contemplating the Peaceful and Wrathful: Stage of Completion Instructions on the Six Bardos.*[1] Presumably composed some time in the late eighth century, the text was dictated by Padmasambhava to his Tibetan consort, Yeshe Tsogyal. Tibetan tradition views Padmasambhava as an emanation of Amitābha, the Buddha of Infinite Light, and refers to him as Guru Rinpoche, or Precious Spiritual Mentor. His name, Padmasambhava, means "born from a lotus," indicating his miraculous birth from a lotus in the midst of a lake in the region of Oḍḍiyāna. Adopted by the king of Oḍḍiyāna, Padmasambhava dedicated his life to the study and practice of esoteric, or Vajrayāna, Buddhism.

In the eighth century, the Tibetan king Trisong Detsen invited Padmasambhava to Tibet to assist the Indian abbot Śāntarakṣita in building the first enduring monastery in that land. In Tibet, Padmasambhava devoted himself to subduing the many malevolent forces that were obstructing the study and practice of Buddhism there, and he gave numerous teachings to his disciples, among whom twenty-five became renowned, accomplished adepts in their own right. When his work in Tibet was completed, tradition says, Padmasambhava departed to the west in a body of pure light to the buddha-field known as the Glorious Copper-colored Mountain, where he resides even to this day.[2]

Padmasambhava concealed many of his teachings in the manner of "spiritual time-capsules" known as "treasures" (*gter ma*; pronounced *terma*) to be gradually revealed over the centuries when human civilization was ready to receive them. The delayed revelation of these teachings parallels the manner in which the Mahāyāna doctrine came to be eventually revealed to the general public several centuries after the passing of the historical Buddha, and the way in which many Buddhist tantras came to be revealed for the first time in India in the centuries following that. Some of Padmasambhava's hidden teachings—known as earth treasures (*sa gter*)—were written down and concealed underground, in caves, or even inside large boulders. Other teachings—known as mind treasures (*dgongs gter*)—were mystically secreted in the mind-streams of his own disciples, awaiting their conscious discovery in the disciples' subsequent lifetimes. During the centuries following his departure to the Glorious Copper-colored Mountain, numerous "treasure revealers" (*gter ston*; pronounced *tertön*), who have generally been regarded as emanations either of Padmasambhava or of his chief disciples, have discovered great numbers of these treasures and have subsequently propagated these teachings.[3]

The concluding words "Samaya. Sealed, sealed, sealed" at the end of sections of this text are unique to hidden treasure texts, or terma. The word *samaya* in this context indicates that those who handle this text should remember their samayas, or tantric pledges. The words "sealed, sealed, sealed" are a warning that if someone other than the treasure revealer should accidently come across these texts while they are still concealed, they should leave the texts alone. These words also warn the treasure revealer who was intended to discover the texts that he or she should make them known only at the appropriate time. Finally, those who read these texts are warned with these words not to show the texts to those who have no faith or to those whose samayas have degenerated.

One of the most renowned treasure revealers in Tibet was Karma Lingpa, who lived in the fourteenth century and is regarded as an emanation of Padmasambhava himself. It was he who discovered the present treatise—a classic example of an earth treasure—in a cave on Gampo Dar Mountain in central Tibet. Dealing with the six transitional processes, or *bardos*, this text quickly became an important treatise of the Nyingma order of

Tibetan Buddhism; as such, it has been widely taught and practiced by Tibetans ever since, but only by those fully initiated into this cycle of Vajrayāna Buddhist teachings. This treatise may also be considered as a companion volume to the well-known *Tibetan Book of the Dead*,[4] for both are included within the same cycle of treasures discovered by Karma Lingpa. *The Tibetan Book of the Dead* chiefly concerns the dying process and the subsequent intermediate state, or bardo,[5] prior to one's next rebirth, and in Tibet it was commonly recited during and after an individual's death to aid that person in making the transition to the next life. The present work is much more extensive in its scope, providing practical meditation instructions pertaining to all six transitional processes, or bardos, namely those of living, dreaming, meditating, dying, the intermediate state following death, and rebirth.

This treasure text was made available to a broader public in the West when, during the early months of 1995, the Venerable Gyatrul Rinpoche, a senior lama of the Payul lineage of the Nyingma order, taught it openly to a group comprising both Buddhists and non-Buddhists at the Orgyen Dorje Den Buddhist center in San Francisco, California. Born in the Gyalrong region of eastern Tibet in 1925, Gyatrul Rinpoche was recognized at a young age by Jamyang Khyentse Lodrö Thaye as the incarnation of Sampa Künkyap, a Payul lineage meditator who spent his life in retreat and who later gave empowerments and transmissions from his retreat cave to multitudes of disciples. After being brought to Payul Domang Monastery, home of his previous incarnation, the young Gyatrul was educated by his tutor, Sangye Gön. During his extensive spiritual training, he received personal instruction on many Buddhist treatises, including the present one, by numerous renowned masters of the Nyingma order, including Tulku Natsok Rangdröl, Payul Chogtrul Rinpoche, Apkong Khenpo, and His Holiness Dudjom Rinpoche. In Tibet he received the oral transmission and instructions on the present treatise from the eminent Lama Norbu Tenzin.

After fleeing from Tibet into exile in India in 1959, Gyatrul Rinpoche continued his spiritual training and served the Tibetan community in India in various ways until 1972, when His Holiness the Dalai Lama sent him to Canada to offer spiritual guidance to Tibetans who had settled there. Since then, he has taught widely throughout North America, establishing numerous Buddhist centers in Oregon, California, New Mexico, and Mexico. He presently moves back and forth between his principle center, Tashi Choeling, near Ashland, Oregon, and his home in Half Moon Bay, California.

When Gyatrul Rinpoche taught this text in 1995, he invited all those with faith in these teachings—whether or not they had tantric initiation or were even Buddhist—to listen to them and to put them into practice. Among the assembled students were several who were suffering from critical illnesses, including AIDS, which made the teachings on the dying process all the more poignant to those listening. He also invites all those who read this book with faith to engage in the practices described here for the benefit of themselves and all sentient beings.

In addition to the main text by Padmasambhava, together with the transcribed, edited, oral commentary given by Gyatrul Rinpoche in 1995, this work also includes translations of other, shorter works that are closely associated with the treatise on the six transitional processes. To facilitate the reader's use of these works, they have been arranged in this book in three separate parts. Part 1 describes the preliminary practices considered to be necessary for engaging in the practices described in the main text. Part 2 consists of the main text itself. And Part 3 contains a number of supplementary prayers. All three parts also contain a transcription of Gyatrul Rinpoche's oral teachings.

The introduction, which takes up the topic of motivation, contains the initial advice and remarks given by Gyatrul Rinpoche before the start of the 1995 teachings. In chapter 1, Gyatrul Rinpoche comments on a text entitled *Preliminary Practices for Subduing Your Own Mind-stream: An Appendix to the Natural Emergence of the Peaceful and the Wrathful from Englightened Awareness: Experiential Instructions on the Transitional Process.*[6] This text was composed by Chöje Lingpa,

Karma Lingpa's principle disciple, and was written down by Guru Nyida Özer. Although Tibetan tradition includes this work as an appendix to the present cycle of teachings, Gyatrul Rinpoche chose to present it first for the benefit of those who are newcomers to Vajrayāna Buddhist practice. The text entails discursive meditations for subduing one's own mind-stream as a necessary prerequisite to engaging in the practices pertaining to the six transitional processes. These discursive meditations concern the suffering of the cycle of existence, the difficulty of obtaining a human life of leisure and endowment, and death and impermanence. The practices of *guru yoga*, the purificatory hundred-syllable mantra of Vajrasattva, and the *maṇḍala* offering are also included in this work by Chöje Lingpa, but they are not translated here, for these practices are included in the following section.

Chapter 2 contains another related text called *The Natural Liberation of the Mind-itself: The Four-Session Yoga of Spiritual Activity of the Secret Mantra Vajrayāna*,[7] composed by Chöje Lingpa and written down by Guru Sūryacandra. Like the preceding work, tradition now includes it in this same cycle of teachings concerning the transitional processes. The first of the four sessions discussed here entails meditations on going for outer, inner, and secret refuge, generating the Mahāyāna spirit of awakening, and cultivating the four immeasurables. The second session is a meditation involving the recitation of the one-hundred syllable mantra of Vajrasattva. In the third session one makes the ritual offering of the maṇḍala, and the fourth session includes a prayer to the lineage of spiritual mentors and a meditation on receiving the four empowerments. If one is engaging in a meditative retreat on the six transitional processes, all the above practices may be performed on a daily basis, together with the practices taught in the main work. If one is incorporating these prayers and meditations in one's daily practice while living an active way of life in the world, these additional recitations may be done intermittently as one wishes.

After these two preliminary chapters comes Part 2 of the book, which presents the main text, *The Profound Dharma of the Natural Liberation through Contemplating the Peaceful and*

Wrathful: Stage of Completion Instructions on the Six Bardos, along with Gyatrul Rinpoche's commentary. Each of the main text's six chapters is presented separately, in chapters 3 through 8 of the present volume. Each of these six chapters takes up one of the six transitional processes, or bardos, starting with the transitional process of living and progressing through the transitional processes of dreaming, meditation, dying, reality-itself, and becoming. Each chapter also describes a different aspect of natural liberation, such as, for example, the natural liberation of confusion, which occurs during the transitional process of dreaming; and the natural liberation of seeing, which occurs during the transitional process of reality-itself. In each chapter, the text gives detailed instructions for practices that are designed to help the practitioner transform each transitional process into a profound opportunity for liberation and enlightenment.

Part 3 of this book contains a number of supplementary prayers, all of which are considered to be part of the cycle of treasures that accompanies the main text. Chapter 9, entitled "Three Prayers Concerning the Transitional Processes,"[8] consists of three prayers. The first is a prayer for recalling the practical instructions of one's spiritual mentor. The second prayer is entitled "The Natural Liberation of All Attainments: A Prayer Concerning the Transitional Process."[9] This prayer itself has two parts: "The Prayer for Liberation through the Narrow Passage of the Transitional Process,"[10] which entails supplications to the five buddhas and their consorts for blessings to transmute the five mental poisons into the five types of primordial wisdom; and "The Prayer for Protection from Fear in the Transitional Process,"[11] which is specifically aimed at transforming the transitional processes of dying so that it becomes an avenue to spiritual awakening. The third prayer in this section is "The Prayer of Calling for Help to the Buddhas and Bodhisattvas,"[12] which calls for the blessings of the buddhas and bodhisattvas when one is at death's door. Padmasambhava is the author of these prayers as well, and they, too, are among the treasures revealed by Karma Linpga.

In chapter 10, the reader will find a prayer of supplication entitled, "The Natural Liberation of the Vast Expanse of the Three Embodiments,"[13] in which one requests the various manifestations of the Buddha for blessings for one's spiritual development along the path. Chapter 11 contains a prayer entitled, "The Natural Liberation of the Three Poisons Without Rejecting Them: A Guru Yoga Prayer to the Three Embodiments."[14] This text is intended to help the practitioner to transmute the three mental poisons into the three embodiments of the Buddha. Both of these prayers are included in the same cycle of teachings as our main text, so their author is Padmasambhava, and they were revealed by Karma Lingpa.

The translation of the root text was prepared in the following way: first Gyatrul Rinpoche went over all these texts with me, line by line, to help me translate them into English. Then he provided an oral commentary to these treatises at Orgyen Dorje Den, reading from the original Tibetan, while I orally translated his commentary and read from the first draft of my English translation. This second reading and commentary enabled me to polish my original translation. Kay Henry, a devoted student of Gyatrul Rinpoche, then volunteered to take on the prodigious task of transcribing the entire oral commentary and coupling this with the textual translations. Then it fell to me to edit the oral commentary, and—together with John Dunne and Sara McClintock, our editors at Wisdom Publications—to prepare the entire work in its present form. I wish to express my deep thanks to Gyatrul Rinpoche for guiding me in the translation of these texts and for his clear and accessible commentary and to Kay Henry, John Dunne, and Sara McClintock, without whom this work could not have been brought to completion. May our efforts be of benefit!

B. Alan Wallace
Santa Barbara, California
Spring 1997

PART ONE

INTRODUCTION

AND

PRELIMINARIES

Introduction: Motivation

IT SEEMS THAT MOST OF YOU have set your minds on attaining buddhahood and you're thinking, "I'm going to become a buddha." But, what's that about? Why would you want to become a buddha? Are you inspired by a patriotic motivation? Do you want to do something for your country? Or is it something for yourself? If it's for yourself, in what way would becoming a buddha be of benefit to you? We want to become buddhas because we are wandering in this cycle of existence, within *saṃsāra*. But what is saṃsāra? A lot of people say, "Oh, it's such a drag to live in San Francisco." Or people say, "Yeah, well, it's even worse in Los Angeles." And other people say, "Well, it's even worse in New York." Is this what "wandering in saṃsāra" is about, going from one city to another? No, that's not the point.

Saṃsāra, this cycle of existence, refers to the six types of sentient existence from the hell realms through the *deva*, or celestial, realms. As we are wandering within these realms, we are subject to the six types of existence, each of which has its own specific type of suffering. In attaining buddhahood, or perfect enlightenment, we gain release from all of these realms. In terms of the temporal well-being to be gained, we achieve the existence of humans or of gods. In terms of the ultimate or everlasting well-being, this is the attainment of enlightenment itself. By achieving that, we gain genuine freedom. Ask yourself, "Do I have that freedom right now?" I don't have it, and I expect that you don't have it either. In order to attain genuine freedom, we strive for enlightenment.

The following is an extensive teaching on each of the six transitional processes, or bardos, that make up our experience in saṃsāra. This teaching is based on the primary text by Padmasambhava called *The Profound Dharma of the Natural Liberation through Contemplating the Peaceful and Wrathful*. The term *natural liberation* can also be translated as *self-liberation*; it is something that occurs automatically, spontaneously, or naturally. In this profound text, Padmasambhava teaches us how to attain this kind of natural liberation within the six transitional processes that make up saṃsāra itself.

Before we can apply these practices, however, it is necessary for us to recognize the suffering of saṃsāra. Each realm of sentient existence has its own specific types of suffering that need to be recognized. The suffering of the deva, or celestial, realm is the anguish that occurs in anticipation of death. For, as death draws nigh, the devas are subject to great misery because they can see where their next, lower rebirth will be. The suffering of the *asuras*, or the demigods, is one of conflict and aggression. With human beings, the suffering to which we are specifically subject is the suffering of birth, aging, sickness, and death. For animals, there is the suffering of foolishness and stupidity. For *pretas,* or spirits, there is the suffering of thirst and hunger. Finally, for the denizens of the hell realms, there is the suffering of extreme heat and extreme cold. Within the context of recognizing these various types of suffering in the cycle of existence, we must also recognize that we have now achieved a human life of leisure and endowment. On the one hand, this means that we now have a human body. But it also includes the fact that we have already encountered one or more spiritual mentors of the Mahāyāna tradition that can lead us to the attainment of enlightenment; and we have obtained Dharma teachings that lay out for us the path to achieve enlightenment in this very lifetime.

Upon recognizing the difficulty of achieving a human life of leisure and endowment and recognizing as well the great significance of such a human life, we then need to pursue this contemplation in terms of recognizing the shortness of this precious human rebirth with which we are presently endowed. When speaking of the types of suffering of the six realms of existence to which we are subject, we can ask, "How does it happen that we experience such suffering whether in a human life or in other lifetimes, in the hell realms, and so forth? Why should we have to suffer in this way? Are we being punished by someone? Is it similar to the brutality of the Communist Chinese regime against the Tibetans? Is it like that? Or is it like the United States government in terms of its brutality against the Native Americans? Is it like that? Are we being punished in the same way as the Tibetans and the Native Americans were being punished?" The answer is, "No, not at all."

How is it that we suffer? We suffer through our engagement in nonvirtuous actions. Suffering is the natural result of nonvirtuous actions. In terms of the relationships between actions and their effects called the law of karma, the result of nonvirtue is suffering and the result of virtue is joy. So it is we ourselves who are punishing ourselves. We ourselves are inflicting the retribution for our acts. We are experiencing the natural consequences of our own acts. There is no external agent who is punishing or rewarding us for them. What do all of you think?

Regarding the situation between the Tibetans and the Communist Chinese regime, had the Tibetans in their previous lives not committed certain unwholesome deeds, then they would not have had to experience the suffering that was inflicted upon them by the Chinese government. Without nonvirtue, there would not have been the ensuing suffering. Similarly, for the Native Americans, when these white, illegal immigrants came over from England, France, and so forth, and took over and perpetrated all the atrocities on the Native Americans here, had those Native Americans not committed unwholesome actions in their previous lives, they too would not have experienced the suffering that was inflicted upon them by these immigrants from Europe. If you believe in karma, then this is the situation. If you don't believe in karma, then anything goes.

In terms of the relationship between actions and their consequences, nothing is ever wasted. No action—be it wholesome or unwholesome, virtuous or nonvirtuous—is without its own consequences. It's very easy to think in our present situation that we can get away with lots of things and that our nonvirtuous actions are insignificant because we won't have to experience their consequences. In fact, this is an error. For example, had the

Native Americans not inflicted injury on other sentient beings in previous lifetimes, then they would not have experienced that suffering themselves. The same thing goes for the Tibetans. The whole cycle perpetuates itself. As white Europeans came over and inflicted great suffering upon the Native Americans, they committed great nonvirtuous actions for which they will experience the consequences in future lives, maybe even right now. In this way the cycle of existence is perpetuated, and it's for this reason that Guru Rinpoche said, "Although my view is as vast as space, when it comes to the nature of actions and their consequences, I am extremely precise, like little particles of flour." If we fail to do likewise, then we're not Buddhists; or at the very least, it's difficult for us to be Buddhists and at the same time to be unconscientious about our behavior.

I have been requested to give these teachings. It is very good to request such teachings, and it's very good for you to put such teachings into practice. It's very good for you to become knowledgeable with regard to these various theories and practices, but you should also know what the purpose of all of this is. What is the purpose of the knowledge? What is the purpose of the practice? If what you actually implement in your life is the eight mundane concerns, then, in fact, you will not be on a path that leads to wisdom.[15] It will not lead to true erudition or to becoming a practitioner. In fact, if you are simply practicing the eight mundane concerns, then you are no different from politicians in America and around the world. They, too, have learned a lot. They are very smart, they're very knowledgeable, and they practice a lot; but what they're practicing is the eight mundane concerns, and you become indistinguishable from them. In learning about and practicing the eight mundane concerns, there is no benefit for your future lives. In comparison, the purpose of the sublime Buddhadharma is that it is of benefit in this and future lives. In terms of whether our Dharma practice is adulterated by or identical with the practice of the eight mundane concerns, we must really look inside ourselves. We must know ourselves and gain this knowledge through introspection. In terms of our hearing, thinking, and meditation, we must check up to ascertain the purity of our own practice. It is useless to point our fingers at other people and say, "Oh, look how that person is going astray and this person is getting involved in the eight mundane concerns." There is no point in this, and, of course, the response we get from these other people when we do it is, "Give me a break" or "Mind your own business." To learn this, we learn about ourselves. Leave other people alone.

Among Tibetan practitioners of Buddhism or among Buddhists around the world, there are many who, in fact, are very much involved in the eight mundane concerns. Insofar as our spiritual practice is adulterated by the eight mundane concerns, then this is like pouring poison into the Middle Way. By allowing our own spiritual practice to be so adulterated and poisoned, the knowledge we acquire of Dharma becomes wasted; and the great effort that we apply in the practice of Dharma also becomes wasted. For this reason, please consider this carefully. Please inspect your own understanding and your own practice to see that it is free of these eight mundane concerns.

MOTIVATION

Whatever type of practice we engage in—be it hearing, thinking or meditation—we need the proper motivation. What kind of motivation? If we review our lives from a very early age, from infancy to the present, and review our actions of body, speech, and mind, we can ask ourselves, "What value did those actions have? In what way were they of any benefit?" They may have had no benefit, or they may have had some mundane benefit. But while producing this small portion of mundane benefit, what these actions were really doing was simply perpetuating our wandering in the cycle of existence. However, in terms of acting as causes for our accomplishing the two embodiments[16] of the Buddha—the Rūpakāya for the sake of others and the Dharmakāya for one's own sake—it seems very likely that these activities until now have done nothing.

Why is this significant? The significance is that all of us die. Whether we want to die or not, this is our destiny; and over this we have no control. We cannot control how we will die. I guarantee completely that I don't have such control. I will not have control at my death, and I suspect it's unlikely that you will have control. On what grounds do I draw this conclusion? Look at our daily lives. To what extent do we have any control over the three poisons of attachment, hatred, and delusion? Don't these poisons dominate our actions from day to day? Even if we have some control over our minds and activities during the daytime, what control do we have at night in the dream-state? Do we have any control at all? If we don't have control in the day or night, on what grounds could we possibly imagine that we will have some control when this life is over and we're wandering in the intermediate state? This is true for all of us. We're equally without control. We don't have any kind of autonomy over our lives, and there are many illustrations of this that we can see around us in human society. For example, people get hooked on cigarette smoking even though they know that it leads to lung cancer as well as various other types of disorders. Their friends and relatives may plead with them, "Please stop, we want you to live a long time," and they may even want to stop; yet they have no control. In a similar fashion, we can become obsessed with alcohol, and then people say, "Oh, please, stop the drinking. It's so harmful." One wants to stop perhaps, but the will power is not there. The control is not there.

Moving closer to Dharma, we find that many people say, "Oh, I'm going to practice Dharma." However, when it gets right down to it, we don't practice Dharma. We just talk about getting to it when future circumstances are more felicitous; but in the meantime, we're awfully busy. I'm not just pointing the finger at you; I feel I'm in the same situation myself. In addition to this, I have students who I heard twenty or more years ago saying, "Well, the first thing is I'm going to get my financial situation secure. I'm going to make money, and then I can do other things." The decades have gone by, and I'm looking at these people. By and large, they are in the same financial situation that they were in then. They haven't gotten the financial security they were looking for. What they have done in the meantime is accummulate a lot of nonvirtue.

These topics are worth our careful consideration. We should hear them and think about them. While knowing this and having gained some understanding of the distinction between virtue and nonvirtue, if you engage in nonvirtue—knowing that it will be detrimental to yourself and others—this is like recognizing that you have a glass of poison and drinking it anyway. The situation is exactly like that. That is, from moment to moment as we engage in activities that are dominated by the three poisons or the five poisons,17 then these actions lead to the perpetuation of our own cycle of existence.

The great spiritual mentors of the past are gone. Impermanence has taken its toll and they have passed away. Similarly, kings, the rich and the poor, the beautiful and the ugly, all perish. All of them are subject to this reality of impermanence and death. Given this reality of human existence, who can guarantee that we will not have to face death? Who can guarantee to save us from the consequences of our own actions? Who can guarantee to save us from the reality of impermanence? There isn't anyone who can give these guarantees, not among humans or gods.

For these reasons, there is the need for genuine Dharma practice, and the time for that is now. There's no putting it off. There can be no excuses. If we succumb to procrastination, we're the ones who lose out. It's not our spiritual mentor. It's not Buddhism. It's not the Dharma center. It's not anything else. We are the losers if we procrastinate in that way. By the way, it's important to recognize that the way of listening to the Dharma is different from the way of attending to other types of teachings. For example, in high school or college, a different mode is required. What is appropriate for these other, secular contexts is not appropriate here. In the context of requesting and listening to Dharma, it is important that you slow down your mind. Let your mind come to rest and attend to the teachings with mindfulness, with introspection.

Returning to the subject of motivation, I have mentioned that you are all welcome to listen to and study these teachings if you have a wholesome motivation. Even those who have not taken refuge in the Buddha, Dharma, and Sangha are welcome to study these teachings if you intend to put them into practice. I respect these people, and I respect people who have taken the vows of refuge and are keeping those vows. I respect both. If there are others who, out of idle curiosity, are just wondering, "Well, what's going on?" I do not respect that attitude; and those people are not welcome to study these teachings either directly or indirectly. Do other things; this is not your business. For those people who have a good motivation, I believe you want to learn the Dharma and you also want to put it into practice, so I'm very glad to accommodate you. I'm very glad to respond to this expressed desire and interest on your part. This, in fact, helps me too. As I face my own death, these teachings are something that is beneficial to me as well.

There are several correct motivations. You can have a very vast motivation that is noble, lofty, and broad as in the Mahāyāna. This is very good. However, even if you simply strive to liberate yourself from suffering, this too is sufficient. However, one should go beyond a motivation that is merely adequate. The motivation that should be generated now is the aspiration for perfect enlightenment both for yourself and for the benefit of others. With that motivation, study these teachings and aspire to put them into practice in meditation. In general, there are three kinds of motivation: wholesome, unwholesome, and ethically neutral motivations. Among these three, it's imperative that we bring forth a virtuous motivation. It's important here that we don't fall into our old habits.

In the West, from infancy on, many of us are always being told how good we are; and we're praised for all kinds of things. As we go through school, we're praised for one thing after another and we end up being spoiled adults. As we grow older, our bodies start to deteriorate, and our previous good looks start to wither away. At that point, many of us may get a little bit nervous about losing that for which people have been praising us for so long, and we apply a great deal of effort to maintain our external good qualities. In the process we tend to get involved with all of the three poisons of the mind: attachment, hatred, and delusion. We may apply all types of means to try to counteract this gradual deterioration of our bodies. Some might even consider plastic surgery. All of this is to try to maintain one's good looks. In any case, all of these efforts that we apply are expressions of our own self-grasping, which is fundamental ignorance; and actions motivated by such self-grasping are inappropriate for these teachings.

Often when Westerners receive teachings, they are very vigorously taking notes during the teachings or they're taping the teachings, so they have them stored when they get home. Then they share them with others; they tell their friends about the teachings; and then, after having done so, they totally disgard them, leaving them in their notes or their tapes in the bathroom together with the toilet paper. This is not useful. Rather than leading to liberation or enlightenment, which is the genuine purpose of these teachings, that kind of disrespect just leads to lower rebirth. You may share these teachings with those who have an earnest desire to put them into practice, at least for the sake of their own genuine benefit, and most nobly for the benefit of all creatures. But you may not share them with those who would treat them without respect or faith. If you teach such people, it will just lead to your own demise and rebirth in a miserable realm.

Please respect the teachings; this is what I ask of you. Of course, if you don't want to heed me, that's your business. Again, you may share the teachings cautiously. In terms of motivation, another point is that you should consider the countless number of sentient beings throughout space who like yourselves yearn for happiness and wish to be free of suffering. Aspire to receive these teachings on the six transitional processes and put them into practice so that all beings throughout space may achieve liberation and perfect enlightenment.

To learn the proper manner in which to listen to Dharma, I suggest that you read the first chapter of the text *The Words of My*

Perfect Teacher. Especially for those who may be somewhat new to Tibetan Buddhism, read this and become familiar with it. There is considerable interest these days in learning *Atiyoga*, which is the culmination of the nine *yānas* of teachings and practice within Buddhism. If you aspire to receive such very deep and advanced teachings, then it would be a disgrace to not know how to listen to Dharma in a proper way. It's a matter of Dharma etiquette. To illustrate this, His Holiness Dudjom Rinpoche once told a story of an old monk who was out traveling and needed a place to stay. He came to one old lady's house and asked her for a night's lodging, which was a common custom in Tibet. She put him up for the night and served him some black tea. However, the tea that she offered him had neither salt nor butter, two things that Tibetans normally put into their tea; so it was two steps away from being really authentic, tasty Tibetan tea. The old monk then tasted the tea, became very displeased, and said, "This tea doesn't even have the taste of salt, let alone butter! Throw this out!" And he threw it out the window. The old lady saw his response and said, "Oh, venerable monk, judging by your response and etiquette, it seems that your deportment doesn't even have the taste of the sixteen mundane types of etiquette, let alone the divine Dharma. So I throw you out!" There are proper ways of listening to the teachings, and this is a matter of Dharma etiquette.

Children are certainly welcome to listen to and study these teachings as well. They get the benefit of receiving the teachings, even if they are not really able to put them into practice at present. It's a similar situation when children attend tantric empowerments. They get the blessings of the initiation even if they do not actually receive or have the responsibility for the samaya. The samayas for children do not degenerate nor are they preserved, so it's a separate case for them. I like kids. Their situation is different, and they don't have oceanlike attachment. They don't have volcano-like pride. As adults, we have more responsibility.

1

Preliminary Practices for Subduing Your Own Mind-stream

NOW WE GO to the preliminary practices, which are the very core of Dharma practice. This is not the time to cut corners. We've been cutting corners since beginningless saṃsāra, and this has led us to perpetuate our own existence in saṃsāra. If we cut corners in the present as we have in the past, then in the future too, we'll simply continue to wander in the cycle of existence. Therefore, it's very important to listen and study well and put the teachings into practice. Without doing that, if you then think that you can teach this to other people, it is a disgrace. You're finished. All of these teachings are Atiyoga teachings, and they're not to be treated lightly or casually in that fashion. For those of you who are planning to skip ahead to the six transitional processes, if you omit the preliminary practices, then you're really making a mistake and you're missing the whole point.

This introduction concerns the preliminary practices for subduing your own mind-stream, and this begins with a prayer.

The Preliminary Practices for Subduing Your Own Mind-stream
With faith and devotion I mentally bow
To the Dharmakāya, the original lord Samantabhadra,
The Sambhogakāya, the victorious peaceful and wrathful deities,
And to the Nirmāṇakāya, Padmasambhava.

First, what is the purpose of the text's having a title or name? There are various reasons for that. First of all, simply by seeing the title of a text, a person who is very well versed in Dharma will have a very clear sense of what the text is about from beginning to end. The title allows such a person to place the text among the three yānas and identify what type of teaching it is.

To take an analogy, it's as if you have a medicine with a label stating its name, ingredients, and benefits. That is the purpose of the title of a text for knowledgeable people. For people who are not so learned, the title of a text will at least give them some idea that it is perhaps a Mahāyāna text. They get some idea of the contents of the text, although they will not have a total grasp of its context and meaning. Thirdly, when you have the title of a text, you will at least know how to find it.

Following the title there is a four-line homage. What's the homage for? Clearly, there are many types of homage: there can be homage to the guru, to the chosen deity, and many others. What's the point of this? There are various reasons for including the homage at the beginning of the text. One is that by presenting the homage, the author is in effect asking for the permission of the enlightened beings to compose the work that follows. It also entails calling for a blessing from the enlightened beings, and specifically that the work in question can be brought to culmination and that it can be completed. It is also used to pray that the teachings that one is about to compose may be of benefit for sentient beings and for the preservation of the Dharma.

Next is what we traditionally call "the commitment to compose the text," through which the author makes a commitment to give these teachings. Once again, what is the reason for the author to make this commitment to compose this work? If this were an author with a modern, worldly mentality, then the composition probably would be made for the sake of profit. This is not the case with these great beings who composed such texts as this. Rather, their motivation was that they would compose such texts for the benefit of sentient beings and for the sake of Dharma. It's like the case of the chosen deity: you chose your chosen deity; and, with that choice there is also the commitment to actualize that deity. In this process when you make this commitment, you may, for example, generate yourself as Mañjuśrī. As Mañjuśrī then you carry forth with the activity. That's one route. Another one is that you simply ask that the blessings of Mañjuśrī might enter into you so that you can carry this work through to its culmination. Another major purpose for the initial commitment is so that the work can be brought to its culmination, that it can be done well, and that it can be done well for the sake of others. Thus, we see that all of this hinges upon one's motivation, and it's important that it's right there from the beginning. Just as we so commonly recite "for the sake of all sentient beings throughout space" and then carry on with whatever practice it is, as we do in our daily practice, so is this the case in composing a text. The motivation is of initial, paramount importance.

> Due to the power of prayers, the experiential instructions
>   on the transitional processes
> Are revealed for the sake of disciples who are training
>   their mind-streams.
> In this there are the preliminary practices, the main practice,
>   and the conclusion;
> And here the gradual instructions in the preliminary
>   practices
> Will be clearly presented for those of inferior intelligence,
> With the introduction and practice in accord with the
>   guru's tradition.

Here, the author is saying that this is not something simply of his own fabrication. It's in accordance with the guru's tradition; and, in saying that, the implication is that it goes back to Vajradhara, the primordial Buddha.

There is a lot of significance in the simple words, "clearly presented." For some texts, you have the root, or primary, text, as well as many commentaries. All of these commentaries are like branches that grow out from the trunk. There may be so many that they actually obscure the root. You get caught up in so many of the details that you lose sight of the root. That can be a problem. There's another problem, though, and that is not being able to understand a text because it is so concise. When it says "clearly presented" here, the implication is that the text will not be so extensive that you lose sight of what it's really about, nor will it be so concise that you can't figure it out at all.

> Here the subject is taught in terms of six general topics: (1) pondering the sufferings of the cycle of existence, (2) the difficulty of obtaining a human life of leisure and endowment, and (3) meditating on death and impermanence are the preliminary practices for subduing your own mind-stream. The preliminary practices for training your own mind-stream include: (4) guru yoga, (5) the hundred-syllable mantra, and finally (6) the spiritual activity of offering the maṇḍala.

PONDERING THE SUFFERINGS OF CYCLIC EXISTENCE

> If you do not ponder the sufferings of the cycle of existence, disillusionment with the cycle of existence will not arise. If disillusionment with the cycle of existence does not arise, whatever Dharma you practice, it cannot be disengaged from this life, and the craving and attachment of this life are not severed. Thus, pondering the sufferings of the cycle of existence is extremely important.

When the text addresses the sufferings of the cycle of existence, this is referring to the first of the Four Noble Truths, the Noble Truth of Suffering. What needs to be done is to recognize the truth of suffering and to recognize the manner in which this suffering is, in fact, suffering. How is it suffering? That, too, needs to be known. Without that, there will be no disillusionment with saṃsāra. Without such meditation, our natural tendency is to be attached to the cycle of existence. Therefore, it's through such meditation that we counteract the grasping onto the cycle of existence. Without such meditation, whatever purportedly spiritual activity we engage in with our bodies and our speech will be ineffectual, because it has no foundation. Thus, it cannot free us from suffering. Without this disillusionment with saṃsāra, even if one engages in some semblance of practicing Dharma, in fact there is no genuine Dharma. In the absence of any genuine Dharma practice, there's no liberation nor is there any enlightenment.

A lot of people may respond, at least internally, that they've heard about the preliminary practices many times already, and that they are thoroughly familiar with them. You may think you know it, but in reality you may not. What would indicate that? You're still attached to saṃsāra. The very fact that you're still attached to this cycle of existence is itself proof that you do not know the preliminaries. You've not gotten the real result from the practice of the preliminaries. You've not turned your mind away from saṃsāra. If you look at the Four Thoughts that Turn the Mind,[18] the sufferings of saṃsāra are discussed there. Just having heard about them or having done a little bit of meditation does not mean you've understood this yet. If you had understood it, you wouldn't still be attached to saṃsāra. It's very straightforward, but here we are; we're still in saṃsāra. We're still attached to saṃsāra, and the reason for that is we haven't fathomed the preliminaries.

First, go by yourself to a place that arouses disillusionment. If possible, go to a deserted place, broken-down ruins, a field of dried grass rustling in the wind, or an eerie place, or else go where there are pathetic ill people, beggars, and so on who were previously prosperous and later fell on hard times. If that is not possible, go by yourself to a place of solitude. In terms of your posture, sit on a comfortable cushion with one leg folded. Plant your right foot on the ground, press your left leg against the ground, rest your right elbow on your right knee, press your palm against your right cheek, and clasp your left knee with your left palm. This posture of despair will lead to stark depression.

Then with your mind ponder the sufferings of the cycle of existence, and with your speech occasionally utter these words, letting them arouse your mindfulness,

"Alas! Alas! Wretched me! This cycle of existence is suffering! Nirvāṇa is joy!" Ponder in this way, "O dear, I am trapped in the sufferings of the cycle of existence, which is like a fire pit, and I am afraid! Ah, now the time has come to escape from within this life. This suffering of the three miserable states of existence is impossible to endure, and it is limitless. Occasions of joy do not occur even for a moment. Now is the time to prepare for a quick escape."

Imagine this: "This cycle of existence is a great fire pit of intense heat. It is deep, broad, and high. In such a terrifying fire pit, I cry out as I am trapped, together with every other sentient being in the cycle of existence." Verbally express this ardently, with a grieving voice: "O dear, I'm afraid in this great fire pit of the cycle of existence. Since beginningless time, I am still burning, and I am afraid." While you are uttering these words of lament, in the space above that pit, imagine your primary spiritual mentor, whose body is adorned with the six types of bone ornaments, and who holds in his hand a hook of light rays. Imagine him saying this to you: "Alas! The joyless cycle of existence is like a fire pit. Now the time has come to escape from it. The sufferings of the three miserable states of existence are limitless, and occasions of joy do not occur even for a moment. Now is the time to escape from the pit of fire."

Simply by hearing these words, the thought arises, "Alas! Long have I been trapped in the fire pit of the sufferings of the cycle of existence. Now, heeding the words of my spiritual mentor, I shall escape from this, and I shall also liberate every one of these sentient beings." As soon as you sincerely bring forth this spirit of awakening, imagine that you are caught by your heart with the hook in your mentor's hand; and you are instantly liberated into the realm of Sukhāvatī. Instantly, a hook of light rays appears in your hand as well, and one by one you save every sentient

being in the fire pit. Earnestly cultivate compassion for
all the sentient beings in the cycle of existence.

When you're meditating in this way, you should apply other
teachings you've received in more extensive presentations of these
preliminary practices in which the individual types of suffering
pertaining to the six realms of existence are all taught. What is
the effect of such meditation? It serves to make your mind turn
away from saṃsāra, and it also helps you progress in the cultivation of the two types of spirit of awakening: the spirit of aspiring
for awakening and the spirit of venturing toward awakening.

Continually reflect in that way upon the fire pit of the
cycle of existence, and ponder all the sufferings of the cycle
of existence. Day and night, bear this in mind without
being distracted. A sūtra states, "Joy is never present on the
tip of the needle of the cycle of existence." Thus, meditate
on the problems of the cycle of existence until disillusionment arises. Once your mind has turned away from the
cycle of existence on which you have been meditating, you
will ascertain the need for Dharma; and meditative experience will arise as there is no craving for this life.

If your mind does not turn away from the cycle of
existence, meditation is pointless. Meditate on this for
three days, and then return. By meditating on this, for
the time being, your mind will withdraw from the cycle
of existence, and ultimately it will ascend to nirvāṇa.
Practice this! The meditation on the sufferings of the
cycle of existence is the first session in the *Natural
Liberation through Contemplating: Experiential
Instructions on the Transitional Processes.*

When the text uses the term "all the sufferings of the cycle of
existence," this refers to the suffering of every type of sentient
being within saṃsāra throughout the six realms. Once your mind
is turned away from saṃsāra, then phrases like "I will practice

Dharma" or "I need to practice Dharma" or "I want to practice Dharma" will really be true. Your aspiration will be authentic, and it will lead you to the genuine practices of hearing, thinking, and meditation.

Whether you're meditating in retreat or at home, this is the place to start. This type of meditation lays a foundation; and, if you cultivate this well, what follows from it is very meaningful. You'll have good results if you establish a solid foundation in this type of meditation to turn your mind away from saṃsāra. If you do this, you won't be like the person who is always eagerly anticipating "what's next" in terms of the practices, as if you are watching a movie and are wondering how it will turn out. Rather, you will have a firm foundation, and you will progress well. However long we have been practicing Dharma, whether it's for twenty years, ten years or eight years—or like in my case, about sixty or sixty-five years—we can look at what is actually arising in our minds right now. What have we realized? Spiritual realization has still not arisen in many peoples' minds, and this is due to failing to comprehend the fundamental point that we're not yet enlightened. This is the reason why we've not accomplished our own ends. Why have we been unsuccessful in accomplishing our own self-interest? Because we've not sufficiently laid this foundation.

If we're looking for peace of mind, we should look to such practice, for it is by this means that the mind comes to equilibrium. The spirit of awakening arises from this type of meditation, and it also leads to the attenuation of our own mental afflictions. When Dharma practitioners find that their minds are really transforming, it's because they've established a firm foundation in such meditations as this. It is through this that Dharma actually arises in the mind. Otherwise, without this, one might be very arrogant about one's knowledge and experience and so forth. This attitude is like the rack of antlers on a deer—it reaches out in an impressive display. However, all of that is an indication that the Dharma has fallen into one's mouth and not into one's heart.

Padmasambhava says, "Meditate on this for three days and then return." A number of you have been meditating on this for quite a bit longer than three days. However, this is something you can meditate on for three days, three months, or three years. After you become a buddha, you don't need to meditate on it any more. Through this practice, the mind turns away from saṃsāra. Through the practice of hearing, thinking, and meditation, you eventually do achieve nirvāṇa. How is it that the nature of saṃsāra is suffering? What does that mean? The first point is to recognize the very nature of saṃsāra itself. On that basis, you seek out the causes of saṃsāra. In this process, it's very important to distinguish between the genuine causes of happiness and the genuine causes of sorrow or suffering. These you need to know for yourself, so identifying the causes of happiness and sorrow is most important. It's not enough just to say, "Oh, I don't like suffering" or "I don't like saṃsāra."

When we speak of saṃsāra, it seems to be something bad. What is saṃsāra? What do you point to when you want to identify saṃsāra? Who is saṃsāra? If you're wondering who saṃsāra is, you can point to yourself. Each of us is our own saṃsāra. Is it the same or different from ourselves? It's not to be found anywhere else apart from our own existence. We are the ones who experience suffering; we are the ones who experience joy. Moreover, we are the ones who create our own saṃsāra. Is saṃsāra created? Yes it is, and we're the ones who create it. How does this take place? With such mental afflictions as the three poisons of attachment, hatred, and delusion, we create saṃsāra. The nature of all of these poisons is delusion. That is what creates our saṃsāra.

All of us here have attachment. We grasp onto one thing after another. All of us are subject to jealousy, we all have hatred, and we all have pride; and the nature of all of these poisons is delusion. This is what we have. We possess a composite of these five poisons. The nature of these is grasping onto a real "self," whereas, in fact, no real inherent self exists. That's one form of delusion. Another form of delusion is the dualistic grasping onto the real existence of subject versus object. Those are the nature of delusion, which is itself the nature of all of the five poisons.

We are now endowed with a body created out of the four or five elements, and this body itself is the basis of suffering. On this basis, we engage in various types of nonvirtues. Within a tenfold classification, there are three nonvirtues of the body, four of the speech, and three of the mind. Of course, there are not only ten nonvirtues, but these ten lead to a great variety of other nonvirtues. Engaging in nonvirtue leads to rebirth in various miserable states of existence. Depending upon the intensity of the motivation, such nonvirtue may lead to rebirth in one of the eight hot hells or eight cold hells. Also, such deeds may lead to rebirth as a preta, or spirit. They may lead to rebirth as an animal, of which there are countless different species. Within the human realm we see a tremendous diversity of individuals. Beyond the human realm are the asuras, or demigods, who are especially characterized by the pain of aggression and competition. Finally, there are the devas, or gods, who experience intense suffering when their lives are about to come to an end.

Diversity is especially evident in the human realm. Even in one family, there are tremendous differences even from one member to another in terms of their merit, lifespan, and their degree of suffering. All of these variations in human life and in these other life forms are a result of our own previous actions. We are the ones who have created this. We are the creators. In terms of the wide variety of sentient beings, we can look at the people gathered here. On the one hand, there are the obvious differences between men and women; and there are other differences in the ways you appear and so on.

We ourselves are the creators of our own suffering. This being the case, it's very difficult to find any people in positions of authority, like kings or world leaders, who are without suffering or without the five poisons. Even among lamas, it's difficult to find. The greatest lamas are really inconceivable; but most of the rest have suffering and are still subject to the five poisons. Whether one is powerful or rich, pretty or handsome, there are no grounds for being puffed up about one's position. If one becomes filled with self-importance, this simply leads to one's own disgrace. Even if you're in a position of great authority like a president or a king, if you become arrogant about this while you're still subject to suffering and to these five poisons, this just leads to your own disgrace. Moreover, if after a while spiritual teachers develop a sense that they are really quite special, then they too are making a very big mistake.

All of the previous instances mentioned can lead to disgrace if you're not careful. The way to be careful is to check up on your own mind. If you're not conscientious about that, you're bound to fall into disgrace. Even if you're acting under the guise of serving sentient beings with a motivation of altruism or for the sake of Dharma, if you're not checking up on your own mind, then the chances are that you'll come to resemble the subject of a Tibetan aphorism that speaks of people presenting an outer semblance of being of service, while inwardly they're conniving to get things only for their own self-interest. What's coming out your mouth is altruistic, but what's inside is really still self-centered. If one operates in that devious way, it actually leads to disgrace for sentient beings, and it's a disgrace for Dharma as well. By presenting an outer semblance of being of service while in fact trying to twist things for your own benefit, you wind up damaging your own self-interest. If you try to deceive people, you may, in fact, be effective for a couple of months; but after a while, they'll catch on. The buddhas and bodhisattvas are all-knowing, so you can't deceive them at all! There's no tricking the buddhas and bodhisattvas, nor can we trick the Dharma protectors or the various spirits who accompany them.

There's one person, though, who's been tricked; and that's yourself. If you're trying to trick other people, the first person you can be sure you're deceiving is yourself. The result of this is that you lose. If you feel you are a compassionate person, it's most important, first of all, to look to see whether you really in fact do have compassion. At the beginning, it's very difficult. Insofar as we have strong self-grasping, that really precludes compassion. Therefore, look carefully. Buddhas and bodhisattvas have abandoned this self-grasping tendency and genuinely strive for the welfare of others.

When I was a little boy, I used to lie to my own spiritual mentors. I would fib to them and make up stories, and they would listen and say, "Oh, I see, I see," as if they were admiring everything I was saying. I would feel that I had tricked them, whereas in fact they knew all along what was going on. They were just leading me on. Later on in India, there were great lamas with whom I had contact, including His Holiness Karmapa, His Holiness the Dalai Lama, His Holiness Dudjom Rinpoche, and so on. When speaking to such lamas then, even if they are saying, "Oh yes, oh yes," as if they're agreeing with us and accepting everything we're saying, if we are lying, this simply leads to our own disgrace. From their perspective, what they're seeing is that all composite phenomena are impermanent. They are viewing the world in light of the ten analogies of the world being like an illusion, like a reflection in a mirror, and so on. Some of these lamas are actual masters of Atiyoga and are living the experience of the Great Perfection. The point of all this is that, if one tries to deceive others, it really is only one's own loss. In India and Tibet there were a lot of people who lied to the great lamas. A lot of aristocrats would go to His Holiness the Dalai Lama and tell all kinds of stories; and they would think they had succeeded. However, all they really succeeded in doing was to bring disgrace upon their own heads. Be careful about how you speak. It's important not to deceive. On the other hand, you don't have to be so honest that you run off at the mouth, telling everything that you've seen or heard and so forth. You don't need to do that either. Sometimes you can just be quiet.

When we look at the situation of the six realms of existence and consider that we are the ones who create this, it makes us look like we're really intelligent and powerful. In a way, yes; in a way, no. When we are judging other people, we say, "He did this. She did that. They did this. I'm good, but they did this." There is some satisfaction when we point out others' faults and put them in their place. However, for the person who is listening to us as we're slandering another person, we are falling into disgrace. Other people will see the kind of person we are, getting a thrill out of slandering other people. It seems as if we have some inconceivable power in being able to create these various realms of saṃsāra.

PONDERING THE DIFFICULTY OF OBTAINING A HUMAN LIFE OF LEISURE AND ENDOWMENT

> If the difficulty of obtaining a human life of leisure and endowment is not pondered, one will not think of Dharma, so such reflection is extremely important. In terms of location, go where there are insects, ants, and many kinds of animals. As for your posture, sit cross-legged, and place your hands in the *mudrā* of meditative equipoise.

The reference to "leisure and endowment" is to the eight types of leisure and ten types of endowment with which we are presently endowed. It is this life that makes the difference. This present body is very difficult to achieve. With regard to this body, we are in an unusual situation in these modern times. Nowadays women commonly kill their own children when they're in the womb. Not long ago an American woman in the South drove her vehicle into a lake and killed her two children; and people were stunned at how anyone could do that. They were so amazed. I don't find that amazing at all. There was another woman who threw her children off a bridge, and people were amazed at how a mother could do that. From my perspective, this is not amazing at all. Some women have had abortions three or four times. When that's so common, why is it so amazing that a woman should wait a little bit and kill her children when they're older? What's the big difference?

The human life with which we are presently endowed can serve as a cause for achieving buddhahood. It can be a cause for us to effectively serve the needs of others and to relieve them from suffering. This is the potential that we have with this present body. When we consider the qualities of buddhahood, these may seem amazing. That's fine, but we should recognize that this present body acts as a cause for achieving those amazing qualities of buddhahood. Similarly, in terms of the spirit of awakening, we may hold in awe the great love and compassion that saturates that mind state. Once again, recognize that the spirit of awakening is something that can be cultivated with this body. To learn more about the preciousness and rarity of this human life of leisure and endowment, simply go back to the Four Thoughts that Turn the Mind. It's going back to the A B C's, but until you completely get it, keep on going back to it.

> With your mind, ponder in this way: "Oh dear! The acquisition of a human life is just for now. If I can't bring Dharma to it now, it will be very difficult to obtain it later. Moreover, it is not enough that I alone have obtained a human life, for these sentient beings of the three realms have long wandered in the miserable states of existence. Oh compassion!"
>
> Verbally utter these words in a melodious voice and let them arouse your mindfulness: "Alas! Alas! Wretched me! The procurement of a precious human life is just for now. If I fail to accomplish any Dharma in this life, it will be difficult to obtain a human life later on. Alas for those who have taken birth in the three miserable states of existence!"
>
> Arouse your mindfulness with those words and meditate on the following: "Throughout the vast universe as far as the extent of space, sentient beings are screaming with pain in the hell realms, pretas are enduring the incapacitating miseries of hunger and thirst; and all animals—including tigers, leopards, black bears, brown bears, dogs, foxes, wolves, yaks, goats, and sheep—devour one another. Under the soil, red ants, black ants, scorpions, spiders, and every kind of insect that fills the earth kill each other. In the water, incalculable aquatic animals including fish, frogs, and tadpoles kill one another. And in the sky, vultures, kites, hawks, eagles, sparrows, crows, doves, magpies, warblers, and so on

that fill the sky kill and devour each other. Even the winged insects that fill the sky and earth devour each other alive, making sounds of anguish."

Within this cycle of existence, there are general types of suffering to which all sentient beings are subject. Then there are specific sufferings pertaining to the various realms of existence in which one might be reborn. Generally speaking, the intensity of the suffering, the manner in which the suffering is experienced, and the duration of suffering are created by one's own actions. One's own karma is the determining factor.

Imagine the whole sky and the earth moving and trembling, fearful and vast. Then ponder this: "Within their midst, I am alone upon a high, rocky peak, with no companion. I alone have obtained human life, and I am on the verge of falling down. Oh dear! Amidst such a multitude of denizens of the hell realms, pretas, and animals, I alone have obtained human life. Has this present, unique situation just been my good luck, or has it arisen by the power of virtue? Having obtained this, which is so difficult to acquire, now if I were pointlessly to fall back empty-handed, I would have to experience such overwhelming suffering down there. What a waste! Although I have now obtained that which is difficult to acquire, there is no time to waste, for now I shall certainly fall down there soon. Now what is the best way to avoid falling down there? Where is it? Oh dear! Wretched me! Oh, I am afraid!"

Earnestly utter these words of misery: "Oh dear, I'm afraid! Oh dear, I'm afraid! There are so many sentient beings in the miserable states of existence. The attainment of human life is so rare. And I shall fall down there so soon. That which is difficult to find is easily destroyed. What can I do to be liberated? If there is a way, I shall follow it."

Human life is "difficult to find" but "easily destroyed." It is very difficult to bring about the causes that lead to obtaining a human life of leisure and endowment. Yet once it's accomplished, it's very easy to lose. There are many causes leading to its destruction. One needs to bring forth a very powerful resolve to do whatever can be done to obtain human life again.

> While you are uttering these words of lamentation, like before, imagine that your primary spiritual mentor appears in the sky above you, displaying the mudrā of bestowing protection. Imagine that he utters these words to you: "Alas! The attainment of a human life of leisure and endowment, which is difficult to find, has been obtained only now, and it is not permanent. Soon you are about to fall to a miserable state of existence. If something of great significance is not accomplished with this now, it will be very difficult to find human life later. Look at the number of sentient beings to see whether it is rare or not. In dependence upon this human life, accomplish buddhahood!"

The reference to "something of great significance," pertains both to one's own ends, as well as serving the needs of others. There is no point in doing nothing with this life to accomplish either of these and then wondering if there is hope of getting the same situation in the future.

> As soon as you hear these words, consider, "Alas! Amongst such a multitude of sentient beings, I alone have obtained human life, which is so difficult to attain. Now I shall liberate myself from the sufferings of the cycle of existence, then I shall free every one of those sentient beings down there. Now there is no time for distractions, for I shall swiftly bring them to the state of buddhahood." As soon as you bring forth the spirit of awakening with those thoughts, imagine that the essence of light-rays from your spiritual mentor's heart strikes

you, instantly causing you to reach the realm of Sukhāvatī. Then incalculable rays of light emerge from your own heart, and bring every single sentient being to the realm of Sukhāvatī. Cultivate powerful compassion for all sentient beings.

This is like a wake-up call, saying, "Look what you have to do right now; look at your present opportunity." It's not uncommon to find people who say they want to work for the sake of other sentient beings and that they're acting out of altruism. But while they're trying to help other people, they really haven't even helped themselves yet. They're still subject to their own delusions. It's really like the blind leading the blind. Until you relieve your own mind from afflictions, you're not very well equipped to serve the needs of others effectively. Some people may agree that if they really focus on trying to help other people now, it's like the blind trying to lead the blind. Actually, we really should try to help other people. I'm not saying that trying to help others is wrong. That's fine. But the degree and quality of service that we can offer now is sometimes quite artificial, so I am suggesting that we see if we can render more genuine and effective service to others.

To illustrate this, there is a story of a great lama in Tibet. Various lamas would come to him, and he'd greet them. When one monk visited him, he asked what he knew about a certain lama. The monk told him, "Oh, he's doing great work. He's built stūpas, printed Dharma books, and established monasteries and temples." Upon hearing this, the lama said, "Oh, that's good, but isn't it great to practice genuine Dharma." On another occasion, he asked about another lama. The monk responded, "Oh, he's doing such good work. He's teaching the Dharma, and he has many disciples." The lama said, "That's very good, but how good it is to practice genuine Dharma." On another occasion, he asked about yet another lama; and the monk responded, "Oh, he's in very strict retreat, reciting mantras." The old lama said, "Oh, that's very good, but how good it is to practice genuine Dharma." On another occasion, he asked about another lama.

The monk responded, "Ah, him, he sits around, he puts his robe over his head and cries all the time." And the old lama said, "Oh, he's practicing genuine Dharma."

Don't think that this man had fallen into some chronic depression. He was weeping out of compassion. If you truly want to serve the needs of others, such genuine compassion is necessary, and there must be genuine wisdom as well. This enables you to be of effective, genuine service to others. In contrast, when we lack such compassion and wisdom and put on some pretense of trying to serve others, the chances are that we will wind up serving our own self-interest, while presenting an outer semblance of being purely altruistic.

We can take another analogy of spiders spinning their webs. They look like they're doing something so beautiful and intricate, but in fact they are just waiting to catch other insects and eat them. Whenever we start mixing Dharma and mundane things, like the eight mundane concerns, we run into this danger. When we lead our lives like a spider spinning a web, eventually we will be caught in our own webs.

> In that way meditate continually on the difficulty of obtaining human life. Your spiritual mentor should also explain in detail the reasons for the difficulty of obtaining human life. In short, *A Guide to the Bodhisattva Way of Life* states:

>> These leisures and endowments, so difficult to obtain, have been acquired, and they bring about the welfare of people. If one fails to take this favorable opportunity into consideration, how could this occasion occur again?

> A sūtra states:

>> It is possible that peas thrown against a wall might stick there, but they all fall to the ground.

Likewise, to see how difficult (human rebirth) is to obtain, look at the number of sentient beings.

A sūtra states:

> Śāriputra asked the Lord, 'Lord, how many beings are there in hell? And how many pretas, animals, demigods, gods, and humans are there?' The Lord replied, 'Śāriputra, the number of those in hell are like the earth; the number of pretas is like the grains of sand in a city built of sand; the number of animals is like the grain used in making alcohol; the number of demigods is like the flakes of snow in a blizzard; and the number of gods and humans is like the dust that can stay on the surface of a fingernail.'

Thus, you should know that this is very difficult to obtain. A sūtra states:

> The appearance of a buddha is rare and difficult to find, and birth as a human being is also very difficult to obtain. Such friends, faith, and the opportunity to listen to Dharma may not be obtained even in a hundred eons.

If it is difficult to obtain a human life of leisure and endowment, it should go without saying that the appearance of a buddha is also very rare and difficult to find. The reference to "friends," is to spiritual friends and holy beings such as bodhisattvas and so on; and the reference to "faith," is faith that serves as a cause for achieving enlightenment. They "may not be obtained even in a hundred eons."

> Thus, meditate in that way on the difficulty of obtaining a human life of leisure and endowment until your mind

turns away from the cycle of existence. If human life is so difficult to obtain, you must by all means imbue this present, unique opportunity with Dharma. Cultivate sincere compassion for these people who have obtained a pure human life but return from it empty-handed. If compassion does not arise when you see these worldly beings, the experience has not arisen. If sincere compassion is brought forth and enthusiasm increases, the experience has arisen. If enthusiasm does not increase, meditation is pointless. Meditate on this for three days, and then return!

The opportunity of Dharma is like living in a region of famine and suddenly coming upon a feast. If you came to a banquet, ate nothing, and then headed back into the wasteland, this would be really crazy. Similarly, we've been wandering in the cycle of existence for an immeasurably long period, and now we're in a situation in which we have access to causes for ourselves and others to achieve enlightenment. It would be madness to pass up this opportunity.

If you respond with jealousy, pride, anger, and the like when you see worldly beings engaging in various kinds of misdeeds, you still lack a genuine experience of Dharma. If sincere compassion is brought forth and perseverance[19] increases, such an experience has arisen. These are signs of Dharma having really arisen in one's mind-stream. In order for such sincere compassion to arise, focus on the fact that others experience joy and suffering just as you do, and that we all continue to suffer because we do not know the true causes of suffering and the true causes of happiness.

When people hear about Atiyoga, the Great Perfection, their eyes get really big and they listen very eagerly. Whereas, when the topic turns to the rarity and the preciousness of a human life, people show indifference. This is not a helpful attitude. When it comes to the cultivation of the Four Thoughts that Turn the Mind, our tendency is to kind of cover these over, like a cat covering its droppings in the sand. Now is the time to uncover these teachings and use them. In this modern age elderly men and women frequently try to conceal their age, and they really like it when other people tell them, "Oh, you look so young." It's all a sham. They're not young, they're old. What they should be doing is preparing for their death.

In terms of Dharma practice, it's very often the case that our friends and companions wind up being the greatest hindrances. On the one hand, spiritual friends may be our greatest aids; but they can also hinder us in our practice. Even our interrelationship with a spiritual teacher may be a hindrance to our practice. When we get obsessed with thinking, "The teacher said this" and "the teacher said that," it becomes a hindrance. Therefore, it's possible to accumulate causes for lower rebirth through our relationships with our teachers and friends. At the very least, try not to obstruct each other in your spiritual practice. If you can help each other, that's great; but, in any case, be careful not to hinder each other. In India, Tibet, and the United States I've seen many occasions in which companions obstruct each other in their spiritual practice. The bottom line is that it's really your own responsibility. You have to take control of yourself and show some backbone. For mundane things, we can be really very stubborn like donkeys, so it's time to be stubborn and have backbone when it comes to Dharma as well!

The extraordinary opportunity of Dharma is here and now. We are right now in the midst of a great Dharma banquet. It's a grave error to think that you're such a special person that only other people and not you need to practice this. I've heard people take this attitude in Tibet. Some lamas say, "Oh, I don't need to do it, but you people should do it." But we may ask such people, "Do you really have the power to overcome your afflictions and the sources of your suffering?" More often than not, such people are simply expressing their own egotism and foolishness.

By meditating like this on the difficulty of obtaining a human life of leisure and endowment, in the future you will obtain a human life, you will be freed from craving for this life, you will not think of anything but Dharma, and finally you will become a buddha. Practice this! The meditation on the difficulty of obtaining a human life of leisure and endowment is the second session in the *Natural Liberation through Contemplating: Experiential Instructions on the Transitional Processes.*

MEDITATING ON DEATH AND IMPERMANENCE

If you do not think about death and impermanence, the awareness that there is no time to waste will not arise in your mind-stream. If the awareness that there is no time to waste does not arise in your mind-stream, you will succumb to laziness and lassitude, and you will not think of Dharma. You will apply yourself to the activities of this life, and will indulge in indolence and complacency. If you slip into death with this ordinary attitude, your precious human life will have been squandered; so meditating on death and impermanence is extremely important. Once the awareness of impermanence has arisen in your mind-stream, you will have no time for lassitude. Earnestly bearing death in mind, Dharma will arise automatically; so meditate on impermanence.

On the one hand, we can say we all know that we're going to die. That's not news. However, we have not realized that the time of our death is totally unpredictable. We have not truly fathomed the reality of our own death. To take an example of a person who really understood the significance of death, recall the story of a meditator who had a small thornbush near the opening of the cave in which he practiced. One day as he was going to get some water, the thornbush scratched him on the way out, and he thought, "Oh, I need to cut that shrub so I don't get scratched every time I come in and out." As soon as that thought arose, he thought, "Ah, but if I spend my time doing that, might I die first? I guess I don't have time to do that." Gradually the thornbush grew bigger and bigger; and each time he went out, it scratched him. Again he would think, "Oh, I need to cut it," and then he would catch himself with the thought, "But, I don't have time." This went on and on; and eventually this meditator became a siddha, and the thornbush became a very, very large thornbush. So they both grew to maturity. From one perspective, you can say that the thornbush acted as a hindrance. It was an obstacle to his comfort. On the other hand, it acted to arouse his awareness of impermanence and thereby helped him in his practice.

That story stands in contrast to the nowadays common attitude of thinking, "It is very important to practice Dharma, but I have so many other important things to do." This attitude is an indication that we have not yet fathomed the reality of suffering. We have not yet meditated sufficiently on the significance of a human life of leisure and endowment, and we have not penetrated the reality of impermanence. Rather, with this type of mentality, we grasp onto that which is impermanent as being permanent and that which is unstable as being stable. As a result of this casual attitude, we don't get around to practicing Dharma; and, as a result of that, we don't achieve liberation. In the meantime, whatever Dharma we do practice ends up being artificial.

When people adopt this attitude, after a while they find that they're not making progress in their spiritual practice as they had hoped. Then it's common for them to conclude, "Oh, well, Buddhism isn't very effective." The problem is not that the Buddhadharma is ineffective, but rather that our mode of practice is ineffective. If you don't know how take medicine or if you don't take it at all, there's no way that you can validly conclude that the medicine doesn't work. The problem is one of not knowing how to take the essence of Dharma, and the associated problem is that one is subject to pride and to a sense of self-grasping. When these mental states are dominant, it's as if we imagine ourselves being in a very high place from which we look down on Dharma. If we can turn that around and place our ego beneath Dharma, then we naturally get good results.

The point of the practice is to subdue our own mind-streams. Generally speaking, and especially in the West, it is very common for people to think that, as soon as you become a Buddhist, this should somehow bring about an extraordinary transformation, like becoming a bodhisattva overnight. This isn't true for anything else in the world. For example, when entering school, you don't suddenly become a doctor or anything else. This occurs only gradually. However, not being aware of this, people sometimes point to a person and say, "Oh, this person's been a Buddhist for many years. How can he (or she) have done such and such?" This whole business of "many years" is not a big deal. We've been reinforcing our mental afflictions for many, many lifetimes. We're dealing with a veritable ocean of mental afflictions. Practicing Dharma for many years is all very well, but don't expect extraordinary, radical transformation even if you have practiced for a long time. Transformations take place little by little. It's misguided to expect that astonishing transformations will occur if you become a Buddhist and practice Dharma for a little while.

Even though you may have been a Buddhist for a long time, faults may persist; you must continue in your practice at your own pace. If a Buddhist who has been practicing for many years still engages in nonvirtues, is this a fault of Buddhism? I think not. These are simply human problems for which the Buddhadharma provides remedies. It's not a fault of Buddhism any more than it's the fault of, let's say, Christianity when some Christians who've been practicing their religion for many years also show certain faults. I feel this is not a fault of Christianity; these are simply human faults. Similarly, this is true for Hinduism, and so forth.

This whole attitude that spiritual practice or the practice of Buddhism in particular is some kind of a "push-button" procedure is in error, of course. Non-Buddhists are in error when they impose their expectations upon Buddhists, thinking that they must have achieved some very rapid, amazing spiritual progress. People who impose such expectations and judgments from the outside should come on in and test the water for themselves. Step in, try it, and see whether it's so easy to become a bodhisattva overnight just by snapping your fingers.

Whether or not we purify our mind-streams depends upon the cultivation of the Four Thoughts that Turn the Mind and meditation upon the Four Noble Truths. This is crucial for purifying the mind. It is from these contemplations, too, that the spirit of awakening arises. Be it a genuine spirit of awakening or even some facsimile, it arises from such meditations. Likewise, the degree of faith that we have in the Buddha, Dharma, Sangha, and so on stems from our understanding of the Four Thoughts that Turn the Mind and the Four Noble Truths. If you lack this understanding, you have no foundation for Dharma practice.

With regard to khenpos, tulkus, lamas, monks, teachers, and so forth, if such people truly have the spirit of awakening, this indicates that they already have a thorough understanding of the Four Thoughts that Turn the Mind and of the Four Noble Truths. If they have this, it implies that they are without attachment for their own side and aversion to others. It implies, too, that they are endowed with compassion and faith. Even though there are lamas, teachers, khenpos, tulkus, and so forth who have such qualities and such purity, it's very difficult for us to be able to see it and ascertain it for ourselves. What we tend to see is faults. Because we ourselves have faults, we tend to see faults in others. Therefore, even if we were to encounter a pure person, it would be very difficult for us to recognize that person as being pure. For example, even if Buddha Śākyamuni were to arrive right now, the chances are we would be able to find fault with him. Or if Padmasambhava were to walk in the door right now and we watched his behavior, we might conclude, "Oh, he's a playboy." Or if Buddha Śākyamuni were to arrive, we might think, "Oh, a skinhead!" We have all these preset conceptual constructs. These projections come from our own faults. If it's possible for us to perceive faults in beings who are utterly pure, then it goes without question that we will become really fixated on faults of other people who may, in fact, have some faults. Rumors abound. For example, there was a story some time ago that His Holiness the Dalai Lama had some Western woman as a girlfriend, which, of course, is a complete fabrication. In fact, it seems His Holiness never even met the woman in question. However, such rumors have been passed around, whether by the

Communists or due to some kind of a sectarian rivalry, who knows? This type of mud-slinging can come from sectarianism, from Communism, or from politics. The point is, though, that each of us needs to free ourselves from faults. From the perspective of His Holiness and any other sane person, people who start such rumors are simply viewed with compassion.

Other people's faults are not really our business, and we don't need to concern ourselves with them. It is most important for us to focus on the Four Thoughts that Turn the Mind, for these actually liberate ourselves and others. We need to rid ourselves of the casual attitude that we're going to be around indefinitely, and to transform our minds so that we have no time for the eight mundane concerns. When the text says "you will apply yourself to activities of this life," it refers specifically to these eight worldly concerns. Wouldn't it be a great loss if we were to miss such an opportunity to practice the Dharma and then simply lose it without a trace? If somebody steals a thousand dollars from you, you would feel, "Oh, I've lost so much! What a loss! What a tragedy! What a waste!" We're presently endowed with this life that can act as a cause for joy, both in this lifetime as well as in future lifetimes, and yet we don't value this opportunity as much as we value money. Moreover, sometimes we even help waste each other's time through engaging in nonvirtue and so forth.

Sometimes entering Dharma is like coming to a door without having a key and wondering, "How do I get in?" By meditating on death and impermanence, the door of Dharma opens by itself.

> Meditate in places such as this: Go by yourself, with no companions, up to a remote region where there are no people passing by, a disagreeable and depressing place where there are dark, craggy peaks of piled-up rock and bits of rubble as your companions, where the wind makes a rustling sound in the grass, with the sun rolling down from the sky, and mountain creeks thundering downward. Or else go to charnel grounds where there are a lot of human corpses lying around, with little

fragments of legs and arms, flesh, bones, and skin, where foxes are howling, ravens are stalking around, owls are making their rattling calls, the wind is moaning, and foxes and wolves are pulling back and forth on the corpses. Go by yourself to such a place that is terrifying, depressing, creepy, and frightening. Or if that is not possible, imagine such a place. The place makes a great difference, for by going to such a spot and meditating, an awareness of impermanence will arise automatically. So, it is very important.

Here in the West, we make a big deal about sunsets and so forth. Another way of looking at a sunset is that it's just another sign of your life passing by. Also, in America cemeteries tend to be really cheerful and nice places with lots of flowers and so forth. If you really want to find something closer to the charnel grounds mentioned in the text, you can go to India.

Once you have gone there, sit in a cross-legged posture, and clasp the bottom of your knees with your palms, or else sit in the posture of despair like before. Withdraw your mind and earnestly follow this line of thought: "Oh dear! What is this? In terms of the external universe, the world is impermanent. These seasons are passing with each moment. Summer and winter, autumn and spring, and so on gradually change and pass on. And even during this single day, morning, afternoon, and night change and pass on. Time does not remain still even from one period to the next, but passes on. Sentient beings, who are the inhabitants of the universe, are impermanent. My own father and mother, old men and women, my countrymen, neighbors, companions of my own age, and all my enemies and friends are also impermanent; and one by one they will die. People in different phases of life, from infancy, childhood, adulthood, old age, until death, do not remain the same for even a moment, but change and gradually pass on. All sentient beings who have been born are near death. There are those who were present last year but are gone this year, those who were alive this year but gone yesterday, and those who were here in the morning but gone by nightfall. All are of the nature of impermanence. Now death will soon come to me, too. Such is the swift passing of numbers of years, months, and days. Will there be causes for me to remain in this present body until next year? Let alone that, given the absence of assurance in my own life, will I die tomorrow or the day after? As there is no certainty concerning the time of death, there is no time for me to remain as usual; so if my human life were to dwindle away in the course of idling away the time, what a waste that would be! I am sure of the certainty of death. While I have not died yet, there is no one who has escaped death, so death is certain. Since the body is a composite, death is again certain; and since this life passes on without remaining even a moment, death is certain. Like a creek flowing down a steep mountainside, or like an animal that is being led to the slaughter, I am steadfastly approaching death.

Even in the course of one hour, you can see the minutes ticking by. As a person grows up, one is called an infant, a young child, an adolescent, and so forth. These are labels for the process of change moving toward death. All of us right now are alive, but everyone will die and become a corpse. In a way, we're already corpses in the preparation, so our present environment is already a cemetery of sorts. Consequently, do you really need to go elsewhere? In terms of Vajrayāna, the six types of consciousness are discussed as being a charnel ground. The White House, in Washington, D.C., is one more charnel ground. Nowadays, the Potala, His Holiness the Dalai Lama's palace in Lhasa, is also a charnel ground.

When the text says "remain as usual," it means remaining

with one's earlier habituations regarding the three nonvirtues of the body, the four of the speech, and the three of the mind.

> While death is certain, the time of death is unpredictable. As there is no guarantee that my life will continue for any given period, the time of death is unpredictable. Moreover, as there are very many circumstances resulting in death, the time of death is unpredictable. Moreover, as the body has no essence, the time of death is unpredictable. So there is no time to idle away the years.
>
> When I am beginning to die, no one will be able to hold me back, there will be no defense, no one will help me. The wealth I have accumulated will not help at death; my children, wife, and assembled relatives will not help me at death; and not even my own body will help at death. My body itself will be left behind, cremated, and will drift upwards in the form of ashes. Even the ashes will be carried away by the wind, and there is no telling where they will go. The wealth I have accumulated will be left behind, and I shall not be able to take even a single needle with me. I will be separated from each of my assembled relatives, for now I must head out on a long road on which I shall not meet with them again. I shall not be able to bring even a single companion with me. Now I am about to come to the time when I must helplessly proceed alone, with no companion, so how can there be any time to remain in lassitude? How can there be any time for the activities of this life? Oh dear! From today onward I shall practice virtue, and right from today I shall reject sin. Then when I face death, my mind will be at ease, and thereafter I shall reach the path. Wretched me! Oh what fear!

Not even Amitāyus, the Buddha of Long Life, can help you at death; and if he can't help you, who else can? Even people of great power and influence can do nothing to hold you back from death. Even having millions of dollars will not help you at the point of death. Even having a lot of wives, all of them beautiful, still would not help you.

It has been the custom in India and elsewhere to cremate dead bodies. In Tibet, it was also very common to cut up corpses and give them to vultures to eat. Here in America, it's more common to bury them in the ground so that they become food for worms. Whatever you do with the body, it finally decomposes. Even if you've accumulated a whole world full of wealth, there's nothing you can take with you. You usually develop a lot of attachment for your possessions; and, by so doing, you can accumulate causes for lower rebirth. However, not "a single needle" can be taken with you after death. Right now, we're knocking on the portal of death.

> Pondering in that way, utter these words many times in a mournful voice such that they vividly arouse your mindfulness: "Alas! Alas! Wretched me! Composite things are impermanent. The days and nights are stealing away my life. The time of death is unpredictable. How fortunate that I have not yet died! Now death is about to arrive."

For beings who are in one of the miserable states of existence, death may not be such a bad prospect. It might actually be preferable, because they may be released from that realm. Within human existence, I am aware of people who have been tortured in prisons and have spent many years in prisons where their lives are a continual stream of misery. From my own personal experience, such people really look forward to death because it will bring an end to the suffering they're having to experience in life. However, if such people have lived nonvirtuous lives, then their release from this type of suffering might just make way for even worse suffering. There's no guarantee. On the other hand, if their lives on the whole have been virtuous, then when they die in prison, this wouldn't really be such a bad thing. Generally speaking, the rest of us, who are not in concentration camps and are not being tortured, fear death.

Vividly arouse your mindfulness by uttering these words, and mentally imagine the following: "I have arrived in a land without having any idea where I have gone. That area faces north. It is dark in color. There are no movements or voices of humans. Water is flowing down with a rushing sound. The wind is howling. The grass is rustling. The sun is rolling down over the mountain peaks. Mountains of rock glisten in purple hues. Ravens are croaking. I have arrived in such a place, without having any idea as to where I am. I have no friend or companion. I have never been here before. I must wander in a daze, with no sense of where I am bound. Verbally I utter these words: 'Alas! Wretched me! Oh dear! Alas! Wretched me! Oh dear! With no companion I am wandering alone in an empty land. I have no idea of where I am bound. Where is my homeland? Where are my father and mother? Where are my children and possessions? When will I arrive at my homeland? Alas! Wretched me! I'm so depressed.' Speaking those words out loud, I aimlessly wander about in a daze. After a while, I come to the edge of a ravine and fall over. With arms flailing, after a while I grab onto a clump of grass on the face of the cliff. Tightly holding onto to it, I tremble with fear. Looking down, there is a bottomless abyss; and looking up, I am aware of the sky. The rock is slick like a mirror and immense. The wind is howling. Upon falling into such a predicament, a white rat emerges from a crack in the rock to the right of the clump of grass, snips off a blade from the clump of grass and carries it away. A black rat comes out from a crack in the rock to the left, snips off a blade from the clump of grass and carries it away. The two do this alternately, and the clump of grass gets smaller and smaller. I find no way to resist against the rats, and I'm terrified of dying. I quake with fright and horror, and I think, 'Now death is upon me. There's no place to escape. I have no Dharma, for in the past I did not think of dying. I'm afraid of the place I am bound. It never occurred to me that I would die today, but now death will descend on me at once. Now, from today onward, I will be separated from my homeland, children, possessions, relatives, compatriots, neighbors, classmates, and friends; and I shall never meet with them again. The belongings I've accumulated will be left behind; and from today onward I must go on a long journey to an unfamiliar place that I've never experienced before. Oh, what is the best way to be freed from this fear? Where is it? What shall I do? Oh dear!'"

The analogy of the rats eating the grass symbolizes the days and nights snipping away the duration of our lives. When we have the the perfect opportunity to practice Dharma and yet fail to take advantage of it, it is because we fail to think about dying.

Thinking thus, clearly utter these words out loud: "Oh dear, I'm afraid! Oh dear, death is approaching! Now death is coming soon. I must go alone, with no companion. I must go far away. I must go to an unknown place. I must cross over a great pass. What can I do to be free? If there is a way, I shall do it. Oh dear, I'm afraid!" While you are crying out these words, imagine in the sky above you, your own primary spiritual mentor upon a lotus and moon, holding a *ḍamaru* and bell. He is dancing about, wearing the six kinds of bone ornaments. Imagine him saying this to you: "Alas! This composite entity is impermanent and will soon be destroyed. The external four seasons are impermanent, they change, and pass on. The elderly, enemies, and friends die and part ways. Youths and adults change with each year, month, and day. This life swiftly passes by like a stream flowing down a steep mountain. You were foolish to go on without knowing you would die. Now impermanence and death are about to arrive. There is no way to avert this death. Look at this present to see whether there is a way to avert it. Now there is no time to waste—revere your spiritual mentor!" As soon as you hear these words, consider, "Alas! Before encountering such a death there was Dharma for me to practice, but until now I have not practiced Dharma. How I regret it! Now whether I am to live or whether I am to die, the jewel of the spiritual mentor knows. If the precious spiritual mentor has compassion, why doesn't he liberate me from this great precipice? My father, precious spiritual mentor, knows."

If we do not practice Dharma, we will regret it. What do you think about this? Do you think the text is being redundant about the nature of death and impermanence? Is this a problem of Buddhism that it emphasizes death? It's not Buddhism's problem; it's our problem. Buddhism is simply calling attention to some salient characteristics of our existence. This is our problem and the problem of all sentient beings. As sentient beings, we are subject to death and impermanence.

Once I was teaching on this theme and the whole issue of the suffering of saṃsāra in Los Angeles, and people asked, "Is this what Buddhism is really about? Is it just about suffering? Is it a religion of suffering?" No, this is not a characteristic of Buddhism. This is a description of the very nature of our daily lives. If we allow our lives to be dominated by attachment, with no thought of death, this desperate type of death is the natural result. To counteract that, the time has come to engage in these main sequential practices of hearing, thinking, and meditation. The gist of this instruction is to get rid of your mental afflictions and cultivate virtue.

> Simply by bringing forth powerful faith and devotion with such sincere reflection, imagine that an essence of light-rays from the spiritual mentor's heart strikes you; and at the same time that the clump of grass is gone, that rays of light instantly lift you up and you arrive in Sukhāvatī. Then incalculable rays of light emanate from your heart and bring every single sentient being of the

three realms to Sukhāvatī. Powerfully cultivate compassion for all sentient beings. The spiritual mentor should also give a detailed explanation of the reasons for death and impermanence. In that way ponder death and impermanence and bring forth a sense of disillusionment.

In short, a sūtra states:

> A place in which composites are permanent is not be found. All composites are impermanent, but do not grieve, Ānanda.

The *Descent into Lankā Sūtra* states:

> Human life is like a stream swiftly flowing down a steep mountain.

Mahāyāna Yoga states:

> Wherever you go, a region where there is no death is not found on the mountain peaks, nor in the depths of the ocean. This body is subject to destruction, like a clay pot. It is like something borrowed, and there is nothing in it that is immutable.

The body is like something borrowed from the four elements. It's just on loan.

The Set of Aphorisms states:

> Some are seen to die in the womb, and some die at the spot where they are born; likewise, some die in infancy, some when they are old, some when they are young, and some die upon reaching adulthood. They all gradually proceed on to

death, and who can maintain the assurance of staying alive with the comment, 'This person is young'?

It's all very well to say, "This person is young" or "This person is healthy." However, where is there any guarantee that a person who is young and healthy will even be alive tomorrow?

A sūtra states:

Like a prisoner being led to his execution, with each step we approach death.

Nāgārjuna says:

Many are the causes contributing to death, and few are the causes contributing to life. Even the causes supporting life may turn into circumstances leading to death. So always strive in the Dharma.

It often happens that conditions intended to support life turn into the circumstances leading to death. For example, people sometimes take medication to try to get over disease, and the medication ends up killing them. Likewise, people do other things to try to protect their lives, and those very acts sometimes lead to their demise.

The *Crown Jewels Sūtra* states:

Friends, while this life is impermanent, passing swiftly like a brook crashing down a steep mountain, foolish people do not realize it, and the unwise are intoxicated by the vanities of desires.

The term "vanities of desires" refers specifically to our attachment to the eight mundane concerns and they include feelings of pomposity and self-importance that commonly arise when we feel we're on top of the world.

A sūtra states:

> The *māra* of the lord of death is like someone waiting in ambush. Birth, aging, sickness, and death are like the revolutions of a water mill. In this world, there is no one—neither the great nor the humble, the poor nor the rich—who does not fall into the hands of the lord of death.

And:

> Each one of the elderly who died in the past constantly acquired children and possessions, but their progeny and wealth were of little benefit to them in their next lives.

Generations upon generations of people—including our grandparents, their grandparents, their grandparents, and so on—have applied themselves throughout the whole course of their lives to the eight mundane concerns, to the acquisition of material goods, to children, and so forth. Each generation does this, but each one leaves all its possessions and wealth to the next generation. Not only are these acquisitions of no benefit to these people at death, but they can actually hurt them. In the process of accumulating these possessions, people commonly engage in many nonvirtues. This has been true in the past, and it is true in the present. Among us, many people in our present generation are applying themselves to these same goals and will also end up the same as those in the past. We, too, shall die.

With all these references to children, some people may be thinking, "I don't have any children, so I'm not the person being addressed here." If you think you're so smart, then practice Dharma.

"Thus, as we are impermanent and pass on without pausing even for an instant, there is no time for remaining in laziness." In this way cite many quotes from the sūtras and tantras and bring forth disillusionment. By meditating on problems of such impermanence and death, you will experientially understand that all the affairs of the world are impermanent; and in particular, your mind-stream will become calm, enthusiasm for Dharma will arise, and so forth.

We shouldn't be satisfied simply with one very small teaching but instead should think at length about the many types of suffering in the cycle of existence and the significance and reality of death. Think about it in many ways and draw on many sources to enrich your understanding and awareness of it. All of the Buddha's teachings from the pinnacle teachings of the Atiyoga down to the most basic fundamentals of the Hīnayāna are designed to bring us liberation. Nevertheless, many of you really wake up and listen with a lot of interest only when Atiyoga, or the Great Perfection, is taught. However, you need to focus on these teachings first. First you must establish a good foundation by turning your mind away from the cycle of existence. Meditate on impermanence and the nature of actions and their consequences—the law of karma. By meditating upon these, a fine foundation will be established for the more advanced teachings and practices, and the afflictions of jealousy, attachment, aversion, and so forth will be calmed.

All the eighty-four thousand collections of the Buddha's teachings and, more specifically, all the six hundred and forty thousand Atiyoga tantras, are designed to protect us from the sufferings of the cycle of existence. This suffering is not a fabrication. The suffering to which we are subject and the suffering that is of the nature of the cycle of existence are not insignificant or trifling. This is why we need to focus on it and to recognize the full depth and extent of the suffering to which we are subject. Upon recognizing this, our attachment will gradually decline. With the attenuation of attachment, aversion will also decline. It's through such gradual progress that we can expect to achieve liberation.

You may wonder whether you need to study all the eighty-four thousand collections of teachings or all the six hundred and forty thousand Atiyoga tantras. If you have the time, the enthusiasm, and the ability to do so, that's good. But by and large, we don't have time for that, so we need to focus on their essence. One way to grasp the essence of these teachings is, first of all, to contemplate the Four Thoughts that Turn the Mind. Then, if you are to enter into the practice of Vajrayāna, you must receive Vajrayāna teachings, empowerment, and so on. You meditate upon a specific chosen deity. If you meditate well on one chosen deity, this acts as a key to all the rest. Thus, you don't need to engage in a wide variety of practices. Do one well, and it will act as a key to the rest. You will find teachings on emptiness in the Atiyoga teachings, and the realization of emptiness is the primary cause of achieving buddhahood.

> If the desires of this life increase and you cannot remain in solitude even though you have meditated on impermanence, continue meditating until the experience arises. This is the vital essence of all Dharmas. If you do not have success in this, meditative experience will not arise, so it is important that you apply yourself to this. Anyone of superior or inferior faculties will be liberated with this point, so diligence in this is important. Meditate until you weep tears of compassion at the sight of sentient beings who are unmindful of death. Meditate on this for three days, and then return.

> By meditating in that way, in the near term you will attain bountiful happiness, and finally you will become a buddha. Practice this! The meditation on death and impermanence is the third session in the *Natural Liberation through Contemplating: Experiential Instructions on the Transitional Processes.*

> Those three are the preliminaries for subduing your

own mind-stream. At the outset it is extremely important that you gain certainty concerning these three. If you do not gain a foothold in them, you will slip in all other Dharmas. Until the awareness of impermanence constantly and vividly arises as if your heart had been pierced by the arrows of those points, continue meditating. Samaya.

Practice this! May the preliminary practices for subduing your own mind-stream not vanish until the cycle of existence is empty. These "Preliminary Practices for Subduing Your Own Mind-stream" in the *Natural Liberation through Contemplating: Experiential Instructions on the Six Transitional Processes* are teachings of the tradition of Chöje, the spiritual son of the tertön Karma Lingpa. Due to this, which was put in writing by Guru Nyida Özer, may the revelation of the Buddha grow and flourish in all times and places, and may they long be preserved.

Maṇgalam bhavatu!
(May there be virtues!)

2

The Natural Liberation of the Mind-itself: The Four-Session Yoga of Spiritual Activity of the Secret Mantra Vajrayāna

THE PRECEDING TEACHINGS DISCUSS the common preliminaries, and now we move on to the uncommon, or extraordinary, preliminaries.

> In the *Natural Liberation through Contemplating the Peaceful and Wrathful* it is well to practice in accordance with these preliminary practices for training your own mind-stream.

The following practice, which is written in beautiful metered verse in Tibetan, would commonly be recited in the monasteries in Tibet. When I was a young boy, early in the morning monks would come around chanting this. It was a way to prevent people from sleeping in, and they had a special way of chanting it which was very melodious.

> Alas! Wretched me! O fortunate child of good breeding![20]
> Without succumbing to the influence of ignorance and
>   delusion,
> Bring forth the power of enthusiasm and get up now!
> From beginningless time until now
> You may have remained fast asleep due to ignorance,
> But now do not sleep; apply your body, speech, and
>   mind to the Dharma.

If there were real benefit in leading a lethargic way of life, we should already have benefited by now because we've had plenty of experience doing that since beginningless time. Enough is enough. Now is the time to set aside sleep and apply ourselves to the Dharma. Why not just sleep in, hang out, and live a casual life? Since beginningless time, we have succumbed to such foolishness; and the result is that we've developed behavorial patterns to cover up our own faults and point our fingers at other people's faults. Sometimes we even see faults in others where there aren't any faults at all. In this way we remain subject to the sufferings of birth, aging, sickness, and death.

> Are you unaware of the sufferings of birth, aging, sickness,
>   and death?
> There is no permanent circumstance even today.
> The time has come to bring forth enthusiasm for practice.
> Now alone is the occasion for accomplishing eternal bliss;
> It is no time for remaining with an attitude of lassitude.

This "attitude of lassitude" is one of procrastination, thinking, "Well, I really can't get around to Dharma today, but later on when circumstances are more conducive, I will really apply myself to it. In the meantime, I've got more pressing concerns." Now there is no time for such procrastination; rather focus on the essence of the practice, especially emphasizing the Four Thoughts that Turn the Mind.

> Think of death, and bring your practice to its culmination.
> There is no time to waste in life, and the circumstances
>   that lead to death are beyond imagination.
> Then if you fail to achieve the confidence of fearlessness,
> What is the point of your being alive?

In the innumerable circumstances that lead to death, our lives are like a flame flickering in the wind that can be blown out at any time. There is especially no time to waste in turning around the habit of finding fault in others and covering up our own faults. The point of Dharma is, first of all, to encounter the fear of death and then to surmount that fear. There one finds the fruit of Dharma. If we fail even to progress toward that, what is the point of our existence? What gives our human life meaning? We may as well be animals. What's the difference? If we fail to achieve such confidence through the application of Dharma, then we don't accomplish our own self-interest and we simply forget about the interest of others.

> Phenomena are identityless, empty, and free of conceptual
>   elaboration,
> Like an illusion, a mirage, a dream, a reflection,
> A city of *gandharvas*, and an echo.
> Know that the phenomena of the cycle of existence and
>   of liberation
> Are like the ten illusory analogies of known objects,
>   including
> The moon in water, a bubble, an optical illusion, and a
>   phantom.

Counteract your inborn grasping to the true existence of yourself and other phenomena as if everything had its own intrinsic identity. All phenomena of saṃsāra and nirvāṇa, including ourselves, are like these ten analogies.

> Phenomena are by nature unborn,
> They are unpreserved and unceasing, without going or
>   coming.
> Nonobjective and signless, they are inconceivable and
>   inexpressible.
> The time has come to fathom that reality.

There is no way to grasp any phenomena completely in terms of the three times—past, present, and future—or in any other way by means of either words or thought.

> *Namo gurubhyaḥ! Namo devebhyaḥ! Namo ḍākinībhyaḥ!*
> Alas! Alas! The impermanent phenomena of the cycle of
>   existence

Are an inescapable, deep ocean of karma.
Alas for every sentient being who is afflicted by karma!
Bless us that the ocean of suffering may dry up!

If we look at our own situation in this cycle of existence, we can ask, "Why do we suffer? What is it about this deep ocean of karma that makes it inescapable?" The reason it's inescapable is that we have made it inescapable for ourselves. By engaging in nonvirtuous actions and grasping onto the self as something very precious, we bring great disgrace upon ourselves. Karma simply means action, but specifically action that is imbued with a deluded sense of self, of the objects of actions, and so forth. When we suffer, we need to know that fundamentally we have brought our suffering upon ourselves through our previous actions in this or in previous lifetimes. Finally, it is not a matter of pointing our fingers at others and blaming them for the suffering we experience.

The "ocean of suffering," refers especially to the ocean of our own mental afflictions, so the prayer that this ocean of suffering may dry up refers to the extinction of the ocean of our own mental afflictions. The way to make this ocean dry up is through such practices as hearing, thinking, and meditation.

At the death of Mao Tse Tung, His Holiness the Dalai Lama spoke of his passing before a large crowd of Tibetans and he had a large religious ceremony done on Mao's behalf. He said that now that Mao had passed away from life, he was to be viewed with compassion. In fact, when His Holiness was speaking of Mao's death, there were tears in his eyes because of his great compassion for this man. He asked the Tibetan people to dedicate the virtue of their practice to Mao's benefit. What had Mao done to deserve this kind of attention and compassion from His Holiness? What he had done was systematically destroy the monasteries, the statues, and the books of Dharma in Tibet. He had done his utmost to annihilate all of the representations of Buddha and Dharma in Tibet. In terms of the people of Tibet, Mao had perpetrated genocide, and tremendous suffering was inflicted fundamentally due to his policies. Not only was this suffering inflicted upon the people of Tibet, but upon the people of China as well. A tremendous amount of suffering can be traced back to Mao and his regime. When we hear about such a person or government that inflicts such great suffering, our natural response is one of anger; whereas, when His Holiness the Dalai Lama views this, he simply realizes that this was the Tibetans' karma, and people who engage in such terribly detrimental actions are worthy of our compassion.

When we judge people as usual, saying, "That's my enemy" or "this is a bad person," we're constructing other people in these ways. When we conceive of others in this fashion, we reap the harvest from our own thoughts. What we send out, we receive back. Was His Holiness's response to Mao's death faulty or virtuous? It was a virtuous response. When the spirit of awakening truly ripens in one's mind-stream, that is the type of response that arises—a response characteristic of a true follower of the Buddha. You may think it's naive, but that's how a Buddhist should respond.

> Beings who are afflicted by ignorance and karma
> Engage in deeds of suffering due to their desire for happiness.
> Alas for every sentient being who is unskilled in methods!

Every sentient being wishes for happiness, and everyone wishes to be free of suffering. Yet, however passionately one may desire these fruits of happiness and freedom from suffering, they cannot be attained without knowing the effective methods for bringing about such results. Beings who are ignorant of these methods are worthy of compassion.

> Bless us that mental afflictions, karma, and obscurations may be purified!
> In this prison of selfish desires and dualistic grasping,
> We are like a deer that returns to a snare in which it has already been trapped.

If a deer gets caught in a snare, it's not likely that it will be caught again in the same snare. It will learn from its mistakes. In this regard, we are more foolish than deer because, in terms of selfish desires and the dualistic grasping of "I am," we fall into the same trap again and again. We repeatedly suffer without learning how to avoid returning to the same snare.

> Alas for every sentient being who is subject to ignorance and delusion!
> Bless us that we may emerge from the pit of the cycle of existence!
> In these six inescapable cities of karma[21]
> It is as if we move from one blade of a water mill to the next.
> Pity every sentient being in this inescapable cycle of existence!
> Bless us that the entrances of birth into the six realms may be cut off!

When the Buddha Śākyamuni first turned the Wheel of Dharma, he began by teaching the Four Noble Truths. The gist of the Four Noble Truths concerns the nature of actions and their consequences, with advice on how to avoid actions that lead to suffering and how to engage in actions that lead to the cessation of suffering. Most people do not heed this advice. All the eighty-four thousand collections of teachings of the Buddha address this same theme. After the Buddha there have been many great disciples, sages, and contemplatives in his tradition who have composed their own works by the thousands. They, too, tell us what actions lead to misery and bondage and what actions lead to joy and freedom. But most people still don't listen. Likewise, Padmasambhava came to Tibet and he taught how to avoid suffering and to find immutable happiness. His twenty-five great disciples and the one hundred and eight treasure-revealers again showed the way to liberation. Our present spiritual mentors are also showing us the path leading to joy and the path leading to suffering. We often feel that we know better than these mentors, that we know what's really best, what things are helpful to people, and what things will help to preserve the Dharma. So we come up with various excuses for not following the counsel of our spiritual mentors.

The great enlightened beings are like people who have eyes in comparison with we who are blind. Enlightened beings know what needs to be avoided and what needs to be practiced for our own well-being and for the well-being of others. These enlightened beings are endowed with the two types of knowledge: ontological and phenomenological.[22] They are like adults, and we are like children. Yet, we still tend to hold stubbornly to our own views and opinions. People say that donkeys are really stubborn, but even donkeys can't compare to us. We can check for ourselves to see whether the above comments are true. We don't need to blindly accept them as dogma. Instead of being "force fed," we can observe our response and behavior and see for ourselves. Is it true that we are stuck in old behavioral patterns and excuses?

Many of us have taken various tantric pledges. We are told what entails an infraction of these pledges, how to keep them, what benefits arise by keeping them, and what the disadvantages are of allowing them to degenerate. All of this is to help us. Unfortunately, often people do not even accomplish their own self-interest with respect to the pledges that they've taken. We may wonder about obstacles and interferences that arise in the course of our practice. When we break our pledges or damage the relationships with our spiritual mentor, chosen deity, Dharma protectors, ḍākinīs, and so on, problems and intereferences to our practice occur as swift retribution for our misdeeds. It's not the spiritual mentors or the buddhas who are punishing us, but the Dharma protectors. They bring immediate retribution. What are Dharma protectors protecting? They're trying to protect us from nonvirtue, and the way they do that is to attempt to bring us back to Dharma when we go off on the wrong track. By experiencing the suffering of such obstacles, we are protected from having to experience the long-term karmic consequences of our misdeeds, such as taking rebirth in some miserable state of existence. This is the task of the protectors, and actions we take against our pledges are the origin of a lot of the obstacles that we experience in the course of our practice. Therefore, when we encounter obstacles, there's no reason to wonder, "Why me?" Instead, think, and see how the obstacles relate to your own behavior.

There are two types of protectors: supramundane, or the thoroughly enlightened protectors, and mundane, or unenlighted, protectors. The latter are simply sentient beings who are committed to preserving the Buddha's Dharma and to guarding those who are following this Dharma. It's the mundane protectors who inflict retributions on us for our misdeeds.

> However much we witness the sufferings of birth, aging, sickness, and death,
> We fear not, but remain undaunted.
> This life of leisure and endowment runs out in the course of our distractions.
> Bless us that we may be mindful of impermanence and death!

In the face of birth, aging, sickness, and death, it's as if we have such courage that we can just bear all this suffering and thereby justify idling away the hours, days, months, and years.

> Not knowing that impermanent things are unreliable,
> We still crave and cling to this cycle of existence.
> Human life passes in suffering while we yearn for joy.
> Bless us that we may cease craving the cycle of existence!

Both students and teachers may still cling to saṃsāra, and due to this attachment, we fail to sow the actual seeds of joy.

> The inanimate physical world is impermanent and is destroyed by fire and water.
> The sentient beings of the animate world are impermanent, our minds being separated from our bodies [at death].

The seasons of summer, winter, autumn, and spring are
impermanent.
Bless us that disillusionment may arise from the depths
of our hearts!

This is a brief reference to Buddhist cosmology, which discusses
the course of cosmic evolution in terms of the creation of world
systems and their destruction by fire, water, and so forth.

Last year, this year, and the beginnings and ends of the
seasons,
And every moment of the days and nights are imperma-
nent.
If this is well considered, we will see that death will
reach us.
Bless us that we may rise to courage in our practice.
While this life of leisure and endowment is very hard to
obtain,
Alas for those who are without Dharma and return
empty-handed
When struck by the malady of the lord of death.
Bless us that there will arise in our mind-streams the
awareness that there is no time to waste!
Alas! Wretched me! Precious Compassionate One!
May the Victor,[23] endowed with merciful compassion,
Bless us right now that we may be delivered
From the sufferings of the six states of existence!

Throughout our entire existence in the cycle of existence, we're
not overlooked by the buddhas. Rather, the buddhas, bodhisattvas, and our spiritual mentors have explained to us the
nature of saṃsāra and the way to be free of suffering. It's not that
they haven't told us, but rather that we have ignored their counsel. We are like people who, when the sun rises, turn their faces
to the west, so there's no mystery as to why the sun of the buddhas' wisdom doesn't shine in our faces.

GOING FOR OUTER, INNER, AND SECRET REFUGE

> I bow and take refuge in the spiritual mentors
> Who constantly bear in mind
> The limitless sentient beings of the three realms[24] and six
>   states of existence,
> In the past, the present, and the future.
> I bow and take refuge in the buddhas,
> The blessed *sugatas*[25] of the ten directions and the four
>   times,
> The foremost among people, endowed with the signs and
>   symbols of spiritual awakening,
> Whose enlightened deeds are inexhaustible and as vast as
>   space.

When taking refuge in the Buddha, you should bear in mind that you are not simply taking refuge in Buddha Śākyamuni, the historical Buddha, but in the buddhas of the past, present, and future throughout the ten directions. In terms of the sugatas of the four times, the fourth time is utterly transcendent time.

> I bow and take refuge in the sublime Dharmas,
> The Dharma of ultimate truth, free of attachment to
>   quietism,
> The irreversible path of the three yānas,
> The scriptures, treasures, oral transmissions, and practical
>   instructions.

The three yānas are the Hīnayāna, Mahāyāna and Vajrayāna. The scriptures are also called *kama* (Tib. *bka' ma*), while the treasures are called terma (Tib. *gter ma*). The term oral transmissions is clear, and later contemplatives and scholars gave practical instructions associated with the scriptures and the treasures.

> I bow and take refuge in the sanghas,
> The field of supreme assemblies who dwell on the

unmistaken path,

The assembly of *āryas*, [26] who are utterly free of the
taints of mental afflictions,

The bodhisattvas, *śrāvakas*, and *pratyekabuddhas*, who are
the supreme upholders of the Victor's revelation.

I bow and take refuge in the spiritual mentors,

Who are of the very nature of all the buddhas of the
three times,

The chiefs of all the secret, unsurpassable maṇḍalas,

Who, with blessings and compassion, guide all beings.

I bow and take refuge in the chosen deities,

Whom the Dharmakāya, unborn and free of the
extremes of conceptual elaboration,

Emanates as peaceful and wrathful deities for the sake of
the world,

Bestowing the supreme and common *siddhis*.

The relationship between the unborn Dharmakāya and the emanations of the peaceful and wrathful deities is like that of the sun
and the rays emanating from it. The peaceful and wrathful deities
bestow the supreme and common siddhis only when they are
actualized, or realized.

I bow and take refuge in the assembly of ḍākinīs,

Who move in the space of reality-itself with the power of
compassion,

Who bestow supreme bliss from a pure abode,

And grant siddhis to those who maintain their samayas.

The Tibetan term for ḍākinī is *khandro-ma*. *Kha* means space, *dro*
is to go, and *ma* indicates the feminine gender. Literally, a ḍākinī is
a female space-goer. "Space" here refers to the absolute nature of
reality. Ḍākinīs have realized that ultimate truth, they dwell and
function in the awareness of that reality, and they never waver from
it. That's the etymology of the term *ḍākinī*: they move about in the
space of reality-itself, the absolute nature of reality.

Are all female buddhas ḍākinīs? The wisdom aspect of any buddha is a ḍākinī, and the method aspect of a buddha is personified as a *ḍāka*, the male counterpart of a ḍākinī. In terms of the deity and consort, the male deity is the embodiment of the method aspect of enlightenment, and the consort is the embodiment of the wisdom aspect of enlightenment.

> I take refuge in the originally pure essence, nature, and compassion
>> In primordial emptiness, free of conceptual elaboration;
> And I take refuge in the state of nongrasping, which transcends the intellect,
> In the nature of the great, vast expanse of homogenous perfection.

In this case, that which is taking refuge and that in which one takes refuge both transcend the intellect as well as any sense of subject versus object.

> I take refuge in unmediated, nonconceptual, natural clarity,
> The identity of the five primordial embodiments of the nature of spontaneity,
> In the *vajra* strand[27] of the clear light of my own awareness
> In the maṇḍala of the *bindu* of clear and empty absolute reality and awareness.
> I take refuge in the unceasing, naturally creative power of the omnipresent Compassionate One,
> The appearing and liberating, unceasing, playful rays of the creative power of awareness,
> Which, from the experience of nonconceptuality, dispel the darkness in the minds of beings
> During the three times, without beginning or end.

To understand the full import of these two verses, you must study more elaborate teachings on Mahāmudrā and Atiyoga, specifically concerning the Breakthrough and the Leap-over phases of Atiyoga practice. Only then will you see what is meant by the above terms.

What are the demarcations among the outer, inner, and secret refuge? The outer refuge is in one's spiritual mentors, and the Buddha, Dharma and Sangha. The inner refuge is again in one's spiritual mentor, one's chosen deity, and the ḍākinī. Finally, the secret refuge is "taking refuge in the experience of nongrasping which transcends the intellect."

GENERATING THE MAHĀYĀNA SPIRIT OF AWAKENING

Alas! All phenomena are empty and identityless.
Pity every sentient being who fails to realize this!
So that these beings worthy of compassion may attain enlightenment,
I shall dedicate my body, speech, and mind to virtue.
For the sake of all sentient beings in the six states of existence,
From now until enlightenment is attained,
I shall generate the spirit of supreme enlightenment,
Not only for myself, but for all beings.
Pity all those who are without Dharma, who shackle themselves
In the immeasurable ocean of suffering!
So that these beings worthy of compassion may be brought to joy,
I shall generate the spirit of supreme enlightenment.
All limitless sentient beings and I
Are primordially of the nature of the Buddha.
I shall generate the spirit of supreme enlightenment
As a great being to know that
We are indeed of the nature of the Buddha.

The ocean of the world's cycle of existence is like an illusion.
No composites are permanent.
Their nature is empty and identityless.

> But these children who fail to realize that
> Wander through the twelve links of dependent origina-
>   tion in the cycle of becoming.
> So that those stuck in the swamp of name and form
> May attain buddhahood, I shall dedicate
> My body, speech, and mind to virtue.

"Name and form" together comprise one of the twelve links of dependent origination. "Name" specifically refers to consciousness, and "form" refers to the body. We become "stuck in the swamp of name and form" through attachment to the cycle of existence. Thus, we are like an elephant who likes to bathe in a swamp. It likes the feel of the mud against its skin, but then it gets in over its head and loses its foothold, sinking down. The elephant got in there in the first place because of its attachment to the mud. This getting stuck is also like a bee that is attracted to an insect-eating flower. It comes to the flower because it's attracted to the nectar, but once it gets inside, the flower closes in over it.

> In the Buddha, Dharma, and supreme assembly
> I take refuge until enlightenment.
> By my merit of practicing generosity and so forth,
> May I accomplish buddhahood for the benefit of the
>   world.

"Practicing generosity and so forth," refers to all types of virtue. There are three types of generosity: the giving of material things, the giving of protection or fearlessness, and the giving of Dharma.

> May I become a spiritual mentor to guide
> All limitless beings without exception.

A spiritual mentor is not only a person who wears yellow or maroon robes or one who sits upon a Dharma throne. A genuine spiritual mentor is one who has developed the spirit of awakening and has become a bodhisattva.

CULTIVATING THE FOUR IMMEASURABLES

> May all sentient beings be endowed with happiness!
> May everyone be free of suffering and its causes!
> May we be endowed with sorrow-free joy!
> May we dwell in equanimity free of attachment and
> hatred!

The first line here pertains to the cultivation of immeasurable loving-kindness, the second to immeasurable compassion, the third to immeasurable sympathetic joy, and the fourth line to immeasurable equanimity. If you would like to have a more detailed understanding of the Four Immeasurables, look to Śāntideva's classic text, *A Guide to the Bodhisattva Way of Life*. If you can cultivate these, it will bring very tangible benefit to your own mind-stream.

RECITING THE ONE HUNDRED SYLLABLES TO PURIFY SINS AND OBSCURATIONS

Now we move on to the Vajrasattva practice of reciting the "one hundred syllables" to purify sins and obscurations. There are two types of obscurations. The more subtle class of obscurations is called *cognitive obscurations* or *obscurations of knowledge*, which are principally the latent propensities for mental afflictions. Grosser than these are the *afflictive obscurations*, such as anger, attachment, delusion, and so forth. The Vajrasattva practice is designed to purify these two types of obscurations.

> On a lotus and moon seat on the crown of my head
> Is the form of my spiritual mentor as Vajrasattva.
> The color of his body is like crystal, and at his heart
> The hundred syllables surround a HŪM upon a moon-
> disc.
> A stream of ambrosia descends through my Brahma
> aperture,

Purifying my infractions, sins, and obscurations.
I pray that right now the Glorious Lord Vajrasattva
May bestow a stream of ambrosia of primordial wisdom
To purify the sins and obscurations
Of myself and of every sentient being in the world.

OM VAJRASATTVA SAMAYAM ANUPĀLAYA VAJRASATTVA
TVENOPATIṢṬHA DṚDHO ME BHAVA SUTOṢYO ME
BHAVA SUPOṢYO ME BHAVA ANURAKTO ME BHAVA
SARVA SIDDHIM ME PRAYACCHA SARVA KARMASU CA
ME CITTAM ŚRĪYAM KURU HŪM HA HA HA HA HOḤ
BHAGAVAN SARVATATHĀGATA VAJRA MĀ ME MUÑCA
VAJRA BHAVA MAHĀSAMAYA SATTVA ĀḤ

This is an extremely important practice. It's dealt with quite concisely here, but much more elaborate instructions can be found in other teachings on the preliminary practices. This practice is of very tangible benefit. There are other teachings on Atiyoga and so forth that we may consider more esoteric or advanced, but it's questionable how deeply benfited we can be by those and how much we can truly enter into the experience of the Great Perfection. Here, though, is something of practical benefit. If you are familiar with this practice, it's good to share it with others who may be beginners. By such a practice as this, the two types of obscurations can be purified. Once all of your obscurations have been completely purified, you are a buddha; and that means you have realized the Great Perfection.

Due to ignorance, delusion, and stupidity,
I have transgressed my samayas, and they have degenerated.
O spiritual mentor, protector, protect me!
Glorious Lord Vajradhara,
Merciful being of great compassion,
Lord of the world, protect us!
Please cleanse and purify the whole mass
Of sins, obscurations, faults, downfalls, and taints.

By this virtue, may I now
Swiftly actualize Vajrasattva
And quickly bring every sentient being
Without exception to that state.
O Vajrasattva, may we become exactly
Like your form, with your retinue, life span, pure realm,
And with your supreme, excellent signs.

OFFERING THE MAṆḌALA

Once you have begun purifying the two types of obscurations, there is the task of accumulating the two collections of merit and of knowledge for one's own benefit and the benefit of others. The welfare of others is accomplished in the realization of the Rūpakāya, or form embodiment, of the Buddha; and it is toward accomplishing that end that one offers the maṇḍala.

> OṂ VAJRA BHŪMI ĀḤ HŪṂ.
> The basis becomes the powerful golden ground.
> OṂ VAJRA REKHE ĀḤ HŪṂ.
> On the periphery is a surrounding jeweled iron fence.
> In the center is the supreme king of mountains,
> Majestic in its composition from the five kinds of precious
>   substances.
> Lovely in shape, beautiful, and delightful to behold,
> Seven golden mountains are surrounded by seven con-
>   centric seas.
> In the east is the continent Videha, in the south,
>   Jambudvīpa,
> The west is adorned by Godānīya,
> And in the north is the great Uttarakuru;
> With the eight sub-continents of Deha and Videha,
> Cāmara and Aparacāmara,
> Śāṭhā and Uttaramantriṇa,
> Kurava and Kaurava,
> The sun, the moon, Rāhu and Kālāgni,

And this bounty of wealth and enjoyments of gods and
humans
I offer to the precious spiritual mentor and his retinue.
Out of compassion, please accept this for the sake of the
world.

This is one of the various recitations of the maṇḍala offering. It's
important to realize that the physical offering of the maṇḍala
with its base and heaps of grains of rice and so on is simply the
physical support for the actual offering of the maṇḍala. In terms
of your visualization, imagine all of the objects of the offerings—
your spiritual mentor, the Buddha refuge, Dharma refuge, and
Sangha refuge—as being boundless in nature. To these vast
objects of refuge, you bring offerings that are correspondingly as
vast as the clouds of offerings of Samantabhadra. In your mind's
eye, you should imagine these offerings as being immeasurable. It
is said that the maṇḍala is best offered without any sense of reified objectification. That is, as you make the offering, there arises
to your mind no intrinsically existent recipient of the offering
and no intrinsically existent offering, nor do you as the offerer
have any intrinsic existence. Thus, these three—the object, the
act of offering together with the substance that is being offered,
and yourself as the offerer—lack inherent existence, and all of
these are of the same nature.

OṂ ĀḤ HŪṂ
The palace of the animate and inanimate galaxy is cov-
ered with
Clouds of vast offerings of Mount Meru and the
continents.
All the immeasurable enjoyments of gods and humans
I offer to the Nirmāṇakāya realm of the precious spiritual
mentor.
Look upon this with your merciful compassion and
accept this,
And may all beings be born in the Nirmāṇakāya realm!

This "galaxy" is the billionfold world system that is commonly mentioned in Buddhist cosmology. "Animate" refers to sentient beings, and "inanimate" refers to the inanimate environment. You imagine this galaxy totally pervaded by clouds of offerings, as massive and extensive as you can.

Make sure that your offering includes the entire environment, together with the mountains, soil, plants, lakes, streams, oceans, and so forth, imagined in their purified form. Likewise, in terms of the animate environment, all sentient beings—female, male, all of their enjoyments, their wealth, their prosperity, and their happiness—are offered. Imagine all the objects of your own attachment and desire in their purified form, and you offer them to the Nirmāṇakāya realm of the spiritual mentor and the objects of refuge. You can do this type of practice not only when you're sitting in formal meditation, but also when you're engaging in ordinary daily activities, like driving a car.

> OM ĀḤ HŪM
> The palace of the pure channels and elements of my own body
> Is adorned with the splendor and radiance of the five
>   faculties.
> These pristine sense elements and bases
> I offer to the Sambhogakāya realm of the precious spiritual
>   mentor.
> Look upon this with your merciful compassion and
>   accept this,
> And may all beings be born in the Sambhogakāya realm!

Just as in the previous case in which the the earth is adorned with the sun, moon, and so forth, here the body is adorned with the pure channels and elements, including earth, water, and so on. When offering to the Sambhogakāya realm, one offers the pure channels, elements, and essential fluids within the body.

> OM ĀḤ HŪM
> In the palace of the pure Dharmakāya dwells

The mind-itself in the sphere of nonobjectivity, emptiness
and clarity, and nongrasping.
This originally pure, innate, primordial wisdom
I offer to the Dharmakāya realm of the precious spiritual
mentor.
Look upon this with your merciful compassion and
accept this,
And may all beings be born in the Dharmakāya realm!

The phrase "originally pure," refers to the original purity of the
mind-itself, and not some temporary or adventitious purity. In
this original offering, the outer environment is offered to the
Nirmāṇakāya, the channels and elements of your own body are
offered to the Sambhogakāya, and the mind-itself—this mind of
primordial wisdom—is offered to the Dharmakāya realm.

In another practice you offer the channels of the body in their
purified form to the Nirmāṇakāya realm, the vital energies in the
body are offered to the Sambhogakāya realm, and the essential
fluids are offered to the Dharmakāya realm. The secret-level
offering pertains to the essence of awareness, the nature of awareness, and the pervasive compassion of awareness. The essence is
offered to the Dharmakāya; the nature is offered to the
Sambhogakāya; and the pervasive compassion is offered to the
Nirmāṇakāya. All of these offerings act as causes for our achieving those three embodiments of the Buddha.

There are two general modes of offering the maṇḍala. One is
the offering the maṇḍala of actualization, and the other is offering
the maṇḍala of offering. There are various recitations for this, such
as the thirty-seven part maṇḍala offering, and there are two ways of
doing this. In the maṇḍala offering of actualization the eastern
direction faces yourself. The full maṇḍala is created; and once it is
actualized, it is set aside. It then becomes a representation that has
been actualized for an initiation. In making a maṇḍala offering
simply as an offering, the east faces away from you, and the different continents and so on are presented according to that orientation. Once it is offered, the maṇḍala is collapsed outwards.

As I mentioned, there are various liturgies for offering the maṇḍala, some with thirty-seven parts, some with two lines, and some with four lines; so you can do this practice with various degrees of elaboration. The purpose of the maṇḍala offering is to lessen the tendency of "I need" and "I want," thereby counteracting our tendency toward grasping. Bear in mind, too, that the maṇḍala offering is not simply this formal offering with the liturgy; rather, all offerings are included in offering the maṇḍala. Even the practice of Cutting Through, in which you offer your own body, is an offering of the maṇḍala of your own body. Generally speaking, all the four types of generosity are expressions of the offering of the maṇḍala as well.

The practice of offering the maṇḍala is prevalent throughout all spiritual orders of Tibetan Buddhism, including the Gelug. The Gelug tradition has many versions of this, and they are very widely practiced. Within Gelug literature, it is found, for example, in the writings on the stages of the path. It's also taught extensively in the Kagyü and Sakya orders. Therefore, it's important when you practice that you don't simply go through an external ritual of setting up little mounds of rice, but be aware of the great significance of offering the maṇḍala. Extensive discussions of the nature and the significance of offering the maṇḍala are found in the teachings on the preliminary practices.

OṂ ĀḤ HŪṂ
By offering this fine and pleasing maṇḍala,
May obstacles not arise on the path to enlightenment,
May the intention of the sugatas of the three times be
    realized,
And without being confused in the cycle of existence or
    dwelling in quietism,
May beings throughout space be liberated!
OṂ ĀḤ HŪṂ MAHĀGURU DEVA ḌĀKINĪ RATNA
    MAṆḌALA PŪJA MEGHA SAMUDRĀ SPHARAṆA SAMAYA
    ĀḤ HŪṂ

Prayer to the Lineage

OṂ ĀḤ HŪṂ

By offering this fine and pleasing maṇḍala,
May obstacles not arise on the path to enlightenment,
May the intention of the sugatas of the three times be realized,
And without being confused in the cycle of existence or dwelling in quietism,
May beings throughout space transcend!
To the Dharmakāya Samantabhadra, the original Lord,
To the Victor Vajradhara, the nature of the six (buddha families),
And to the supreme-minded Vajrasattva, foremost of guides—
I pray to the lineage of the Victor's contemplation.
To the Vidyādhara Garab, supreme emanated being,
To Guru Śrī Siṃha, foremost spiritual son of the Victor,
To the immortal Padmasambhava, achiever of the vajra body,
To the ḍākinī Yeshe Tsogyal, vessel of the secret mantra—
I pray to the lineage of the Vidyādhara's knowledge.

The first Atiyoga lineage is from Samantabhadra to Vajrasattva. The the second lineage follows the line from Garab Dorje, through Śrī Siṃha, Padmasambhava, and Yeshe Tsogyal. Yeshe Tsogyal is the mistress of this lineage of the secret mantra.

To Karma Lingpa, the master of profound treasures,
To the one named Chöje, his supreme heart son,
To the one named Sūryacandra, protector of the world in degenerate times—
I pray to the lineage of individuals with authoritative oral teachings.
To the master of Dharma, the Chinese monk named Namkha,

To Sönam Özer, who realized the meaning of the two stages,

To the venerable Puṇya Śrī, who perfected the two accumulations,

To Sönam Chökyongwa, who spontaneously accomplished the two aims,

To Natsok Rangsardröl, the supreme guide of the three times,

To Künga Drakpey Pal, protector of beings of the three realms,

To Dongak Tendzin Je, who personified the three types of embodiments,

To Trinley Lhündrup Tsal, who progressed through the four visions,

To Gyurmey Dorje Dey, lord of the four embodiments,

To Lochen Dharmaśrī, who revealed the meanings of the four empowerments,

To Rinchen Nampargyal, son of the victors,

To Padma Tendzin, supreme Nirmāṇakāya being,

To Karma Vijaya, preserver of the heritage of the Vidyādharas,

To Trinley Chökyi Drön, of inborn bliss and emptiness,

To Dorje Ziji Tsal, who possessed the seven oral lineages,

To Gyurmey Ngedön Wang, who directly perceived reality-itself,

To Düdjom Drodül Ling, treasure of ripening, liberation, and the expanse,

To the peaceful and wrathful chosen deities, of indivisible appearance and emptiness,

To the oceanic assembly of ḍākinīs, dharma protectors, and samaya-preservers,[28]

I pray to the assembly of deities of the three roots.

The above is a list of many of the great beings in this lineage. It would take too long to give you a clear idea of the accomplishments of each of those beings. However, you may be able to learn about some of them from other texts in English translation.[29]

> O spiritual mentors of the oral lineage, who offer whatever training is needed,
> If your teachings were to fall into decline,
> It would be to the sorrow of contemplatives born in this era,
> So please lead all beings from the swamp of the cycle of existence.
> If we call upon you with a roar of anguish,
> Please think of your earlier solemn promise.
> From the expanse of the space of the absolute nature, reveal your countenance, with its signs and symbols of enlightenment,
> And lead all beings from the swamp of the cycle of existence.

The phrase "reveal your countenance," is a request for the Buddha to appear in this pure vision in which various emanations of the Buddha appear endowed with all the signs and symbols of enlightenment.

> With the resounding brahmā words of emptiness,
> May the entrance to the treasury of your mind be opened,
> And with the outpouring of light rays of your wisdom and compassion,
> Please lead all beings from the swamp of the cycle of existence.

The first line above refers to the Buddha's speech and literally means "empty words." This is speech that is endowed with the sixty qualities of a Buddha's speech. It does not mean empty words in the sense of nonsensical or misleading words.

> Now liberate every being of this final era!
> Now grant the stream of the four pristine empowerments!

Now liberate the four continua[30] of confusing mental
   afflictions!
Please lead all beings from the swamp of the cycle of
   existence!
Now bestow the fruition of the four embodiments of the
   sugatas!
May I become a spiritual mentor to guide
All limitless, parent sentient beings throughout space.
Please lead all beings from the swamp of the cycle of
   existence.

Genuine spiritual mentors take birth and live for the sake of
other sentient beings. They have come into the world just as
Buddha Śākyamuni did, to be of service to others, but it's up to
us whether or not we listen to them. Similarly, Padmasambhava
made a promise to live and teach for the benefit of the world.
There are examples of such lamas nowadays, including His
Holiness the Dalai Lama, Gyalwa Karmapa, and Kyabje Dudjom
Rinpoche. All these great beings made solemn vows in past lives
to be of service, and they are fulfilling their promise for those
who are living now.

There are also lamas of this stature living in Tibet today, such as
Khenpo Jigmey Phüntsok, who came to North America in 1993.
He is one of these great beings who has taken birth once again in
fulfillment of his own vow to be of service. If we are to fulfill our
own ends, it's important that we listen and be receptive to what
such fine teachers have to say. Great beings in the past have already
appeared—like Buddha Śākyamuni, Padmasambhava, and so on—
but at that time we either weren't present or we weren't listening to
them. We do the opposite of what they advise, so we remain in the
cycle of saṃsāra. If we continue to turn away from the counsel of
these great beings, we will continue to wander in the future.
There's no forseeable end to this self-perpetuating cycle, so we
could continue wandering in saṃsāra for eons. The teachings
offered by these great beings can bring us to perfect enlightenment
in this one life. We presently have this opportunity, and we have

the ability to carry this practice through to its culmination. It's our choice whether or not we put these teachings into practice to realize their potential as they are applied to our lives.

THE CONTEMPLATION OF RECEIVING THE FOUR EMPOWERMENTS

From the crown of the head of the spiritual mentor with consort
White OM together with light rays
Descends to the point between my eyebrows.
Upon receiving the vase empowerment, physical obscurations are purified.
Please grant me the siddhis of the body.

Receiving this first empowerment establishes in us the seeds for achieving the Nirmāṇakāya, and it empowers us to practice the stage of generation.

From the throat of the spiritual mentor with consort
Red ĀḤ together with light rays
Descends upon my taste faculty.
Upon receiving the secret empowerment, verbal obscurations are purified.
Please grant me the siddhis of speech.

This establishes in us the seeds for accomplishing the Sambhogakāya and the sixty qualities of a buddha's speech.

From the heart of the spiritual mentor with consort
Dark blue HŪM together with light rays
Descends upon the center of my heart.
Upon receiving the primordial wisdom empowerment, mental obscurations are purified.
Please grant me the siddhis of the mind.

This third empowerment is for the purification of all obscurations of the mind, and it sows the seeds for accomplishing the Dharmakāya.

> From the navel of the spiritual mentor with consort
> Red HRĪḤ together with light rays
> Descends upon the center of my navel.
> The obscuration of grasping onto the three doors as different is purified.
> And I receive the fourth, indivisible, inborn empowerment.

With this fourth empowerment, we are enabled to accomplish the four embodiments of a buddha, the fourth being the svabhāvakāya, also called the jñānakāya, the embodiment of primordial wisdom.

> Glorious, precious, primary spiritual mentor,
> Constantly, inseparably remain
> In the center of the lotus of my heart,
> And look after me out of your great kindness!
> Please grant me the siddhis of body, speech, and mind.
> Glorious spiritual mentor, may we become exactly
> Like your form, with your retinue, life span, pure realm,
> And with your supreme, excellent signs.

Colophon

It is appropriate to append this practice for training your own mind-stream to the preliminary practices of the *Profound Dharma of Natural Liberation through Contemplating the Peaceful and Wrathful*. This spiritual activity of the unsurpassable Mahāyāna is the advice of Chöje Lingpa, the principle spiritual son of the treasure revealer Karma Lingpa; and it was put into writing by Guru Sūryacandra.

Sarvaṃ mangalam!

PART TWO

THE PROFOUND DHARMA OF THE NATURAL LIBERATION THROUGH CONTEMPLATING THE PEACEFUL AND WRATHFUL: STAGE OF COMPLETION INSTRUCTIONS on the Six Bardos

3

The Natural Liberation of the Foundation: Experiential Instructions on the Transitional Process of Living

> Homage to the original Protector, the birthless Samantabhadra,
> To the peaceful and wrathful Sambhogakāya deities, who are his unceasing creative expressions,
> To the limitless emanations of various appearing and liberating Nirmāṇakāyas—
> To the peaceful and wrathful deities of the three embodiments.
> For the benefit of future beings of a degenerate era,
> I, Padmasambhava, untainted by a womb,
> Have synthesized all the contemplations of the Victor
> And have established them as the six kinds of bardos.
>
> All of them are contingent upon fundamental practice,[31]
> So I reveal this natural liberation through contemplating
> The experiential instructions of the essential teachings on the bardos.
> Oh, people of the future, practice in this way!
> Samaya.

When the author, Padmasambhava, says he is "untainted by a womb," he means he is not tainted by birth from a womb, for he was born from a lotus blossom. When he says, "Oh, people of the future," he is referring to all of us who are wandering in the cycle of existence and are still unfree.

> Among all phenomena of saṃsāra and nirvāṇa, there are none that are not included within the six bardos, or

transitional processes. The way to put them into practice is taught by way of three principal topics: (1) two kinds of preliminary practice that bring forth the meditative state for those in whom it has not arisen, (2) instructions on the actual practice for the training of those in whom the meditative state has arisen, and (3) the subsequent stage for enhancing that.

This subsequent, concluding, stage is for the purpose of clearing away obstacles, for bringing in blessings, and for enhancing the practice.

In the preliminary practices, there are the instructions for training your own mind-stream, which have four parts: instructions on refuge and the spirit of awakening; instructions on the hundred syllables that purify sins; instructions on guru yoga, which allows one to receive blessings; and instructions on the Dharma practice of the maṇḍala, which perfects the two accumulations.

The "hundred syllables that purify sins" refers to the hundred-syllable mantra of Vajrasattva. The instructions on guru yoga are to enhance the blessings for those who have already received them and to bring blessings for those who have not yet done so. Regarding the maṇḍala practice, the "two accumulations" refers to the accumulations of merit and of wisdom.

The instructions for subduing your own mind-stream have three parts: pondering the difficulty of obtaining a human life of leisure and endowment, pondering the sufferings of saṃsāra, and meditating on death and impermanence. These sevenfold preliminary practices are to be put into practice. In that way, you meditate on and establish the preliminary practices until the experience of them arises.

Within the preliminary practices, the second part pertains to subduing your mind-stream. The sevenfold preliminary practices include the first set of four and the second set of three. We should practice "until the experience of them arises." For example, you should continue meditating on the sufferings of saṃsāra until your mind turns away from saṃsāra. Similarly, continue in the meditation on death and impermanence until you gain certainty about these realities. In other words, practice until you get results.

Many of you may feel you are very familiar with the Four Thoughts that Turn the Mind. Moveover, some of you have made a hundred thousand recitations of one practice after another. Some of you may have completed the sets of preliminary practices even two or three times, and yet still your minds have not really changed. The transformation for which these were designed has not taken place; or in some cases, it took place but then your mind reverted back to its old ways. You still remain obsessed with saṃsāra. You still remain obsessed with mundane desires and so on. Clinging and attachment continue. In particular, there are some older Dharma practitioners who initially brought about a positive transformation through their practice; but as time went on they regressed so that they are now no better off than they were in the first place.

> In the practice of the actual stages, there are six parts: instructions on the transitional process of living, involving the natural liberation of the foundation (practical instructions that are like a swallow entering its nest); instructions on the transitional process of dreaming, involving the natural liberation of confusion (practical instructions that are like holding aloft a lamp in a dark room); instructions on the transitional process of meditative stabilization, involving the natural liberation of awareness (practical instructions that are like a lost child finding its mother); instructions on the transitional process of dying, involving the natural liberation of recalling the transference of consciousness (practical

instructions that are like dispatching the sealed commands of the king), instructions on the transitional process of reality-itself, involving the natural liberation of seeing (practical instructions that are like a child crawling up on its mother's lap), and instructions on the transitional process of becoming, involving the natural liberation of becoming (practical instructions that are like joining a broken water canal with a channel).

The practice of the transitional process of living is like a swallow entering its nest. If you watch how a swallow prepares its nest, first of all, it examines its environment to make sure that there is water nearby. Then it finds a safe spot to build a nest in which to raise its young. When that is found, it builds its nest and can raise its chicks, for it doesn't have to worry about anything else.

Like that analogy, the first phase of the practice is hearing and learning the teachings. The second stage is thinking about the teachings, and finally there is the stage of meditation. By setting forth in a very systematic fashion—first hearing, then thinking, then meditating—you get everything straight; so when you begin meditating, you are able to do so effectively without having to fuss with anything else. If a little bird has the sense to do that, we as human beings should have the same sense to prepare well in our spiritual practice. If you think, "Well, I'm a human being, I'm smart," then use your intelligence to prepare well for your spiritual practice.

The instructions on the second transitional process concern the transitional process of dreaming, which involves the natural liberation of confusion. These instructions are like holding a lamp aloft in a dark room. If you go into a dark room, obviously it's very hard to move around because you can't see anything; but if a companion comes with you and holds up a light, then you can see perfectly well. Like that analogy, for the practice of Dharma it is very important to engage in the systematic practice of hearing, thinking, and meditation. By so doing, obstacles in your spiritual practice are dispelled, and you cultivate the qualities of mindfulness, introspection, and conscientiousness.

Third, the instructions on the transitional process of meditative stabilization, involving the natural liberation of awareness, entail practical instructions that are like a lost child encountering its mother. The analogy here is of child who has lost track of his mother. Not knowing where she is, he searches around, experiencing much grief and unhappiness. Finally, however, he meets his mother. As soon as the mother and the stranded child encounter each other, there is no doubt from the child's side that this is his mother; and there's no doubt from the mother's side either. There is total recognition from both sides. In a similar fashion, it is important that we practice this systematic procedure of hearing, thinking, and meditation. In so doing, we must first gain realization of the two types of identitylessness, namely personal identitylessness and phenomenal identitylessness. By engaging in such meditation, we come to recognize our own nature, and this is like the analogy of the lost child recognizing his mother.

This analogy pertains to the practice of Atiyoga in general. Many people reading this may not have taken the Buddhist vows of refuge, and that's fine. You are still welcome to read these teachings. If you have the desire to attain enlightenment in this very lifetime, you are welcome to enter into this practice. If you do so and practice according to the instructions, I guarantee that this will be for your benefit. I guarantee that this will lead to your own liberation. I offer this guarantee, not on the basis of my own experience or some great realization that I have, but rather because of the lineage and origins of these teachings. These teachings originate from the Buddha Samantabhadra. They were composed by Guru Rinpoche, Padmasambhava. It's upon the basis of the depth of the realization of Samantabhadra, Guru Rinpoche, and of the lineage that runs from them to the present time that I tell you it is utterly certain that, if you put these teachings into practice, it will result in your own liberation. You may practice this whether or not you have taken the vows of refuge. The reason I want to extend this to all of you is because we are all subject to death. We all will die. For those of us who have gathered to receive these teachings in person, where will we go when we leave? Where are we heading off to? Are we going off to Russia? Are we going off to war? Do we have some other big agenda? Clearly not. Our agenda is that we have the five poisons of our own minds, and these are our true adversaries. This practice enables us to become warriors who can overcome the afflictions of our own minds. By so doing, we gain liberation. If you wish to attain enlightenment, you are welcome to practice these teachings.

Fourth are the instructions on the transitional process of dying, involving the natural liberation of recalling the transference of consciousness. These practical instructions are like dispatching the sealed commands of the king. If a king sends an emissary with his sealed commands, then it is the emissary's responsibility to dispatch these commands, and to do exactly as the king has commanded. Similarly, when each of us is in the process of dying, even if we have not gained realization in the two stages of generation and completion; and even if we have not gained realization of the Great Perfection; if we have these teachings on the transference of consciousness, this is like having received the commands of the king. That is, these teachings will suffice to carry us through the dying process in a very meaningful and helpful way. Beginning now, we should engage in the reflections upon the Four Thoughts that Turn the Mind and prepare our minds so that we can really take advantage of these teachings during the time of our own dying process. Thinking about death, we can ask, "Well, do you need a visa? Do you need a passport to cross the border?" The answer is, "No, you are ready to go right now. With or without a visa, you're ready to go." However, what we're not ready to do right now is to die with freedom, so these teachings are offered to give us that opportunity.

Next, the instructions on the transitional process of reality-itself involves the natural liberation of seeing. These practical instructions are like a child crawling up on its mother's lap. This analogy pertains to the gradual training in realizing the two types of identitylessness, receiving the mentor's introduction to the nature of awareness and engaging in the two stages of Atiyoga—namely the Breakthrough to original purity and the Leap-over into spontaneous presence. By so doing, some people may attain liberation in the course of this life, before dying. Others may attain liberation during the dying process; others may attain liberation during the transitional process following death; and others may attain liberation at the time of conception. However one gains realization, this is like a child crawling up onto its mother's lap. As in the previous analogy of the child recognizing his mother, there is a recognition that is utterly free of doubt. Whether you think of this as crawling into the lap of Samantabhadra, or crawling into the lap of awareness, this is the route to follow.

The final instructions concern the transitional process of becoming, involving the natural liberation of becoming. These practical instructions are like mending a break in a water canal. That analogy pertains to our present situation of wandering within the cycle of existence, failing to recognize our own nature. In the meantime, we grasp onto that which is not "I" as being "I" and that which is not truly existent as being truly existent. By succumbing to such confusion, it's as if we sever the canal that provides the connection between Samantabhadra and ourselves. By engaging in this practice, we reconnect ourselves to this source. It's like laying a pipe to connect a spring to a field you wish to irrigate. From the perspective of ignorance, it looks as if we are trying to reestablish a connection between Samantabhadra and ourselves. However, in terms of reality, Samantabhadra and we are of the same nature. Consequently, the process here is one of recognizing our own nature as being the same as that of Samantabhadra. This concludes the outline of the six transitional processes.

As mentioned previously, the first of the six transitional processes—namely the transitional process of living, involving the natural liberation of the foundation—consists of practical instructions that are like a swallow entering its nest. Like the swallow surveying the environment before building its nest, for these higher practices, including the stages of generation or completion, the Breakthrough to original purity, and the Leap-over into spontaneous presence, the preparation is essential. What does that mean in terms of practice? We need to train ourselves well in the Four Thoughts that Turn the Mind and the Four Noble Truths and, by so doing, to turn our minds away from the attractions of the cycle of existence. This does not mean, by the way, that as you progress in this training, you should reject your husband or wife. What you should reject are the three poisons of the mind, and what you're turning away from is saṃsāra. In the process, you do in fact get a new lover, and that is liberation. This becomes your true love.

QUIESCENCE

Settling the Body, Speech, and Mind in their Natural States

> For the practice of the instructions on the transitional process of living (practical instructions that are like a dove entering its nest, which are for cutting through outer and inner superimpositions), there is an establishment of the foundation consciousness, and the first of three parts is the settling of the body in its natural state.

The point of this practice is to prepare for our own dying process so that when death is imminent, we are well prepared for it, we can gladly accept it, and be ready to go to a Pure Land. That is the point of these teachings. In order to follow these instructions on the transitional process of living, the first crucial point is that of settling the body in its natural state.

> *Settling the body in its natural state.* If you do not know how to place your body in a good posture, the genuine meditative state will not arise in your mind-stream, or even if it does, it will run into problems; so the posture is important. When the body is straight and erect, the channels are straight; when the channels are straight, the vital energies are straight; when the vital energies remain straight, awareness settles in its natural state; and the meditative state occurs naturally.

The meditative state arises when the posture is settled in that way because of the dependence of the mind upon the vital energies within the body and their dependence upon the channels and so on. Upon learning about the proper posture, with its seven attributes of Vairocana, including folding the legs in the full-lotus position, you may be thinking, "Well, that's not only excruciating, but it's simply impossible for me," or "I have a physical impairment that makes that posture impossible. So does that mean that the meditation is hopeless for me?" The answer is, "No, it is not hopeless." Go ahead and proceed. Have faith, do the best you can, and this can lead to perfectly good results. Don't quit simply because you can't sit in that special posture.

> Thus, to settle the body in its natural state in terms of physical activity, novices or beginners should completely dispense with all external, mundane activities, such as farming. Inwardly, also suspend spiritual practices such as prostrations and circumambulations. Secretly, meditate firmly and unwaveringly in the appropriate posture, without any bodily movement at all. That is because the meditative state must arise once the body is settled in its natural state.

Outwardly, simplify your life. Inwardly, the meditative state arises as a natural result of sitting in the proper posture.

> The actual *adhisāra*[32] of the body is imbued with the seven physical attributes of Vairocana: the legs are placed in the *vajrāsana*, the hands are positioned beneath the navel in the *mudrā* of meditative equipoise, the spine is straight like an arrow, the abdomen is pressed against the spine, the neck is slightly inclined, the tip of the tongue is pressed against the palate, and without meditating on anything, the eyes gaze fixedly in the space at the level of the tip of the nose. Position your body faultlessly with these seven attributes. If you know how to establish the

adhisāra naturally, the meditative state will naturally happen.

Settling the speech in its natural state. In settling the speech in its natural state, there are also three parts: outwardly, dispense completely with all conversation and idle, confusing speech and remain silent; inwardly, suspend dispersive movement and spiritual activities and remain silent; secretly, stop the activities of recitations and mantras. Settle your speech naturally in silence, like a lute with its strings cut.

Settling the mind in its natural state. In settling the mind in its natural state, there are also three parts: while keeping the body and speech as they were before, let your mind be lucid, without engaging any thoughts concerning earlier or later deceptive appearances of the three times; inwardly, settle the mind evenly without engaging in any good thoughts, such as deity meditation; secretly, settle the mind in its natural state by letting it be just as it is, steadily, clearly, and lucidly in the space in front of you, in the mind's own mode of existence, without bringing to mind any of the mentally engaging thoughts of the view and meditation which entail mental grasping. Do that for three days.

In this phase of the practice you do not bring to mind any thoughts of the view—the Atiyoga view or the view of emptiness and so on. That is, now you are not to ponder the two types of identitylessness or engage in the discursive examination of the nature of the arising, presence and disappearance of thoughts. Now simply allow the mind to settle in its own natural state without any such mental grasping. Practice the above instructions for three days.

Some of you may wonder how you are to "settle the mind in its natural state by letting it be just as it is, steadily, clearly, and lucidly in the space in front of you in the mind's own mode of existence." It is this ordinary awareness of the present that is the nature of the mind, which is of the very nature of both saṃsāra and nirvāṇa. It is not physical in nature, and it's not contaminated by the three times: the past, the present, and the future. It is not something that is benefited or harmed by such conceptualizations of the three times. This natural state of the mind is intrinsic to the mind. It is its own natural state, not something created, and it did not become as it is due to some special tradition. Rather, this is the natural, innate nature of the mind. This is what emerges when the mind is allowed to rest in its own natural state without being disturbed. What is this nature? The inborn nature of the mind is one of spontaneous presence.

One can say that the mind is not something that is existent as a thing. It does not have a form, nor is it a physical substance. It has never been seen as a real existent thing by any buddha. On the other hand, the mind is also not nonexistent. Just as the mind does not accord with the extreme view of existence, neither does it accord with the extreme view of nonexistence, or nihilism. This mind is the basis of all of saṃsāra and nirvāṇa. Its primordial nature is that of the Dharmakāya. The mind's qualities are those of the two form embodiments: the Sambhogakāya and the Nirmāṇakāya. In terms of the path, there are three qualities that are cultivated in meditation: namely bliss, clarity, and nonconceptuality. These are salient features of the path to enlightenment, and these correspond one by one to the three embodiments of the Buddha. However, if grasping occurs toward these three qualities—bliss, clarity, and nonconceptuality—as they arise, then the same qualities simply lead to a perpetuation of the cycle of existence. On the other hand, if one does not respond to these qualities with grasping, then bliss, clarity, and nonconceptuality give rise respectively to the three embodiments: the Nirmāṇakāya, the Sambhogakāya, and the Dharmakāya.

> Our so-called mind, which is continually aware, busy, and recalling all kinds of things, acts as the basis of the

whole of saṃsāra and nirvāṇa; so it is given the name foundation. The root of all joy and sorrow is your own mind, so it is important first of all to establish this. The mind of a novice is like a wild horse. To illustrate this, to catch a wild horse, if you chase after it aggressively, it will be frightened and will not be caught. So by enticing it in various ways and gently holding it, it will be caught and can be put to work. Likewise, if this wild mind is controlled aggressively, more and more thoughts will flow out, and obstacles will arise that produce numerous problems such as an imbalance of the heart vital energy. By gently settling the mind in its natural state, using various techniques, genuine quiescence will arise in your mind-stream.

This mind that is called the foundation is the basis of both joy and sorrow. We are novices in this practice. So, it is *our* minds that are like wild horses. Here, you must be cautious about taking a very aggressive approach to subduing the mind. If you have no experienced spiritual mentor or you are not following a good practice, then you may take too forceful an approach in trying to still the mind. If you do that to a horse, it will rear up, neigh, and start bucking. Likewise, the mind responds very similarly when it is restrained too aggressively, and it responds with increased conceptual agitation. If you persist in that aggressive approach to subduing the mind, instead of succeeding, you will simply create mental and physical problems for yourself. For these reasons a gradual path is taught, starting by first subduing the mind by means of the Four Thoughts that Turn the Mind and then gradually entering into this practice. As Padmasambhava states here, by settling the mind using various techniques, genuine quiescence will arise in your mind-stream.

Concerning this mind, we might ask, "What is this mind? Who has it? Is it something that somebody else has? Is it something special?" The answer is "no"; the mind is something we all have. If you think your mind is already peaceful, check again. If your mind is frequently subjugated by any of the three poisons of attachment, hatred, or delusion, this clearly indicates that the mind is not peaceful. The mind is like the current of a river. Sometimes it comes under the domination of anger, attachment, pride, and so forth. The mind that is discussed here is just this ongoing stream of consciousness that is subject to these afflictions.

The Actual Practice of Quiescence

Instructions on quiescence with signs. First cultivate your motivation by thinking, "May all sentient beings throughout space achieve perfect awakening. In order that this may happen, in this very life, at this very time, and upon this very cushion, may I achieve this precious, unsurpassable state. In order to fulfill the needs of beings, however they may be trained, I shall cultivate the Mahāyāna Dharma. In conjunction with guru yoga, settle your body, speech, and mind in their natural states. Know that positioning the body with the seven attributes of Vairocana serves as the basis for all meditative objects. While maintaining them, place in front of you a small object such as a stick or pebble. Gaze at it steadily without closing your eyes, and at the same time place your attention upon it steadily, clearly, and lucidly, without being distracted by anything else. Do not strenuously thrust your attention at it. Vividly settle your awareness simply on the unwavering meditative support without succumbing to any ordinary distractions. Remain clear, gently release into a sense of comfort, and relax a bit. Meanwhile, rest the mind naturally, unwaveringly, and steadily upon that meditative support, without entering into the dispersal of thoughts. The text *Transforming Compassion into the Path* states, "Meditate in clarity and joy, cutting off mental dispersion, during many short sessions."

Do not thrust the spear of your attention at the meditative object. For example, you may focus your attention in meditation as if you were an archer strenuously aiming the arrow at your target. That's not the way to focus your mind here, for that entails too much striving and intensity. Rather, simply rest your mind lightly on the object. Dudjom Lingpa illustrated this point with the comment, "Rest your gaze simply so that you don't lose your awareness of space." You lose your awareness of space when your eyes start wandering around and you're looking at different things. Focus just to the extent that your visual awareness of space is not lost, but no more vigorously than that.

> By having short sessions, you do not succumb to the prob-
> lems of laxity and excitation; and by having many sessions,
> a faultless meditative state arises, so train in that way.

For beginners like ourselves, it's very difficult to have long meditative sessions of high quality; so it's better to have as many sessions of short duration as we can throughout the day. By so doing, you avoid the problem of laxity, which is a sinking sensation in your awareness when clarity is lost. This is one major problem in meditation. A second one is excitation, which occurs when you've completely lost control of your mind and it's just brimming over with various types of thoughts pertaining to the past, present, and future. At such times the mind is like a bubbling cauldron of thoughts, and this also causes insomnia. In order to avoid those two problems of laxity and excitation, have many short sessions; and in this way, Padmasambhava says, a faultless meditative state will arise. Therefore, this is a very practical way to avoid obstacles.

> When bringing the session to a close, do not rise from it
> abruptly; rather, with a sense of conscientiousness, gently
> integrate it with your behavior and transform this into
> the path. Let all your conduct be like that of a person
> with a concussion who is afraid of getting bumped, and

conscientiously lead your life in a meditative fashion. Do that for three days.

A person who has a concussion does not jump around, but moves very carefully. Likewise, when you arise from meditation, avoid doing so abruptly. Try to maintain the meditative state, including mindfulness, introspection, and conscientiousness, and integrate it into your subsequent awareness. What's the significance of doing this at the conclusion of the meditation session? By sustaining these qualities of mindfulness, introspection, and conscientiousness, we can gradually gain control over our minds throughout the course of the day. On that basis, we can also learn to control it throughout the night, and eventually through the transitional process following death. Thus, this practice leads to the ability to gain control over the mind at all times, both during and following this lifetime.

The importance of sustaining this meditative state beyond the formal meditation session is not confined just to this practice. This is important for all types of meditative practice: the stage of generation, the stage of completion, and so forth. The process is like growing up. We didn't suddenly transform from being children to adults. Rather we were carefully nurtured from day to day, year to year, and matured gradually, until we came to be as we are now.

> Next, place your body in the proper posture and so on, like before. For your meditative object, vividly direct your attention simply, without wavering, to a white, radiant, clear, limpid bindu at the point between your eyebrows. About the size of a white pea, it appears but is without an inherent nature. Gently release in clarity and joy, and settle your mind in its natural state. Do not be interrupted by thoughts. Meditate just like that, with many sessions of short duration, as before. Engage in that meditation for three days or as your own experience dictates. Whatever experiences occur from time to time, examine them.

The phrase translated here as the "point between the eyebrows," literally refers to the little curl of hair between the eyebrows, which is one of the signs of enlightenment of a Buddha. If you have one of those, you're in really good shape. If you don't, then visualize a white bindu at the point between the eyebrows where you will have that curl when you become a Buddha.

When freeing yourself from the interruptions of compulsive thinking, you must disengage from all thoughts, both good and bad. Don't slack off if the distracting thoughts are nice ones. Rather, avoid being interrupted by thoughts at all. Regarding the instruction "engage in that meditation for three days or as your own experience dictates": if you can gain this realization in one day, that's wonderful. If you can get it one hour, that's just fine. On the other hand, you may need to spend one year doing this practice before genuine experience arises, if you're really honest about it. Therefore, you may want to continue in this practice for a year or for however long it takes until the sought-after experience arises. This reminds me of an experience of mine that occurred a long time ago in Ashland. Someone visited me there and informed me that six months earlier he had attained buddhahood, but in the meantime he had lost it—which is always a disappointment! Genuine experience is not like that. It's not an exalted state that you achieve for a while and then lose without a trace. The stability that is sought here arises from the mind. It is to be cultivated and sustained, not experienced like a flash in the pan.

> Next, practice the other points as previously stated. Then clearly and vividly visualize your own body as hollow, like an inflated balloon.[33] At the level of your heart visualize a radiant bindu the size of an average butter lamp of the nature of unified vital energy and mind. Its color is blue and clear, and its feel is hot. It does not touch the back and it does not touch the chest; rather imagine it at the position of the heart. Instantly, direct your consciousness at that. Clearly and joyfully cut off mental dispersion. When there is distraction, visualize the meditative object.

If your consciousness becomes agitated and the meditative object is not maintained, the element of the vital energy has become dominant; so eat nutritious food, release the meditative object a little bit, and relax. Meanwhile, moment by moment maintain mindfulness and conscientiousness, without being distracted toward ordinary things. On the whole, releasing is most important, so naturally release your mind and see that there is simply no wavering.

In this practice imagine your body to be clear on the inside and the outside, and hollow. The bindu is right in the center of your torso. If you become agitated, this means the vital energy is surging up to some extent. To counteract that, the author says to "eat nutritious food." This means rich food. Don't eat a lot of it, but eat some rich food, release the meditative object a little bit, and relax. But do not relax to the extent that you forget the object.

You should prevent the attention from wavering, but it is most important to release the mind. The statement "releasing is most important" is for people in whom the "wind" element has become dominant. These people need to lighten up a bit, relax, and release the mind. People with different types of metabolisms should take this into account in their meditative practice. For example, if you have a lot of heat in your body, meditate in a cool area. If the wind element is dominant, it's important to direct your awareness downwards. If you tend to have a lot of torpidity in your body and mind, it's important to elevate your gaze and your attention. Whenever you start to veer off to one extreme or another, counterbalance that in your meditative technique.

Moreover, if depression or sadness arises, your consciousness has become distorted, so meditate on the disadvantages of saṃsāra, the difficulty of obtaining a human life of leisure and endowment, and impermanence, and cultivate reverence and devotion for your spiritual mentor or your lama. Take satisfaction, thinking, "Now I have obtained a human life of leisure and endowment, I have met with the precious teaching, and I have come upon such a profound path." Consider, "If I do not strive now, I shall slip up, and I hate to think what would follow after that." Cultivate enthusiasm and delight. Those who do so will find that quiescence arises in their mind-streams.

Here the author touches on the major topics of the Four Thoughts that Turn the Mind. That's just the part that needs to be done. When your consciousness has become "distorted," or crooked, you should straighten it back into shape by meditating on the disadvantages of saṃsāra.

If it does not arise in that way, vividly imagine in the space in front of you the body of Vajrasattva, about one hand-span in height. Although he appears, he is without an inherent nature. Like a polished crystal, he is white, clear, and of the nature of light. Focus your awareness at his heart, and visualize clearly and vividly, with many short sessions as before. Regarding this, the *Sūtra Synthesizing the Contemplations of the Buddha* says there are inexpressible benefits simply from recalling Vajrasattva. Alternatively, focus your awareness in the space in front of you on the body of Bhagavan Śākyamuni, shimmering with golden light. The *King of Samādhi Sūtra* says that there are also incalculable benefits in this meditative object. Or you may lucidly direct your attention, simply without wavering, in the space in front of you on the white syllable HRĪḤ with a *visarga*,[34] at the heart of clear, shimmering white Ārya Avalokiteśvara. The *Sūtra of Basket Weaving* says that this, too, has incalculable benefits.

With those meditative objects, thoughts will evenly decrease. At first thoughts will increase, and there will be more coming and going in excitation. That is a sign that the meditative state has begun to arise. At that time, you may become disgruntled with the meditation and succumb to lassitude. There is also a danger that you may give up, thinking, "The meditation isn't coming along for me. Thoughts in the meditation have just gotten more and more coarse!" Without getting frustrated, gently engage in applying the instructions. That increase of thoughts is the beginning of meditation. Previously, even though thoughts were spinning on unceasingly, there was no sentry of mindfulness, so they naturally flowed out. As their increase is detected by the sentry of mindfulness, they are recognized. This is a desirable sign that the meditative state is arising, so gently recognize the thoughts. Even if you impede them, they will not stop. Without following after them, focus on the meditative object. By so doing, thoughts will become more and more subtle, and they will decrease in number.

Using the above meditative object, thoughts gradually thin out and become more and more subtle. In the beginning stages the mind may appear to be more agitated than it was before meditating. In fact, it was agitated already, but you simply weren't aware of it. Now, for the first time, you are gaining cognizance of how chaotic your mind has been all along. You're actually making progress.

The word "gently" here also has the connotation of "slowly." I've gotten to be known for my general advice to go, "slowly, slowly," so lethargic people defend their lifestyle by saying, "Well, I'm practicing just like Rinpoche said, 'slowly, slowly.'" That's not quite what I mean. What I do mean is that you should gradually proceed in the practice with perseverance. That's what needs to be done here. This initial sign of the apparently increased excitation of the mind is like a brook rapidly cascading down the side of a mountain. Even if you try to stop those thoughts, you will not succeed. That's simply how the mind behaves in the early stages of the meditation.

Even though you are meditating on the object as before, if detrimental habitual thoughts suddenly pop up, focus right on that compulsive ideation as your meditative support. Whatever detrimental, habitual propensities of attachment and hatred arise, recognize them; and in a relaxed way release the mind right upon them. Each time a thought arises, recognize it immediately and release it so that it naturally vanishes. If two thoughts arise, recognize them. Do not follow after anything that appears, but let it arise and be released. At times, focus on the meditative object; and at times, let thoughts arise and vanish. While not fabricating anything in their wake, relax and release. By alternately practicing like that, the chain of compulsive ideation will become disconnected, and thoughts will become fragmented. Thus, detrimental thoughts will become fewer and fewer, and fine stability will arise. Meditate in that way for three days or as your experience dictates. If genuine quiescence with those objects arises in your mind-stream, train in seeking out awareness. On the whole, since it is difficult to subdue this harmful habituation to latent propensities, it is important to use numerous methods to settle the mind in its natural state.

While you're meditating, if thoughts of attachment or hatred arise, focus right on the very object of that attachment or hatred. Let that be the object of your meditation. Rest your awareness right on those thoughts as they arise. In the early stages of the meditation, the thoughts seem to appear in a continual stream, but as you progress in the meditation, gradually these thoughts start to thin out. They become more subtle, fewer in number, and you start to detect intervals between the thoughts rather than an unceasing stream of them. Here is the proper sequence. First of all, let genuine quiescence arise. Strive for that until it actually arises, and thereafter engage in the next phase of the meditation, which entails seeking out the nature of awareness.

All of the practices to which we've been introduced, including the preliminary practices and these various techniques for cultivating quiescence, are designed to help us gain control of our own minds. That's the crucial point. I mentioned that it is important not to take an aggressive approach to subduing the mind, for it gets very agitated when we do so. The reason for this is the mind's beginningless habituation to the various poisons of the mind, including attachment, hatred, and delusion. This is why, as Padmasambhava says here, it is important to use a variety of techniques to subdue the mind.

A central feature of this entire training is the self-liberation, or natural liberation, of awareness. The meaning is that the afflictions of the mind release, or unravel, themselves, like a snake unraveling itself out of its own knots. This natural liberation occurs by itself, not by some other agent. It is important to recognize the difference between natural liberation and primordial liberation. In terms of primordial liberation, there are no knots to be untied, and there's nothing to release; for the mind is primordially liberated. It is appropriate to speak of natural liberation in terms of the path. However, ultimately, the mind is primordially liberated.

The training in the vital energies. Maintaining the body in the posture bearing the seven attributes of Vairocana, let the spine be erect and straight, and press the hands against the ground. While so doing, completely exhale three times, once through the right nostril, once through the left, and once from the middle. Simultaneously imagine that sins and obscurations are purified, and that the sins are discharged from your nostrils in the form of scorpions and are then incinerated in the roaring flames of the fire of primordial wisdom in the space in front of you. This expels the toxins of the vital energies. Then together with your inhalation, while swallowing your saliva once, scrunch down beneath the navel; and without thinking of any meditative object, rest your awareness in clarity. When you can do so no more, completely exhale. Do that for three days.

In case you do not have three nostrils and you're wondering about that third one—the middle one—this simply means you should exhale through both nostrils. Quite a few Tibetan practitioners take snuff, and when they are exhaling, some of the snuff comes flying out, so the visualization may be easier for them. The text suggests imagining sins "in the form of scorpions," but this is only one possibility. For instance, if you have a special predilection for cockroaches, you can imagine cockroaches coming out of your nose.

Training in the unborn vajra-recitation of the three syllables. Expel the residual vital energy and position your body as before. Now when you inhale, imagine the physical blessings of all the buddhas of the three times being drawn in in the form of a white syllable OM. Then push the upper vital energy down, draw the lower vital energy up, and gather them together beneath the navel.

In the midst of the "closed amulet" of the upper and lower vital energies, imagine the essence of the speech of all the buddhas of the three times in the nature of a clear, empty, vivid red syllable ĀH, which appears but is without an inherent nature. Place your awareness there as long as you can.

When you can do so no longer, exhale and simultaneously imagine the essence of the mind of all the buddhas of the three times issuing forth in the form of a blue syllable HŪM, and think of them as a continuous stream of emanations of Nirmāṇakāyas for the sake of the world.

In that way, sustain your attention, with unwavering awareness, on the inhalation in the nature of OM, holding the breath in the nature of ĀH, and exhalation in the nature of HŪM. Doing this at all times is called the unborn vajra-recitation. Each day there are twenty-one thousand six hundred movements of the vital energy. Inexpressible virtues result from having a complete series of the same number of unborn vajra-recitations of the three syllables, so practice it continuously. Do that for three days, then do it constantly. All that has been discussed thus far concerns the achievement of quiescence with signs.

Our respiration is, of course, going on throughout the day and the night. Instead of wasting our breath by engaging in idle gossip and so forth, we can apply the vajra-recitation to the respiration, and this is said to be of enormous benefit. Quite frequently people ask me, "Well, what happens if you do the vase breathing?" My response is, "Why don't you just practice, and you'll find out for yourself."

> *Training in quiescence without signs.* Position your body as before. Then, while steadily gazing into the space in front of you, without meditating on anything, steadily concentrate your consciousness, without wavering, in the space in front of you. Increase the stability and then relax again. Occasionally check out, "What is that consciousness that is concentrating?" Steadily concentrate again, and then check it out again. Do that in an alternating fashion. Even if there are problems of laxity and lethargy, that will dispel them. In all your activities, rely upon unwavering mindfulness. Do that for one day.

In the earlier practices of quiescence with signs, there is a meditative object such as a stick or a pebble, but now there is no such object. Now you simply let your visual gaze and mental awareness rest in space in front of you, without looking around. What is there to look at, anyway? At the same time, it's very important, especially for novices, to maintain three qualities: mindfulness, introspection, and conscientiousness.

Increasing the stability means concentrating, or paying attention, more forcefully. Occasionally bear down in the meditation, and then relax again. Don't try to concentrate forcefully all the time; rather, alternate between intense concentration and relaxation. There are various ways to maintain mindfulness throughout the day, one of which is constantly to sustain the awareness of space. Another way to maintain mindfulness is the vajra-recitation. Whatever technique you follow, it's very important that between sessions you don't discard the practice altogether.

> Then position your body as before. Cast your gaze downward, gently release your mind, and without having anything on which to meditate, gently release both your body and mind into their natural state. Having nothing on which to meditate, and without any modification or adulteration, place your attention simply without wavering, in its own natural state, its natural limpidity, its own character, just as it is. Remain in clarity, and rest the mind so that it is loose and free. Alternate between observing who is concentrating inwardly and who is releasing. If it is the mind, ask, "What is that very agent that releases the mind and concentrates the mind?" Steadily observe yourself, and then release again. By so doing, fine stability will arise, and you may even identify awareness. Do that, too, for one day.

What is meant by settling the mind "without any modification or adulteration"? Modifications, or adulterations of awareness, include good and bad thoughts, plans, and all kinds of judgments. You must also practice "without wavering," so if you're simply sitting there with a wandering mind, you're not doing the practice. Let your awareness rest "in its own natural state, its natural limpidity," implying that if you let your awareness become muddled during meditation, you are not practicing correctly.

> Then do as before. Now, alternately concentrate your consciousness tightly, wholly concentrating it without wavering, and then gently release it, evenly resting it in openness. Again concentrate, and again release. In that way, meditate with alternating constriction and release. At times, steadily direct your gaze up into the sky. Steadily focus your awareness with the desire to be without any-

thing on which to meditate. Relax again. At times, steadily, unwaveringly, direct your awareness into the space on your right; at times, direct it to the left; and at times, direct it downward. During each session, rotate the gaze around in those directions.

In this phase of the practice, you experience a sense of space, so you shouldn't need to tell to other people that you "need space"; you'll have space. As you "direct your gaze up into the sky," you elevate your gaze, but without arching your head back. Just gently raise your gaze up into the sky. The fundamental nature of this awareness that you're bringing into this space is the buddha nature, which is like space, boundless and with no instrinsic nature of its own. This is the awareness you are gradually seeking to identify, and this is the awareness that is being so directed.

Occasionally inquire, "What is that awareness of the one who is focusing the interest?" Let the awareness itself steadily observe itself. At times, let your mind come to rest in the center of your heart, and evenly leave it there. At times, evenly focus it in the expanse of the sky and leave it there. Thus, by shifting the gaze in various, alternating ways, the mind settles in its natural state. As an indication of this, if awareness remains evenly, lucidly, and steadily wherever it is placed, quiescence has arisen.

The "expanse of sky," implies a boundless quality of awareness with no demarcations or limits. The term "release" appears in different contexts in this treatise, and it has different meanings in each context. It appears again with regard to the clear light of the transitional process of dreaming and also in the transitional process of meditative stabilization, each time with somewhat different connotations.

The evenly remaining awareness is the buddha nature, or *tathāgatagarbha,* meaning the embryo, or essence, of the Tathāgata, the Buddha. This is the boundless, spacelike nature of our own awareness. However, in our present situation, it's as if we've stuffed it into a crooked pipe that we've thrown into a trash can. This essence of the buddha nature entails the equality of saṃsāra and nirvāṇa. It is the basis of saṃsāra and nirvāṇa, and it transcends the three times of the past, present, and future. So the nature of awareness is beyond the present. Some of you might wonder, "You say that awareness transcends the present, but elsewhere in this text there are references to the 'awareness of the present' or 'present awareness.' How do you reconcile these two statements?'" These are different usages of the term "present." In the former case, "the present" refers to what is occurring now, as opposed to the past or future. In that sense, awareness is beyond the present. The later references to "present awareness," mean awareness that is primordially without beginning and without end. So this awareness is of the primordial present. The distinction here is between conventional and ultimate truth.

This passage concludes with the statement, "Thus, by shifting the gaze in various, alternating ways, the mind settles in its natural state. As an indication of this, if awareness remains evenly, lucidly, and steadily wherever it is placed, quiescence has arisen." Those are indications by which you can know that quiescence has arisen in your own mind-stream. When you have achieved that, you will never need to tell anybody "give me space," and you will never feel lonely. Wherever you place your attention, it will be imbued with the quality of serenity, like a candle flame that is not flickering due to wind.

In the course of your practice, you may experience any of the following three qualities: joy, clarity, and nonconceptuality. If you do not cling to them, they lead to the achievement of the three embodiments of the Buddha: the Nirmāṇakāya, the Sambhogakāya, and the Dharmakāya. If you respond to these experiences with craving, then joy will lead to rebirth in the desire realm, clarity will lead to rebirth in the form realm, and craving for nonconceptuality will lead to rebirth in the formless realm. All of those three realms are within the cycle of existence, so there's no point in practicing meditation in order to achieve any of those three states. The point is "don't grasp onto them."

If awareness becomes muddled and unmindful, that is the problem of laxity, or dimness; so clear it up, inspire it, and shift your gaze. If it becomes distracted and excited, it is important that you lower your gaze and release your awareness. If *samādhi* arises in which there is nothing of which you can say, "This is meditation," and "This is conceptualization," this is the problem of oblivion. So meditate with alternating concentration and release, and recognize who is meditating. Recognize the flaws of quiescence, and eliminate them right away.

As I mentioned earlier, laxity entails a sinking quality of the mind in which mental acuity is lost. This happens when you're "spacing out" and have lost the sharpness, or vividness, of attention. When laxity increases, it turns into lethargy, which is like an overcast sky. As lethargy increases, clarity decreases; so they are inversely related. Moreover, when dimness sets in, the mind has grown dark, and clarity is gone. When the mind becomes muddled in any of those ways, it's devoid of mindfulness, so you must take steps to enhance the clarity of the mind.

Why is the mind subject to becoming muddled, unmindful, lax, dim, and lethargic? First, and generally speaking, this is because we have been accustomed to unwholesome states of mind since beginningless time. But the dwelling in which you're meditating may also lead to laxity and lethargy. Second, the time or season when you meditate may induce laxity and lethargy. Third, if you are meditating with companions who have allowed their tantric pledges to deteriorate, this can hinder your own practice by giving rise to laxity or lethargy. Fourth, your diet may also give rise to these problems. Fifth, if your posture is poor either during or between meditation sessions, this may also induce laxity and lethargy. Finally, if you're meditating in an improper way, the practice itself may be inducing laxity and lethargy. So you have lots of excuses for laxity and lethargy!

In terms of your environment, to avoid laxity and lethargy, it is important that you don't meditate in a basin-like area, such as in a deep valley or any other low or closed-in area. Rather, meditate in a place that's open and spacious. Also avoid places that have been contaminated in various ways, for example, by people who have lived there and have broken their tantric pledges. If you find that your environment seems to be hindering your practice, purify it. You may do this by burning ritual incense, or applying other means of purification. Be careful that you yourself don't contaminate it. In terms of the time for meditating, summer can be a rather lethagic time due to the heat, and spring can give rise to a sense of laziness, which leads to laxity and lethargy. So those are not the optimal seasons to meditate. In Tibet generally there was a preference for meditating in fall and winter.

On a daily basis, the best time to meditate, generally speaking, is the early morning; and second best is in the evening. It is not so good to meditate during the heat of the day for this induces laxity and lethargy. In terms of your food, it's important that you have a proper diet that doesn't make you feel heavy, lethargic, and sleepy. You may also bless the food by reciting prayers or at least reciting OM MAṆI PADME HŪM. By whatever means, make sure your diet is good, and purify your food with blessings and so forth.

In terms of the posture, it is generally best not to meditate lying down if you are prone to laxity and lethargy, because lying down makes you feel like falling asleep. Sit upright and erect, without slouching over. Finally, in terms of the meditative technique itself, for beginners especially, if you try to simply sit there, staring into space, without any meditative object, the technique itself—unskillfully practiced—may lead to drowsiness and mental wandering, so that you lose all track of time. In this way, you may just get caught up in a barrage of internal chatter, or you may actually fall asleep. To counteract that, it's important that you be aware of the correct way to practice. In this particular technique, you are indeed resting your awareness in the space in front; but your awareness must be imbued with the three qualities of mindfulness, introspection, and conscientiousness. If you practice in that way, these problems will be averted.

Laxity, lethargy, and dimness form a degenerating sequence. There is another interrelated sequence of excitation, scatteredness, and guilt. When excitation sets in, you may recall all kinds of things from the past. Memories flood into the mind, you grasp onto them, and you're carried away by them. Not only do you recall things that have happened in the past, but you compound the problem by elaborating upon them. Then the mind leaps off to the future and thinks of all the things you need to do, and then it dwells on things happening in the present. The mind wanders around in agitation throughout the three times. When this continues, it can lead to a sense of discomfort in the heart and anxiety that may be associated with a mental imbalance. Depression may arise, which you physically feel at your heart. Those are the symptoms of excitation.

When scattering sets in, the mind is bombarded with compulsive ideation about things in the past, the present, and the future. The mind is in an uproar of conceptualization, which results in insomnia. This may also result in a feeling of tension in the shoulders or the heart, and you may feel irritable. If scattering continues unabated, this leads to remorse, self-condemnation, and guilt. For example, when you see how poor your meditation is going, you may conclude, "I'm still terrible at meditation. I'm not getting anywhere. I'll never get anywhere, and I've been wasting my time all along. What am I fooling around like this for?" That's phase three. All three of these phases of excitation, scattering, and regret consist of compulsive ideation, where the mind is simply making itself worse. In the meantime, of course, you're not accomplishing quiescence.

There are many other ways that you can create problems in your meditation. For example, when the meditation seems to be going well, you may congratulate yourself with the thought, "I'm doing really great. This practice is sure to lead to success, because I am such a good meditator." All such thoughts are expressions of attachment, clinging, and grasping, which hinder the practice. You may cling, for example, to the joy and clarity that arise in meditation. Clinging is like an odor that clings to clothing even after its source has been removed. Just as the odor clings to the clothing, so does the mind cling to the objects of experience. Grasping occurs particularly when you do not know of higher attainments on the spiritual path. If you are not aware of them, you are bound to grasp onto and identify with your own experiences, thinking, "Well, this is all there is." This attitude impedes further progress along the path. This may be one reason why Hīnayāna practitioners stop themselves from following the Mahāyāna. They're clinging to their own practice, thinking, "This is all there is," and they refuse to look at more advanced, deeper practices. Similarly, within the context of tantra, some people grasp onto the two stages of generation and completion (corresponding to Mahāyoga and Anuyoga) and think, "This is the highest. There is nothing beyond this." Because of that attitude of grasping onto those two stages of practice, they cannot enter the practice of Atiyoga, or the Great Perfection. Thus, grasping can occur in a wide variety of contexts.

Grasping may also occur with regard to your own nationality or race; that is, you may grasp onto your own identity, thinking, "I am Chinese," "I'm American," or "I'm British." All of these cases of identification are expressions of grasping and clinging. In your meditation, whenever you feel you're a good meditator, recognize this as an expression of grasping, clinging, and attachment. Whenever there is grasping onto any of the three qualities of joy, clarity, or nonconceptuality, attachment and clinging are certainly present. This is a hindrance.

Spiritual teachers certainly may have their own flaws and limitations. For example, a teacher may hold a sectarian view, thinking, "The only teachings that are any good are Nyingmapa teachings." Teachers of other schools of Tibetan Buddhism may think that only the Kagyüpa, Gelugpa, or Sakyapa teachings are the pure path, and all other teachings are false. Likewise, some sectarian teachings declare that only Mahāyāna teachings or Hīnayāna teachings are valid. However, it is possible that a flaw may be perceived simply due to a deficiency in the wisdom and intelligence of the students. Therefore, Padmasambhava advises students and teachers alike to avoid the pitfalls of sectarianism and narrowmindedness. If you find that you have a problem with sectarianism, then, first of all, you should receive teachings. Then with good counsel from a genuine spiritual teacher, you should be able to rid yourself of that fault. It is also appropriate and helpful to offer prayers of supplication to your own spiritual mentor and your chosen deity. These are effective ways of clearing out problems and obstacles. In a word, all such problems arise from one source, and that is grasping.

We are all subject to the problem of grasping. It doesn't affect just one or two people; we all have to recognize it and counteract it. Use the teachings you have received to check out your own behavior and your own mind to see to what extent your mind is still subject to the three poisons of attachment, hatred, and delusion. Checking out your own mind is your business. It's not your business to be examining and judging other people. Among Dharma students, there are unfortunately a number who devote themselves to judging other people, but who never get around to examining themselves. Such students are not putting the teachings into practice, but are simply indulging in the eight mundane concerns. So, despite all the teachings they've received, they have actually become worse people. Once again, I emphasize that it's our business to observe our own behavior and to see how much our minds are still subject to attachment, hatred, and delusion. It's not your business to check other people's behavior: when they get up, what type of food they eat, when they go to sleep, how much they meditate, when they go to the bathroom, and all that. In all such matters, we should mind our own business. In one way, Americans have too much freedom, and in another way, they have no freedom. Their overabundant freedom allows them to gossip and slander in all directions. But this is not real freedom. I think you all need to free yourselves. If you want genuine freedom, devote yourselves to genuine spiritual practice.

Flawless quiescence is like an oil lamp that is unmoved by wind. Wherever the awareness is placed, it is unwaveringly present; awareness is vividly clear, without being sullied by laxity, lethargy, or dimness; wherever the awareness is directed, it is steady and sharply pointed; unmoved by adventitious thoughts, it is straight. Thus, a flawless meditative state arises in one's mind-stream; and until this happens, it is important that the mind is settled in its natural state. Without genuine quiescence arising in one's mind-stream, even if awareness is pointed out, it becomes nothing more than an object of intellectual understanding; one is left simply giving lip-service to the view, and there is the danger that one may succumb to dogmatism. Thus, the root of all meditative states depends upon this. For this reason, do not be introduced to awareness too soon, but practice until there occurs a fine experience of stability. Up to this point, the instructions have concerned the practice of quiescence with and without signs. Samaya.

The references to awareness being "sharply pointed" and "straight" pertain to the analogy of a flame that is unmoved by any breeze. The phrase "giving lip-service to the view" literally means "having the view in your mouth," instead of having genuine understanding of the view. "Dogmatism" occurs when you feel, "Well, I've got it," and you can't listen to anybody else. When you say, "Well, I alone have it," what you really have is the view in your mouth, but no genuine insight. Such dogmatism is likely to occur when you receive the teachings on the nature of awareness without first having genuine quiescence.

INSIGHT

Revealing the Nature of Awareness

In that way, until genuine quiescence arises in your mind-stream, use numerous techniques to settle your mind in its natural state. As an analogy, if you wish to look at reflections and the planets and stars in a pool of water, you will not be see them if the water is disturbed by waves and ripples. But you will clearly see them by looking into a pool in which the water is limpid and unmoving. Likewise, when the mind is jolted around by the wind of objects, like a rider on a bucking bronco, even if you are introduced to awareness, you will not identify it; for once the mind is helplessly manipulated by compulsive ideation, it does not see its own nature.

According to the custom of some teaching traditions, you are first introduced to the view, and upon that basis you seek the meditative state. This makes it difficult to identify awareness. In the tradition presented here, you first establish the meditative state, then on that basis you are introduced to the view. This profound point makes it impossible for you not to identify awareness. Therefore, first settle your mind in its natural state, then bring forth genuine quiescence in your mind-stream, and reveal the nature of awareness.

Position your body with the seven attributes like before. Steadily fix your gaze in the space in front of you, into the vacuity at the level of the tip of your nose, without any disorderliness or duplicity. This is the benefit of this gaze: in the center of the hearts of all beings there is the hollow crystal *kati* channel, which is a channel of primordial wisdom. If it points down and is closed off, primordial wisdom is obscured, and delusion grows. Thus, in animals that channel faces downwards and is closed off, so they are foolish and deluded. In humans that channel points horizontally and is slightly open, so human intelligence is bright and our consciousness is clear. In people who have attained siddhis and in bodhisattvas that channel is open and faces upwards, so there arise unimaginable samādhis, primordial wisdom of knowledge, and vast extrasensory perceptions. These occur due to the open quality of that channel of primordial wisdom. Thus, when the eyes are closed, that channel is closed off and points down, so consciousness is dimmed by the delusion of darkness. By steadily fixing the gaze, that channel faces up and opens, which isolates pure awareness from impure awareness. Then clear, thought-free samādhi arises, and numerous pure visions appear. Thus, the gaze is important.

In all treatises other than the *Tantra of the Sun of the Clear Expanse of the Great Perfection* and the *Profound Dharma of the Natural Emergence of the Peaceful and Wrathful from Enlightened Awareness Engaging in the Search for the Mind,* the hollow crystal kati channel is kept secret, and there are no discussions of this special channel of primordial wisdom. This channel is unlike the central channel, the right channel, the left channel, or any of the channels of the five chakras; it is absolutely not the same as any of them. Its shape is like that of a peppercorn that is just about open, there is no blood or lymph inside it, and it is limpid and clear. A special technique for opening this is hidden in the instructions on the natural liberation pertaining to the lower orifice, great bliss, and desire. The lower yānas do not have even the name of this channel.

Thus, while steadily maintaining the gaze, place the awareness unwaveringly, steadily, clearly, nakedly, and fixedly, without having anything on which to meditate, in the sphere of space. When stability increases, examine the consciousness that is stable. Then gently release and relax. Again place it steadily, and steadfastly observe the consciousness of that moment. What is the nature of that mind? Let it steadfastly observe itself. Is it something clear and steady, or is it an emptiness that is nothing? Is there something there to recognize? Look again and again, and report your experience to me! Thus engage in observing its nature. Do that for one day.

Engaging in the Search for the Mind

Perform the adhisāra and the gaze as before. Steadily place your mind in the space in front of you, and let it be present there. Examine well: what is this thing of yours that you have placed here today? Look to see if the one who is placing and the mind that is being placed are one or two. If they were two, there would have to be two minds, so one must be in buddhahood, while the other roams about in the cycle of existence. So carefully, decisively observe whether they exist as two. If there is not more than one, is that one the mind? Observe: what is the reality of the so-called "mind?" It is impossible to find it by searching among external objects.

People seem to have a fascination for seeking out some things but not others. We all have parents, but we tend to ignore our parents. Some of us have a spiritual mentor and we tend to ignore our mentors. There are the causes for enlightenment, but we tend to ignore those; and each of us is endowed with buddha nature, but we tend to ignore that. When we do seek out buddhas, we look for them outside. Where could they be? We look outside in all directions and in various ways for the qualities of buddhahood. But what we are really seeking is ourselves.

When you direct your awareness to the space in front of you, there seems to be someone who is directing it. There seems to be a mind that is focused, and there seems to be a place where the mind has been focused. Therefore, if this mind is being directed, wouldn't that make it some kind of a thing? If so, what kind of a thing is it? What does it mean to direct the mind in the space in front of you? Is it like placing a thing, like a table, in front of you? What kind of a thing is this that you're placing there?

The type of inquiry suggested here is quite similar to the investigation into personal identitylessness. In the present investigation you ask such questions as, "Does the mind have a color? Does it have a form? What kind of a thing is it? Is it a thing that is being placed?" Having pursued that line of inquiry, you ask, "What is it that is placing the mind?" If there were two minds— one being placed and the other being the placer, is one of them already enlightened, while the other one is still roaming about in saṃsāra? If there are two, why stop there? Shouldn't there be a third one that observes the other two? Where do you stop in this infinite regression?

Here's the critical point: experientially inquire into these issues until you come to complete certainty. Even if you practice this meditation a little bit, if you do not gain certain knowledge, you will never gain competence in this training. Some people actually spend years and years engaging in the practices of hearing, thinking, and meditation; and yet they still haven't gained certain knowledge. The reason is that their mode of investigation has not been decisive.

Concerning the mind that is being placed and that which is placing the mind, you must find out what kind of a phenomenon this mind is. Is it a thing? Is it a substance? Is it real? If it is a thing, does it have a color? Does it have a shape? In the process of this type of inquiry, you are also implicitly asking about your own nature. What does this "I" refer to? What is the nature of "I?" The buddhas and bodhisattvas of the past have never ever been able to find the mind in any external object, so it would seem that it doesn't exist as such. In this regard, the mind is unborn; it is unceasing; and it does not remain. External objects include the five elements and the entire environment. Nowhere is the mind to be found out there.

> Let the one who is pondering, "What is the mind like?" observe that very consciousness, and search for it. Steadily observe the consciousness of the meditator, and search for it. Observe: in reality is the so-called "mind" something that exists? If it does, it should have a shape. What sort of a shape does it have? Look nakedly and seek it out. Decisively look to see what sort of a shape it has, whether it is a sphere, a rectangle, a semicircle, or a triangle, and so on. If you say it has one at all, show me that shape! If you say there is nothing to show, tell me whether it is possible for there to be a real shape that cannot be shown. Identify the emptiness of shape.

Looking nakedly means looking directly, without mediation. Padmasambhava says, "If you can find a shape for the mind, show me what it is!" Maybe you can actually find one. Maybe that which all the buddhas and the bodhisattvas of the past have not been able to find you will be able to find. If so, wonderful! With regard to the mind, "emptiness of shape" means there is no shape to be found with this type of inquiry. It doesn't mean that the mind has an empty shape.

> Likewise, let yourself check to see whether it has any color, size, or dimension. If you say it has none of those, then observe whether it is an emptiness that is nothing. If you say it is an emptiness that is nothing, then how could an emptiness that is nothing know how to meditate? What good is it to say you cannot find it? If it is nothing at all, what is it that brings forth hatred? Is there not someone who thinks the mind has not been found? Look steadily right at that. If you do not discover what it is like, carefully check whether the consciousness that wonders where it is is itself the mind. If it is, what is it like? If it exists, there must be a substance and a color, but are they forthcoming? If it were not to exist, you would be like an unconscious corpse; but isn't there someone who thinks? Thus, within the parameters of existence and nonexistence, decisively observe how it is. In that way draw your awareness in and direct it.

In this inquiry, you fall into one extreme if you conclude that the mind does exist and has certain qualities such as shape, color, dimension, and so on. The other extreme is to conclude that the mind is just nothing. The challenge is to navigate your way between those two extremes. The first is the eternalistic extreme of grasping onto the mind as an existent object or thing. But as you veer away from that extreme, you are likely to fall to the opposite extreme of nihilism, thinking that the mind is simply nothing. If you conclude that the mind is nothing, you should ask, "Well, who was it that thought that?" If it's nothing, how can nothing conclude that it doesn't exist?

> Due to differences in intellect, some may report that they find nothing within the parameters of existence and nonexistence. Let them carefully examine the mind that thinks nothing is found. Is there something that is still? Is there a clarity? Is there a still emptiness? Examine! If they report that there is a stillness, that is quiescence, so that is not the mind. Seek out awareness, and come up with its nature.
>
> If they say it is an emptiness, that is one aspect, so let them seek out awareness. If they say there is a consciousness that is sort of still and sort of clear, but inexpressible, they have identified it a little bit, so they should come to certainty and identify it. Let this phase of spiritual practice last for one day or as long as necessary.

For you who are inquiring into the nature of the mind, if you conclude that it is an emptiness, you've gained recognition of some aspect of it. However, you need to go deeper. You need to gain greater certainty in your recognition of the nature of the mind. The task is clear: come to certainty concerning the nature of the mind. The text says this may take one day. That's fine. If it takes one month, that's good. You may finish the task in one half-hour. If you're really sharp, you might finish it in one second or in the duration of one finger-snap. On the other hand, if you're a real slowpoke, you can spend your whole life trying to do it and still not succeed.

Identifying Awareness

> Have all your pupils sit in front of you in the posture bearing the seven attributes of Vairocana. Now place your awareness right in the space in front of you, steadily without modification, fixedly without wavering, and

clearly without a meditative object. While so doing, given the differences in intellect, in some, a nonconceptual, unmediated, conceptually unstructured reality will arise in their mind-streams. In some there will be a steadiness in awareness. In some, there will be a steady, natural luster of emptiness that is not an emptiness that is nothing; and there will arise a realization that this is awareness itself, it is the nature of the mind. In some, there will arise a sense of straightforward emptiness. In some, appearances and the mind will merge: appearances will not be left outside and awareness will not be left inside. There will arise a sense that they have become inseparably equalized. It is impossible that some such kind of experience will fail to occur.

This phase of the training is intended for fully qualified students who have already gained some decisive insight into the nature of the mind, however long this might have taken. This implies that they have established a suitable foundation of the cultivation of quiescence and insight, and they are therefore well prepared to proceed to the next phase of practice aimed at identifying awareness.

In this phase of the practice, there is no target on which to focus the mind and there is no contrived object that is the support of the meditation. There is no fabrication whatsoever. The differences in intellect may refer to different levels of intellectual acuity, of clarity of awareness, or of purity. There are also differences in the ways the kati channel is closed off, partially open, or fully open. However, the essential point is that the pupils are not all the same.

For us now, appearances and awareness seem to be separate. But in this phase of practice, for some people, appearances and the mind merge. No longer does awareness seem to be inside, while appearances are apart, on the outside.

At that time, the spiritual mentor should provide the following instruction: Oh, now steadily observe this consciousness at the time of placing the mind steadfastly and without modification. Oh, once you have calmed the compulsive thoughts in your mind right where they are, and the mind is unmodified, isn't there a motionless stability? Oh, this is called "quiescence," but it is not the nature of the mind. Now, steadily observe the very nature of your own mind that is being still. Is there a resplendent emptiness that is nothing, that is ungrounded in the nature of any substance, shape, or color? That is called the "empty essence." Isn't there a luster of that emptiness that is unceasing, clear, immaculate, soothing, and luminous, as it were? That is called the "luminous nature." Its essential nature is the indivisibility of sheer emptiness, not established as anything, and in its unceasing, vivid luster such awareness is resplendent and brilliant as it were.

This present, unmoving consciousness, which cannot be directly expressed in words, is given the name "awareness." That which thinks is this alone, so it is given the name "mind." It is this that is mindful of all kinds of things, so it is given the name "mindfulness." While it is not seen, it is a special seeing that is clear, steady, unmediated, and steadfast, so it is given the name "insight." It is that which makes distinctions among all specific phenomena, like separating the layers of a mushroom, so it is given the name "discerning wisdom." All terms such as *sugatagarbha*,[35] "sole quintessence," "absolute nature," "primordial wisdom," "the middle way," "ultimate truth," "Mahāmudrā," "Atiyoga," and "emptiness" are names of this alone. This steadfast awareness exists, so it is that which sees form with the eyes, experiences sounds with the ears, smells with the nose, tastes with the tongue, and so on. All the experiencers of such things are just this clear conscious awareness of the present. However, since we have this, and it variously appears as dislike, attachment, hatred, and so on, and because it knows, remembers, and is aware, we are given the name "sentient being."

We should know that all our mental activities, all our cogitations, and all our mental tasks are done with the mind. Discerning wisdom is the ability to distinguish between things, to categorize, and, among other things, to discern the various stages of the path.

Although there is constant, direct mindful awareness, it does not recognize itself, and that is given the name "inborn ignorance." How is it ignorant? Although the eye sees everything out there, it does not reflexively see itself. Likewise, the mind does not see, does not know, and does not cognize itself, so this is called "ignorance." Consciousness that appears to itself is called "awareness" and "primordial wisdom." In short, it is just this clear, steady consciousness that is ordinarily, naturally present right now.

We tend to fail to see our own faults; or, even if we see them, we tend to want to conceal them. If the buddhas themselves did not conceal faults and if Christ did not try to conceal faults, do you really think that we can conceal faults? Other people may find fault in us, and they may denigrate Buddhists and Buddhism. People who denigrate others are simply displaying their own faults. This is not to say that we don't have faults; we do, for we're still on the path. We haven't become buddhas yet, and so we're bound to have faults and limitations. However, people who spend their time looking for faults in other people and then broadcasting them are simply bringing disgrace upon themselves. Moreover, if we do the same thing and spend our time finding fault with other people, this is our own disgrace. If we are following the Hīnayāna path and see faults in others, we may withdraw into our own practice for the sake of achieving liberation. But if we're following the Mahāyāna path and discern faults in others, then the appropriate response is compassion. If we're following the Vajrayāna, engaging in the stages of generation and completion, then we must cultivate a pure view, seeing others in their divine aspects. In this case, others' faults are not an issue, for this pure view saturates our entire awareness of the world.

Furthermore, if we're engaging in the practice of Atiyoga, our view is beyond the parameters of pure and impure. With this view, we experience an equality, or "equal taste," of all phenomena. The very notions of purity and impurity don't even arise. In terms of faults then, we should point to ourselves, for finding fault in others is our own disgrace. His Holiness the Dalai Lama often distinguishes between honorable and dishonorable conduct. Finding fault in others is dishonorable. In terms of virtue and nonvirtue, seeking out faults in others and slandering them is nonvirtuous. Dharma practitioners who do this forsake their vows of refuge, as well as the religion that they're following. For people of high standing who do so, this is a big disgrace; for those of medium standing, this is a medium disgrace; and for those of low standing, this is a small disgrace. In all cases, it's a disgrace. As soon as we start pointing at other people and saying, "You shouldn't do this," we've already gone too far. If we want to find fault, let us find fault with ourselves and work on ourselves.

When hearing about awareness or primordial wisdom, it's very easy to think, "Oh, what kind of a special consciousness is this? What kind of a wonderful thing is it? Where is it? What is it worth? How much would I have to spend to acquire it?" In comparison to awareness, even a trillion dollars is nothing special; it's just paper. Awareness, on the other hand, is the cause of omniscience. The awareness in question is simply natural, ordinary awareness without any type of modification, without any fabrication. It is without beginning; it is without birth, remaining, or cessation. Failing to recognize its nature, we enter into dualistic grasping, grasping onto ourselves, grasping onto others, grasping onto our own personal identity, grasping onto the identity of other phenomena. In this way, we grasp onto that which is nonexistent as being existent. As a result of that, we continue to wander in the cycle of existence.

It is not grounded in the nature of any shape or color, so it is free of the extreme of eternalism. While it is nonexistent, it is a steady, clear, natural luminosity that is not created by anyone, so it is free of the extreme of nihilism. It did not originate from a certain time, nor did it arise from certain causes and conditions, so it is free of the extreme of birth. The mind does not die or cease at a certain time, so it is free of the extreme of cessation. While it is nonexistent, its unimpeded creative power appears in all manner of ways, so it is free of the extreme of singularity. Although it appears in various ways, it is liberated without having any inherent nature, so it is free of the extreme of multiplicity. Thus, it is called the "view that is free of extremes."

It is said to be "free of bias and partiality." This alone is called the "mind of the Buddha." The mind of a sentient being, that which becomes a buddha, that which wanders in the cycle of existence, and that which experiences joy and sorrow are all this alone. If this did not exist, there would be no one to experience saṃsāra or nirvāṇa or any joy and sorrow, which would imply a comatose extreme of nihilism.

The statement that awareness is free of bias implies that it has no extension or dimension in space, and its lack of partiality implies that it transcends space and time. That is, it is not located in the past, present, or future, nor in any direction in terms of north, south, east, west, and so on.

If you recognize the nature of the mind, that is the mind of a buddha. If you fail to recognize its nature, it's the mind of a sentient being. It's all a question of perspective. As an analogy, one person may be identified in many different ways depending on the perspectives from which he is observed.

This alone has been created by no one, but is self-arisen, primordial, and spontaneous, so it is called "primordial wisdom." Such awareness as this does not originate from the profound instructions of a spiritual mentor, nor does it originate from your sharp intelligence. Primordially and originally, the natural character of the mind-itself exists just like that; but previously it has been obscured by inborn ignorance, so you do not recognize or ascertain it, you are not satisfied, and you do not believe. So until now you have remained in confusion. But now grant it to the master of wealth. Know your own nature. Know your own flaws. That is called "identifying the mind."

This "inborn ignorance" is something we all have, and it prevents us from finding the satisfaction we're seeking. It hinders us from belief, and makes us remain in uncertainty and confusion. "The master of wealth" refers to yourself, your own buddha nature, your own awareness, which is like a wish-fulfilling gem. You are the master of this wealth, the wish-fulfilling gem of your own awareness. When the text says "know your own nature" and "know your own flaws," it is suggesting that we don't act like a cat that defecates and then tries to cover it over. Recognize your faults and let them be perfectly obvious to yourself.

If the mind is empty in the sense of being nothing, or primordially nonexistent, who creates the one who wanders in the cycle of existence and who experiences suffering? Once one has become a buddha, whence arises the primordial wisdom of knowledge, the compassion of mercy, and the enlightened activity of deeds? All those are experienced and created solely by this steadfast awareness that is inseparable clarity, awareness, and emptiness. The phrase "the stainless, sole eye of primordial wisdom"[36] refers to this. The phrases "in an instant all phenomena are penetrated and held by great wisdom" and "the variety of phenomena with form arise from the mind" refer to this alone. "It is the experienced

object of discerning, self-cognizing, primordial wisdom"
and there are other authoritative citations.

All phenomena of saṃsāra and nirvāṇa are comprehended by
understanding this one point. As an analogy, if you recognize
that one drop of water is moist, you know that all water is moist.
Likewise, by knowing the nature of awareness, you recognize the
nature of the whole of saṃsāra and nirvāṇa.

Recognize that right now you're endowed with a precious
human life of leisure and endowment. You've encountered quintessential teachings that have the capacity, if put into practice, to
lead you to the attainment of perfect enlightenment in one lifetime. Also, there have been numerous holy beings who've come
to the United States whom you've had the opportunity to meet.
Arouse yourself with the thought, "Now is the time to come to a
firm conviction and to put this into practice." If you still find
yourself wasting time and not practicing, admonish yourself,
thinking, "All right, enough is enough! Now that everything is set
for practice, am I going to turn back now, turn away from all of
this and just fool around?"

There may be some people encountering these teachings who
have not had much background in Buddhism; and for those people, these teachings may seem somewhat strange. You may be wondering, "What's the context for this?" If you don't have a foundation in theory and practice, it would be good for you to establish
that. The quintessence of that is to know what is meant by this
term saṃsāra, the cycle of existence. Briefly stated, we are presently
human beings, but we are subject to other types of birth, such as
an animal. We don't like to hear that or to think about it, but if we
accummulate the causes for it, then whether we like or not, that's
what happens. We may also take rebirth in a hell realm, which we
would like even less than being an animal; or we may take rebirth
as spirit, which we wouldn't like much either. It doesn't matter
what we like; if we engage in nonvirtue, we are prone to such
unfortunate rebirth. If we avoid nonvirtue, we thereby avoid the
result of nonvirtue, which is such miserable types of rebirth.

Even within the realm of human existence, there's a great deal of diversity among human beings in terms of the quality of life. Within human existence, it is worthwhile to be endowed with a precious life of leisure and endowment. On the other hand, to take birth as a demigod is not worthwhile. They have a lot of power, but it's not useful and produces no real satisfaction. Likewise, gods have a great deal of pleasure, but they experience great anguish when they face death and see that they are about to return to lower realms of existence. There are six states of sentient existence, and it's important to recognize the causes and conditions leading to rebirth among these six realms. Teachings on this subject are found in all traditions of Tibetan Buddhism: Sakya, Gelug, Kagyü, and Nyingma. All these have elaborate and thorough teachings on this subject, and they discuss what is permanent and what is impermanent. This raises the question, "Is it possible to be released from being subject to taking birth again and again within samsāra?" The answer is "yes." Due to the kindness of the Buddha and the teachings that he offered, it is possible.

Following some practices within the Buddhadharma, it is possible to attain liberation in two or three eons. According to some other teachings, it's possible to obtain liberation in five or six years. Among Buddhist teachings, there is a great diversity of instructions, taught in accordance with different individuals' faculties. Those with sharp faculties can use more profound and powerful teachings and practices, while those with duller faculties take a slower route. The basic framework of these teachings is the Four Noble Truths, and the foundation is the Four Thoughts that Turn the Mind. A crucial aspect of this foundation is taking refuge. If you don't know the nature of taking refuge, it's difficult to be able to fathom the meaning of entering into this practice.

I would also like to address the issue of prayers of supplication made by spiritual teachers and other Dharma practitioners. If a single person or a community of people has the karma to experience some adversity, is there any benefit in praying for them? If so, does it depend on who's doing the praying? That is, is it effective only if the person making such supplications has great spiritual power or purity? I cannot judge the power of one person's prayers over those of another. What I do know is that the Three Jewels—the Buddha, Dharma and Sangha—do have the power to be able to help people in times of adversity, by removing their obstacles, and so forth. Therefore, because of the power of the Three Jewels, there is certainly benefit in offering prayers for other people's well-being. This is true of everyone's prayers, not only of those of spiritual teachers, so it is very worthwhile to pray for others. Specifically, you may wonder whether there is any benefit in praying for those suffering from natural disasters and so on. My response is that there is certainly benefit in praying for people who are suffering, be they strangers, your loved ones, relatives, or anyone else. Prayers for their benefit contribute to the alleviation of their suffering. The power of those prayers stems from the Three Jewels, but your prayers can be a contributing influence for this benefit. Such prayers can be effective both in removing temporary obstacles, as well as much deeper spiritual obstacles. Bear in mind, too, that praying for the benefit of others is also of benefit to the person making the prayers. Concerning this point, I encourage you to sweep aside your doubts, and know that such prayers are useful and virtuous.

In the preceding section of the text, Padmasambhava discusses the nature of awareness in his own words. In the following section he backs up his words with scriptural citations from the great, most authoritative tantras and other treatises on Atiyoga. His purpose is to instill confidence, certainty, and belief in the reader. In other words, he is showing that his own presentation is not simply his own fabrication, but is based on the deepest insights of the Buddha.

The *Tantra of the Three Phrases of Liberation by Observation* states:

> O Lord of Mysteries, listen! The immaculate
> nature of your own conscious awareness, this
> immaculate emptiness that is ungrounded in

the nature of any substance or color, is the Buddha Samantabhadra. If the nature of your conscious awareness were just emptiness and bliss, it would not be flat emptiness;[37] rather, your own conscious awareness, which is unceasingly distinct and clear, is the Buddha Samantabhadra. The empty nature of your awareness, which is ungrounded in any substance, and this clear and distinct presence of your conscious awareness are indivisibly present; so this is the Buddha Dharmakāya. Your awareness, which is present as a great aggregate of light of indivisible clarity and emptiness, is unborn and deathless, so it is the Buddha of Immutable Light. It may be recognized.

Here, Vajrapāṇi is the one who is supplicated as the "Lord of Mysteries." The above statements about the nature of awareness are useful only for those who have already gained some insight into the earlier practice of seeking out the nature of the mind. Therefore, if you have sought out the nature of your own mind and you've gained insight in this regard, you are primed for these present teachings. If you've not searched for the nature of the mind, these teachings will not be useful to you.

By referring to the nature of awareness as "immaculate emptiness" and as being unceasing, distinct and clear, Padmasambhava avoids both the extreme of nihilism and the extreme of eternalism. When trying to engage in this practice, some Western and Tibetan practitioners sit gazing out in the space in front of them with bulging eyes as if they're going to see something out there. They wonder, "When am I going to see it? Where is it?" and hope to be able to find something they can latch onto. They will not succeed. The gaze is to be directed outwards in the space of front of you, but it's not because there's something to be seen out there. Rather, that mode of directing the gaze is simply part of the technique, which will eventually lead to insight into the indivisibility of the outer space and the inner space. This union of outer and inner space is often referred to in terms of the analogy of a child meeting his mother.

And:

> O Lord of Mysteries, give me your undivided attention! Your own distinct conscious awareness is the Buddha, so you are not to seek for the Buddha elsewhere. Your own distinct, flickering awareness is constantly clear, so for the Buddha Dharmakāya there is no meditation to be accomplished. Your own awareness, the Dharmakāya, is without birth and death, so in terms of action there is no virtue or vice.

The above citation reinforces the previous assertion that your own awareness is not something that you possess or acquire because you have great mental acuity, or because you have a fine teacher. When you read, "so for the Buddha Dharmakāya (your own awareness), there is no meditation to be accomplished," you may think, "Good, then I don't need to practice. I'm fine as I am." That is a suitable conclusion if you are at this stage of practice, but if you're not, you shouldn't think that you can replace meditation with time spent on the telephone, the fax machine, or the computer.

And:

> O Lord! Just this unceasingly distinct, clear, and present awareness of yours is the Buddha. Since it is inseparable from this unceasingly clear awareness of yours, for the Dharmakāya there is nothing on which to meditate. You may recognize that this distinct and clear awareness of yours is the Buddha.

How do we identify our own awareness as the Buddha? Some of us may think of the Buddha as he is depicted in *thangkas*. Buddhas depicted in that way are generally Nirmāṇakāya, embodiments of the Buddha having form, color, and so forth. In contrast, the Dharmakāya, the nature of your own awareness, has no form. If it were to have form, what form would that be? As you investigate the nature of your own awareness, can you find that it has a form? If it does have a form, does it have a color? If so, fine. But if not, it is a mistake to identify your own awareness with embodiments of the Buddha that do have form. Bear in mind the following threefold analogy of the sun pertaining to the Dharmakāya, Sambhogakāya, and Nirmāṇakāya. The sun is like the Dharmakāya, which is the source of emanations. The rays of sunlight emanating out from the sun are like the Sambhogakāya, and the resultant dispelling of darkness is like the Nirmāṇakāya.

In this regard, the illumination and the light rays are not different from the sun; rather, they are of the same nature as the sun. One is an emanation of the other. Likewise, your own awareness as the Dharmakāya, as the Buddha, naturally, spontaneously emanates myriad forms for the sake of sentient beings. From an ultimate perspective, the Buddha is regarded as formless; and from a relative perspective, the Buddha is regarded as having form, including the Sambhogakāya and the Nirmāṇakāya. Nirmāṇakāyas include various forms of the Buddha endowed with the thirty-two symbols and the eighty signs of a buddha, and they are endowed with phenomenological and ontological knowledge. The Tibetan term for buddha is composed of two syllables, the first of which is *sang*, which means to be awakened or to be cleared away. A buddha has awakened from and cleared away all mental afflictions, such as ignorance, attachment, and hatred. The second syllable *gye* means to expand or to come to fulfillment, implying that a buddha has brought to completion all the excellent qualities of enlightenment.

People who can really fathom the depth and significance of these teachings are those who have gained genuine insight into the stage of generation and the stage of completion, implying a high degree of spiritual maturation and insight. Upon hearing these statements about the identity of the Buddha and your own awareness, you may be shocked. If you are, then you should know that there are many aftershocks coming! For example, in the transitional process of the dream-state, the text will explain how you don't even exist at all; and then it will explore other aspects of reality pertaining to the dream-state. So be prepared.

And a passage from the *Tantra of the Lamp of Primordial Wisdom* states:

> O Lord of Mysteries, listen! The fully perfected Buddha dwells in the core of your own heart. The Dharmakāya of clear, unceasing awareness dwells with the conduct of spontaneous primordial wisdom. Lord of Mysteries, the Dharmakāya in the core of your heart is not grounded in signs, so it is present as emptiness.[38] It dwells as unceasing, clear awareness. It is unobstructedly present without obscuration. As it is spontaneous, it is unceasingly present as an impartial basis of appearances. Lord of Mysteries, the empty presence of the Dharmakāya, which is ungrounded in signs, is the immaculate nature of your own conscious awareness. It is ungrounded in the nature of any substance or color, so it is this immaculate, empty presence.

And:

> Lord of Mysteries, the Dharmakāya, which dwells in the core of your heart as unceasing, clear awareness, is this awareness of yours, whose nature is unceasing, distinct, and clear. O Lord of Mysteries, your own awareness, without birth and death, is clear in the equality of the

three times. The body of the Buddha has no
front or back, so primordial wisdom is unob-
structedly clear. The natural luster of primordial
wisdom has no outside or inside, so objects and
consciousness are nondually clear. The primordial wisdom of knowledge has no partiality,[39] so
to the eyes of primordial wisdom the meaning
of all phenomena is uniquely clear.

And:

Lord of Mysteries, the revelation of the
Dharmakāya exists in dependence upon your
body. Its locus is the core of your heart. Its clarity is
the clarity issuing out from your eyes. The Buddha
dwells inside your heart, and though it is enclosed
by the body of flesh and blood, it is not covered.
Thus, unobscured by the body, it is clearly, unob-
structedly present in the three times. That is the
unborn and undying quality of your awareness.

The statement "clarity issuing out from your eyes" pertains to the
channel that connects the heart to the eyes. This clarity is a kind
of luminosity, and since it is beyond the three times of the past,
present, and future, it is unborn and undying.

The locus of your awareness is your heart, so in a way, you're
pregnant with your own Dharmakāya. If you look for your
awareness in the region of your heart, you won't be able to find
it, for awareness is not grounded in form, nor does it exist as a
physical entity. The assertion that the locus of awareness is at the
heart is metaphorical. While it's located in the heart, it is this
same awareness, or Dharmakāya, that illuminates the entirety of
saṃsāra and nirvāṇa, including your dreams. Given the
metaphorical nature of this statement that awareness is located in
the heart, you should not be concerned that your awareness will
be lost if you have a heart transplant. Awareness is not literally

lodged in the heart, nor is it located in the brain, as is commonly thought in the modern West.

> It is unobstructedly present, unobscured by the five bodies of signs.[40] This is the dimensionless quality of the body of the Buddha. In terms of action, it is unobstructedly present, unobscured by the latent propensities of virtue or vice. As the luster of primordial wisdom has no outside or inside, this is the nondual quality in relation to objects and primordial wisdom. Without being obscured by the faults of darkness, it is unobstructedly present.

And:

> Lord of Mysteries, spontaneity is present in the core of your heart as an aggregate of luminosity of your own awareness. It is the unceasing basis of appearances for everything: since your awareness issues forth from your eyes, forms appear so that they are seen unceasingly. Since your awareness issues forth from your nose, smells are unceasingly sensed. The awareness of the one who senses smells is the Dharmakāya. Due to your awareness issuing forth, the male and female genitals come in contact, and joy unceasingly arises. The awareness of the one who experiences joy is also the Dharmakāya. Know its nature!

Chapter 119 of the *Tantra Equal to Space, Which Synthesizes the Definitive Meaning of the Great Perfection* states:

> This Dharmakāya, free of extremes, is not nonexistent, but is mindful and sensible. It is not nihilistic, but is aware and clear. It is not

eternalistic, but is without substance. It is not
dualistic, but is unpaired. It is not a unity, but it
pervades everything.

The statement that the Dharmakāya is "unpaired" means it has no
companion. The nature of awareness, the Dharmakāya, can be
identified. It is the Dharmakāya that experiences all of these types
of experiences—visual, auditory, gustatory, tactile, the experience of
sexual bliss, and so on. However, do not simply equate it with
awareness that jumps around like a monkey from one window of
perception to another. They are not the same. You can speak of
past, present, and future awareness and of your states of awareness
during the day and night. The Dharmakāya is not the same as all
these states of awareness that occur at some times but not at others,
but they can be regarded as qualities of the Dharmakāya. The
nature of the Dharmakāya is the very nature of the entirety of
saṃsāra and nirvāṇa. It doesn't exist as a substance, nor does it have
form. Rather, the Dharmakāya is the embodiment of primordial
wisdom. Please do not conflate conventional reality with ultimate
reality, for they are not the same thing. The instructions concerning
conventional reality can lead us to ultimate truth, but we do not
learn about conventional reality by way of instructions on ultimate
reality. Our present experience right now is conventional, and we
proceed from this to the ultimate. If you simply equate conventional with ultimate reality, you will fail to understand either.

Self-arisen, Unborn, Natural Clarity states:

If you know the reality of this unceasing,
immutable awareness, which is primordially present, that is the contemplation of Vajrasattva.

And:

Because the mind-itself has no birth or death, it
is present without a beginning or an end. Thus,

since it is unchanging in the three times, it is insubstantial and pervasive, and it is therefore like space. Free of the extremes of superimposition and denial,[41] free of existence, without concepts, it is not nonexistent, and is free of nihilism. Free of the extremes of existence and nonexistence, it is self-arisen. As the nature of awareness is without birth and cessation, it is an embodiment of natural clarity. Immaculate and luminous, it has no outside or inside, so it is the self-cognizing Dharmakāya.

This discussion continues on at great length. The *All-Accomplishing Sovereign* states:

> O great being, listen! My nature is thus: my existence is not more than unity; my display is revealed in dual aspects; my origination is to arise as the nine yānas; my synthesis is to be synthesized as the Great Perfection; my being is the spirit of awakening; my dwelling is to dwell in the absolute nature of reality; my clarity is clarity in the space of awareness; my pervasion is to pervade the entire animate and inanimate universe; and my origination is to arise as the entire phenomenal world. Regarding my display, I have no substance of signs. Regarding my sight, I am free of attended objects. Regarding my consciousness, there are no words to describe it. This essence, which does not arise from causes, is free of all verbal designation.

The nine yānas are the nine spiritual vehicles within Buddhism, beginning with the Śrāvakayāna and culminating in the Great Perfection. There are other classifications of eight, nine, and ten yānas, but they all refer to the same systems of Dharma practice.

In their full elaboration there are nine yānas, but they can be synthesized as the Great Perfection. Bear in mind that all references to the "space of awareness" use the word "space" metaphorically. The "entire animate and inanimate universe" includes the whole of saṃsāra and nirvāṇa. "Attended objects" are those that you can see, or objectify. Consciousness is simply ineffable, for it transcends all verbal designations. The *All-Accomplishing Sovereign* continues:

> If you wish to comprehend that reality with certainty, examine it as you would space. That reality is unborn reality-itself. Upon examination, the mind-itself is without cessation; and reality-itself, which is like space, is analogous to space. Reality-itself, which is without an object, is illustrated by nonobjectivity. It is inexpressible in words, but to utter inexpressible words, it is revealed in the nature of nonobjective reality. If the definitive meaning of this is not realized, whatever terms for reality are revealed, you will not encounter me; veering away from me, I am obscured; and the nature of Dharma is not attained.

And:

> The nature of the Spirit of Awakening is the essence of all phenomena without exception. Unborn and pristine, it is without obscurations; free of a path on which to proceed, it is without pitfalls; primordially spontaneous, there is no need for effort.

This discussion continues on at great length. The *Vajra Array Compendium Sūtra of Knowledge* states:

> The meaning of reality-itself is none other than self-arisen, clear, primordial wisdom. Do not

seek out this precious wish-fulfilling jewel; you have it yourself.

The *All-Accomplishing Sovereign* states:

> "Self-arisen primordial wisdom" is self-arisen and arises without causes or conditions. It is unceasingly clear primordial wisdom.

And:

> That essence, having no causes or conditions, has dominion over everything, and it does everything.

And:

> All phenomena are I, so if this nature of mine is known, all phenomena will be known.

And:

> I am the all-accomplishing revealer, the Spirit of Awakening. The Spirit of Awakening is the all-accomplishing sovereign. The buddhas of the three times are created by the Spirit of Awakening. The sentient beings of the three realms are created by the Spirit of Awakening. The animate and inanimate phenomenal world is created by the spirit of awakening.[42]

All such discussions in the sūtras and tantras refer solely to this clear, empty, steady mind of the present. Not knowing this nature of yours is the basis of confusion; it is "ignorance." It is labeled "the ignorance that is the basis of confusion of sentient beings of the three realms." Knowing this nature of yourself is labeled "the

Samantabhadra basis of liberation." When this is present as ethically neutral luminosity and emptiness, it is given the name, "the foundation."

All sentient beings—dogs, human beings, and everyone else—have buddha nature, because we're sentient beings, so we all have the type of mind that's being discussed here.

The basis of saṃsāra and nirvāṇa and all happiness and suffering is none other than this present conscious awareness alone. Due to this being introduced by the spiritual mentor, the pupils knowing their own nature, believing it, and coming to certainty, the foundation is liberated in its own place. So these are the instructions on the transitional process of living called "the natural liberation of the foundation." Know this in that fashion. This has been the first chapter for accomplishing quiescence and being introduced to the insight of the primordial wisdom of awareness. Samaya.

Sealed, sealed, sealed.

4

The Natural Liberation of Confusion: Experiential Instructions on the Transitional Process of Dreaming

The second general topic, the transitional process of dreaming, entails practical instructions, comparable to holding aloft a lamp in a dark room. These instructions pertain to latent predispositions and lead to transforming the clear light into the path. In this topic there are three parts: (1) daytime instructions on the illusory body and the natural liberation of appearances, (2) nighttime instructions on dreaming and the natural liberation of confusion, and (3) concluding instructions on the clear light and the natural liberation of delusion.

INSTRUCTIONS ON THE ILLUSORY BODY

Here there are two parts: the impure illusory body and the pure illusory body.

The Impure Illusory Body

In a solitary place sit on a comfortable cushion, and cultivate the spirit of awakening, thinking, "May all sentient beings throughout space achieve perfect buddhahood! For that purpose, I shall meditate on the natural liberation of appearances through the instructions on the illusory body." Then offer the supplications, "Bless me that I may practice the illusory body. Bless me that I may realize the illusion-like samādhi."

Your own body is an impure illusory body, and you can see for yourself whether or not it is illusory by putting these teachings into practice. The reason for going into solitude is to free yourself of disturbances. But what is it that's disturbing you? You are disturbing you, so if you don't disturb yourself, you're already set. In other words, the emphasis is not on the environment, but on the way you respond to your environment. Our minds are agitated and disturbed by our chasing after the objects of the five senses. If we can control that, we've already accomplished our solitude. If the problem really were located in the five sensory objects, they should also be able to disturb corpses. Therefore, live in a place in which you are not disturbed, which means, in which you stop disturbing yourself.

The first point of the practice is to cultivate a proper motivation. It's not enough just to sit down and then, with a totally mundane motivation, proceed into the meditation. Rather, among the possibilities of having a virtuous, nonvirtuous, or an ethically neutral motivation, it's necessary to bring forth a virtuous motivation, specifically the motivation of the Spirit of Awakening for the sake of all sentient beings. As you bring to mind sentient beings throughout space, bear in mind that every sentient being wishes to experience happiness but doesn't know how to sow the seeds of happiness. Every sentient being wishes to be free of suffering but doesn't know how to avoid the causes of suffering.

The natural liberation of appearances is the natural liberation of everything that appears to your five senses. Prayers of supplication may be offered to your own spiritual mentor or to the Buddha, Dharma, and Sangha, as you wish.

> It is like this: all phenomena are nonexistent, but they appear to exist and are established as various things, like white and red. That which is impermanent is grasped as permanent, and that which is not truly existent is grasped as being truly existent. Although it is said that this cause of the bondage of all beings is like an illusion, due to grasping onto the true existence of deceptive appearances, phenomena now appear as truly existent. These originally

arose from insubstantiality, they now appear even though they are nonexistent, and in the end they will become nothing. Consider that since these things, which are without permanence, stability, or immutability, have no inherent nature, they are like illusions.

Phenomena are designated as virtuous, nonvirtuous, good, bad, and so on. Although they are illusory and not truly existent, we grasp onto them as being truly or really existent. Did the world originate from something that was real and substantial? No, it arose from insubstantiality. The very nature of reality is illusion-like; this is not something we are artificially superimposing on phenomena. Even though things appear as if they were truly existent, they do not really exist in that way. Rather, they are like the images on a television screen: although you see all manner of things on the screen, there is no corresponding reality inside the television.

Then fasten a very clear mirror on a cubit-high post in front of you. Bathe yourself, and look at the mirror-image of your form adorned with ornaments. Praise it and so on, and see if there is a mind-state of pleasure or displeasure. If there is, think to yourself, "Each time there arises pleasure due to praise of this body, which is like a reflection in a mirror, you are confused. This body is simply an appearance due to an aggregation of dependently related causes and conditions, but in reality it has never existed. Why do you grasp onto it as yourself and take pleasure in it?" Meditate for a long time on the reflected body in the mirror.

A cubit is the distance from the elbow to the tip of your hand, but the important point here is simply to have something to prop up a mirror. Since you probably have mirrors all over your house, you don't need to worry about the post at all. However, if you have no wall-mirror, then do as the text suggests. After bathing yourself, whether you're a man or a woman, put on your finery, adorn yourself with jewels and so forth. Then look at your reflection in the mirror. Try to look your best. If you're a little kid, you probably will have a lot more fun making yourself look ugly. As you observe your mental reaction, bear in mind that there are no grounds for either pleasure or displeasure because there is no essence, or reality, in this reflection. If you do experience some pleasure when you praise yourself, realize the confused nature of this response. Just as the reflection in the mirror occurs due to an aggregation of dependently related causes and conditions, so is this true of our own bodies. In the case of the reflection in the mirror, what are these dependently related causes and conditions? In dependence upon the mirror, your body positioned in front of it, and your observation of the mirror, a reflection appears. Similarly, there are causes and conditions from which the body, too, arises; and on the basis of the body, there is mental grasping onto a self. Although we grasp onto the self, there is no self in reality.

It's not enough to try this out once or twice out of curiosity and then forget about it. For this practice to be effective, we need to meditate for a long time on the reflected body in the mirror. This has a strong bearing on our attachment to ourselves, our bodies, and so forth. For example, from the time that we're very young children, many of us have become accustomed to our parents praising us, and we learn to praise ourselves in a similar fashion. As a result, we come to crave more praise, acceptance, and acknowledgment and to fear other peoples' disrespect, contempt, and rejection. Oscillating between hope and fear regarding others' acceptance and rejection, we go to great lengths to gain their respect. We dress up; we try to appear at our best in the way we express ourselves and so forth. In this way, we totally enmesh ourselves in the eight mundane concerns. Craving occurs when we hope to acquire something, and fear arises with the thought that we won't get it. Or if we already have it, we fear that we'll lose it and hope that we can hold onto it. All this hope and fear, desire and aversion come from grasping onto that which is impermanent as being permanent. Out of that confusion, we have big hopes for saṃsāra. If people were as permanent as we conceive of them, nobody would have ever died, and the world wouldn't be big enough to hold all these immortal people. The objects of attachment, anger, hope, and fear all arise from such delusion, which is operative during the waking state and while dreaming.

Then utter abuse and point out numerous failings, and see if there is displeasure. If so, consider, "All praise and abuse are like latent predispositions, and since the body has no essence, the attitudes of pleasure and displeasure are confused." Clearly meditate on the mirror reflection as your mental object. Alternate between praise and abuse, and equalize them. That is one session.

Then for the training in the speech being like an echo, go without any companions to a place where there are echoes. Shout out good and bad words. When the words come back, toward that echo, or sound, there is no grasping onto the empty noise. Likewise practice regarding your own speech, too, as being like an echo.

For the training in thoughts being like a mirage, look at or imagine a mirage. Just as it cannot be found by going in search of it, the assemblage of thoughts that move the mind are also without an inherent nature, like a mirage. That is the second session.

Then imagine that the mirror reflection dissolves into your own body, and meditate on your body as appearing and yet having no inherent nature. At times, consider this, "The Bhagavan, the Great Sage, discussed all phenomena in terms of ten analogies: all composite phenomena are like an illusion, like a dream, like a mirage, like a reflection, like a city of gandharvas, like an echo, like the moon's reflection in water, like a bubble, like an optical illusion, and like a phantom. They are not truly existent." At times, if you have companions, have them speak to you; or if you do not, imagine mentally praising yourself and showing a great deal of respect for yourself. If pleasurable thoughts arise, equalize them in the absence of true existence. Then imagine being abused, robbed, and beaten. If a mental state of displeasure arises, equalize it in the absence of true existence. Meditate on this as being in no way different than praising or abusing a reflection in a mirror. When you are actually praised or abused, equalize it as if it were a reflection in a mirror. If attachment or hatred arises, train in the previous meditation objects for a long time. Thus, if all the eight mundane concerns arise in your mind-stream as being similar to an illusion, you are adept in the practice of the impure illusory body. That is the third session.

The above training parallels the stage in generation, in which you first imagine your chosen deity in the space in front of you, and then you imagine it dissolving into and becoming indivisible with your own body. At that point, your own body naturally arises in the form of the chosen deity. These teachings regarding mirror reflections also pertain to all our experiences in daily life.

The Pure Illusory Body

What's the point of these various phases of the practice of dream yoga, including the first phase of apprehending the dream and, upon that basis, engaging in the practices of emanation and transformation? Is it simply to enable us to fulfill our desires concerning the eight mundane concerns? The answer is, of course, no. The reason for this training is to know the causes of the perpetuation of our own suffering. So the point of these teachings turns out to be the same as the point of the Four Noble Truths and the Four Thoughts that Turn the Mind.

The impure illusory body is not just your own body; rather this training pertains to the entire environment and all of the things in it, the cities, your homes, and so forth. It includes not only the inanimate environment, but also every sentient being in the universe. Why do we need these teachings? It is because we have the tendency to grasp onto our own personal identity, as well as the identity of other phenomena. In this way, we grasp onto that which is nonexistent as being existent; and again there are two types of grasping: grasping onto a personal identity and grasping onto a phenomenal identity. In order to counteract this deluded mental tendency, the Buddha taught the ten analogies of all phenomena as being like illusions, like echoes, like mirages, like reflections, and so forth.

If we can gain an actual realization of the lack of true existence of phenomena, that's excellent; but at the very least, we should gain some understanding of the lack of substantiality of phenomena. One way to do this is with meditation on your body and other phenomena as having an illusory quality. While phenomena are no more substantial than reflections in a mirror, we respond to them by grasping onto that which is nonexistent as being existent. Upon that basis, there arise attachment and hatred. These are our principal responses to the phenomena of our experienced world; and these two responses of attachment and hatred give rise to the whole array of the five poisons. By succumbing to these five poisons, we continue wandering in the various six realms of existence. What is the point or the significance of these various analogies? It's to slow us down so that we can recognize the nature of our own existence and of our activities as being like an illusion or an echo. In short, nonvirtue is the cause of the perpetuation of cyclic existence. First we must recognize the nonvirtue we have committed and recognize its detrimental effects. To counteract those causes, it's important to confess those we have committed and purify them by means of the four remedial powers. This gradually leads to a release from this cycle of existence.

Focusing on the illusory nature of phenomena, seeing them as being dreaml-ike is akin to practice in the stage of generation in which you visualize or imagine yourself as any of the chosen deities, such as Vajrasattva, Avalokiteśvara, Padmasambhava, Śākyamuni, or any other form of the Buddha. In such practice you imagine yourself as living in a pure realm of primordial wisdom; and in that pure realm you imagine a palace that is inhabited by various male and female deities, all of them pure in nature and having an illusion-like existence. In this practice, you regard both yourself and others as being completely pure and having no substantial existence, and you view all phenomena, animate and inanimate, as appearing and yet not being truly existent. That's the general nature of the stage of generation practice. What is the point of this practice? Such training sows the seeds for the accomplishment of omniscience for the sake of oneself and others.

> Cultivate the spirit of awakening as you did before, and position your body in the cross-legged posture. The spiritual mentor should sit upon a throne, adorned with the garb of Vajrasattva. The students should hold a crystal up to their eyes and look at the body of Vajrasattva. By so doing, the body of Vajrasattva, composed of the five kinds of rainbow light, will appear in two, three, or more places. Meditate on that glorious body, which appears but is without an inherent nature, as your mental object. That is the fourth session.

In this practice, if possible, your spiritual mentor sits in the cross-legged posture while wearing the clothing of Vajrasattva. If this is not possible, the mentor may be replaced with a painting, a statue, or a drawing of Vajrasattva. If you don't have any of those, you can simply imagine this. By holding a crystal up to your eyes while looking at the body of Vajrasattva, you see Vajrasattva in several places as a result of the process of refraction. If it is possible for countless buddhas to be present upon a single atom, there should be nothing astonishing in having a number of buddhas appear to your one eye. In terms of all the buddhas being able to fit upon a single atom, it's not that all of the buddhas come in from all directions and try to all crowd onto a single atom. Rather, all of the buddhas may be present upon a single atom, because the nature of a single atom is of the very same nature as the whole of saṃsāra and nirvāṇa. It's in that context that it is said that all of the buddhas can fit upon a single atom. What about the nature of our own awareness? Is that of the same nature as everything else, or is it something separate? If you assume that the nature of your own awareness is something separate, then all the meditations pertaining to the origin, the location, and the disappearance of consciousness and it's relationship to the three times and so forth would be misguided.

> Then let that divine body, a body that appears but is without an inherent nature, clearly arise as your mental object; imagine it dissolving into your own body, and clearly imagine your own body being like that. When you meditate and train yourself in seeing the whole of the animate and inanimate world as being like that, you are adept in the practice of the pure body. During the transitional process, when the peaceful and wrathful bodies appear, you will surely be liberated. Thus, the main part of the practice of the transitional process of living is just this, and the preliminary practice for the transitional process of dreaming and of reality-itself depends on this alone; so strive in this most diligently. In addition, the impure illusory body is crucial to the preliminary practice of the transitional process of becoming, so both of these illusory bodies are main practices of the transitional process. This is the natural liberation of appearances through the instructions on the illusory body. Samaya.

By training yourself in seeing the whole of the animate and inanimate world as being without inherent existence, it is not that you are simply superimposing this upon the world. Instead, this practice merely acts as a catalyst for gaining insight into the nature of reality. It begins as an imaginary process, but it leads to a direct perception of reality.

If you gain realization in this practice of the pure body, then during the transitional process following death, it is certain that you will be liberated. It is best if you can be liberated when the peaceful emanations arise and, if not then, when the wrathful appearances arise. Either way, if you become adept in this practice, without doubt you will gain liberation in the transitional process following death. Therefore, this current practice of the pure illusory body can be regarded as a preliminary practice for the other transitional processs.

This concludes a brief account of the pure illusory body. At this point, if you find that you have not really understood this text and commentary, I suggest that you study other, more elaborate accounts of these topics. The basis of dream yoga is the preceding practices of the impure and pure illusory bodies. The reason for this is that during the dream-state, various latent propensities manifest as the contents of dream. We don't have any control over those while we're dreaming. Thus, by training in this illusory practice during the daytime, we establish a foundation for gaining control over the mind, and that leads to control also during the dreaming process. If we lack both of those, we will certainly have no control when we actually enter into the transitional process following death.

Some people tell me they want to learn about this practice because they want to be able to teach other people. It's a pitfall to listen to teachings and put them into practice so that you can become a teacher. The proper motivation is to put the teachings into practice so that they may be causes of your own and others' liberation from suffering and the cycle of existence. If you practice like that, then when genuine experience has arisen in your mind-stream, you'll be a real teacher. This happens not by wishing to be a teacher, but by cultivating the above motivation.

NIGHTTIME INSTRUCTIONS ON DREAMING AND THE NATURAL LIBERATION OF CONFUSION

Here there are three parts: (a) apprehending the dream-state, (b) emanation and transformation, and (c) dispelling obstacles to dreaming.

Apprehending the Dream-state

Dreaming is induced by latent predispositions, so regard all daytime appearances as being like a dream and like an illusion. Acquire penetrating insight according to the statement in the *Perfection of Wisdom*, "All phenomena are like a dream and like an illusion." In particular, it is crucial to practice the instructions on daytime appearances and the illusory body. At this time, powerfully imagine that your environment, city, house, companions, conversations, and all activities are a dream; and even say out loud "This is a dream." Continually imagine that this is just a dream.

Then when you go to bed in the evening, cultivate the Spirit of Awakening, thinking, "For the sake of all sentient beings throughout space, I shall practice the illusion-like samādhi, and I shall achieve perfect buddhahood. For that purpose, I shall train in dreaming." Then as you lie down, rest on your right shoulder, with your head pointing north, your right hand pressed against your cheek, and your left placed upon your thigh. Clearly imagine your body as your chosen deity.

Your chosen deity may be Vajrasattva, Śākyamuni, or your own primary spiritual mentor, such as His Holiness the Dalai Lama, His Holiness Dudjom Rinpoche, or His Holiness Karmapa. All of these are genuine tulkus, so I feel this is perfectly appropriate. Thinley Norbu Rinpoche, one of the sons of His Holiness Dudjom Rinpoche, has commented that the American notion of a tulku is different from the traditional Buddhist notion of a tulku. Americans have the sense that a tulku is a person who takes birth as a tulku and then lives his or her life serving others. Then, as soon as that life is over, this person zips off to the next life and takes birth again. Then he or she lives that life as a tulku, dies, again doesn't want to waste any time, and zips off to another life. It's hurry, hurry, hurry—a rush-hour traffic approach to tulkuhood. Trinley Norbu remarked that, in contrast to that, the Buddhist view is that the Dharmakāya emanates effortlessly and immeasurably as Sambhogakāyas; and Sambhogakāyas manifest as innumerable Nirmāṇakāyas, like light rays emanating from the sun. All this occurs spontaneously and limitlessly. That view is very different from the out-of-breath, linear movement of one little tulku zipping through time, leap-frogging from one life to another. There are genuine tulkus who are pure, effortless emanations of the Sambhogakāya. Buddha Śākyamuni was a very great tulku. Therefore, buddhas are simply emanations of the Sambhogakāya and Dharmakāya.

There are also many other beings who, by making altruistic prayers, take birth and lead lives of service; and you can say they too are tulkus. Nowadays, in the West especially, when we hear of a lama who has emanated simultaneously as two or even three different people at the same time, we think, "This is astonishing. How could this ever happen?" We ask such questions because we have a narrow and simplistic view of what it means to be a tulku. Do you get astonished that two or even three rays of light come out from the sun at the same time? Like the sun's rays, tulkus are innumerable.

If your visualization is not clear, establish the pride of thinking, "I am the chosen deity." Imagine that on your pillow your head is resting in the lap of your primary spiritual mentor; and vividly focus your attention upon Orgyen Padma at your throat, the size of your thumb joint, with a smiling, lustrous countenance, appearing and yet having no inherent nature. Mentally offer the supplication, "Bless me that I may apprehend the dream-state. Bless me that I may recognize the dream-state as the dream-state." Lie in the sleeping-lion position, and bring forth a powerful yearning to recognize the dream-state as the dream-state; and while so doing, fall asleep without being interrupted by any other thoughts. Even if you do not apprehend it at the first try, repeat this many times, and earnestly do it with powerful yearning.

In the morning when you wake up, forcefully and distinctly consider, "Not a single one of any of the dreams I had last night remains when I wake up. Likewise, not a single one of all these daytime appearances today will appear tonight in my dreams. There is no difference between the dreams of the day and the night, so they are illusions, they are dreams." That is one session.

If you still do not apprehend the dream-state even after practicing that many times, then with the other practices as they were before, imagine yourself as your single, heroic, chosen deity, and clearly, vividly imagine at your throat your chosen deity once again, the size of your thumb joint. Direct your consciousness without forcing it, and fall asleep while envisioning that you will know the dream-state as the dream-state. That is the second session.

If you still find it difficult to apprehend the dream-state doing that, visualize at your throat a four-petaled lotus with OM in its center, AH in front, NU on the right, TA in back, and RA on the left. First direct your interest to the OM in the center; then when you become sleepily dazed, focus your awareness on the AH in front. As you are falling asleep, attend to the NU on the right. When you are more soundly asleep, focus on the TA in back. When you have fallen fast asleep, focus on the RA on the left. While sleeping, focus your interest on OM, and with the anticipation of dreaming, without being interrupted by other thoughts, apprehend the dream-state with your sleeping awareness. That is the third session.

If the seed syllables are unclear and you still do not apprehend the dream-state in that way, focus your attention clearly and vividly on a bindu of light at your throat; and with the anticipation of dreaming, fall asleep and thereby apprehend the dream-state. That is the fourth session.

Meditate by alternating among the meditative objects, and practice with a powerful sense that daytime appearances are dreams. Even the least of practitioners will apprehend the dream-state within one month.

At first, there will be more dreams, then they will become clearer, and then they will be apprehended. In the event of a frightening circumstance, it is easy to recognize, "This is a dream." It is difficult for it to be apprehended spontaneously, but if it is so apprehended, this is stable. If it is not apprehended in any of those ways, there may be an infraction of your tantric pledges, so apply yourself to going for refuge, cultivating the spirit of awakening, restoration through confession, the hundred-syllable mantra, the *gaṇacakra* offering, avoiding contamination, and meditating in the previous way. By so doing, the dream-state will be apprehended in just two or three months, and eventually you will be able to apprehend it regularly.

A nightmare can act as a catalyst for apprehending the dream as a dream. As an analogy, when the Tibetans were terrified at the Chinese invasion of Tibet, many would pray, "Oh, Guru Rinpoche, Guru Rinpoche, look after me! Tārā, look after me! I take refuge!" But when everything is fine, Guru Rinpoche is not in one's mind, Tārā is not in one's mind, and Buddha is not in one's mind. It is similar in the case of dreaming. When a nightmare is experienced, it is easy to recognize this as a dream, but such recognition is more difficult during a normal dream. However, if, by means of sustained, earnest practice, you do recognize the dream-state as such, this is a much more stable achievement.

Restoring a broken vow through confession usually entails a liturgy for purifying the infractions of one's tantric pledges. Such purification can also be accomplished by reciting the hundred-syllable mantra and offering the gaṇacakra feast. In addition, one should be conscientious about avoiding further nonvirtues. In other words, if you still find that you're not succeeding in practice, this may be due to an infraction of a tantric pledge, so apply any or all of the preceding practices to purify that, and then return to the practice. Once you've apprehended the dream, you train in dream emanation and transformation, which is the next phase of this practice.

Training in Dream Emanation and Transformation

> While apprehending the dream-state, consider, "Since this is now a dream-body, it can be transformed in any way." Whatever arises in the dream, be they demonic apparitions, monkeys, people, dogs, and so on, meditatively transform them into your chosen deity. Practice multiplying them by emanation and changing them into anything you like. That is the fifth session.

All subjects and objects in the dream can be transformed. In this phase of the practice you may take a hundred things and transform them into just one, or take one thing and multiply it by a hundred. This is the practice that Milerepa did during the waking state, when he emanated innumerable forms of a certain object. In one particular account, he emanated himself inside a yak horn, without the yak horn getting bigger or him getting smaller. That is an indication that he was extremely well versed in this kind of practice.

> While apprehending the dream-state, by bringing forth a powerful yearning to go to Abhirati in the east or the pure realm of Orgyen in the west, you can go there and request Dharma. To subdue demonic apparitions and so forth, practice emanating yourself as a *garuda* or Hayagrīva or the like, and transform them in any way you wish. In addition, practice condensing many things into one, and multiplying one thing into many. That is the sixth session.

Upon recognizing the dream-state for what it is, you may bring forth the yearning to go to a pure realm; or you may simply view your present environment as already being a pure realm. Whatever experience and understanding you have in the stage of generation practice may be applied here. While dreaming you can imagine the five buddha families, Vajrasattva, Padmasambhava, or Amitābha being present in Abhirati or any other pure realm.

> *Seeing through the dream*: Apprehend the dream-state and go to the bank of a great river. Consider, "Since I am a mental-body in a dream, there is nothing for the river to carry away." By jumping into the river, you will be carried away by a current of bliss and emptiness. At first, because of the clinging of self-grasping, you won't dare, but that won't happen once you have grown accustomed to it. Similarly, by seeing through all such things as fire, precipices, and carnivorous animals, all fears will arise as samādhi. The critical point for all of that is training in daytime appearances and the illusory body and power-fully anticipating the dream-state. When on the verge of sleep, it is important that you direct your attention to whatever you are apprehending at your throat, be it your spiritual mentor, your chosen deity, seed syllables, or a bindu; and it is crucial that this not be interrupted by latent predispositions. That is the seventh session.

While dreaming, you should remember that everything that happens is no more substantial than a dream. There is really no jumper into a raging torrent; there is no jumping; there's no water to jump into. With that realization, you jump into the river. This practice is not only to be applied to jumping into a river, but to any dangerous situation involving any of the four elements. In the dream-state, you could encounter a dangerous animal or any other fearful circumstance, including finding that you're in a hot hell, a cold hell, or being in a preta realm. Therefore, in any fearful situation recognize your own state as simply a mental body, and recognize every aspect of the dream as

156

nothing more than a dream. With this awareness, enter into what ostensibly looks like a dangerous situation. I hasten to emphasize that this is a dream practice. Don't think that you can go to the Golden Gate Bridge and jump off, thinking, "Well, there is no real jumper," because you will terminate your life and create problems for yourself for at least five hundred lifetimes thereafter. Morever, in this dream-state, if you practice correctly, you'll be carried away by a current of bliss and emptiness, which will not likely happen if you jump off the Golden Gate Bridge.

Dispelling Obstacles of Dreaming

Here there are four parts: (i) dispersal through waking, (ii) dispersal through forgetfulness, (iii) dispersal through confusion, and (iv) dispersal through emptiness.

Dispersal through Waking: As soon as novices recognize, "This is a dream!" they wake up and there is dispersal of that recognition.[43] To dispel that, maintain your attention at the level of the heart and below, and focus your mind on a black bindu the size of a pea, called the "syllable of darkness," on the soles of both feet. That will dispel it.

Dispersal through Forgetfulness: This entails apprehending the dream-state, but immediately becoming confused and letting the dream go on as usual. To dispel that, train in the illusory body during the day, and accustom yourself to envisioning the dream-state. Then as you are about to go to sleep, do so with the yearning, "May I know the dream-state as the dream-state, and not become confused." Also cultivate mindfulness, thinking, "Also, when I am apprehending the dream-state, may I not become confused." That will dispel it.

Dispersal through Confusion: If your dreams are solely deceptive appearances of detrimental latent propensities, your awareness becomes diffused and you never recognize the dream-state at all. Therefore, during the daytime powerfully envision dreaming and strongly emphasize the illusory body.[44] Apply yourself to purifying obscurations, practicing fulfillment and confession, and performing the gaṇacakra offering. By forcefully practicing *prāṇāyāma* with the vital energies, and continuing in all this, the problem will be dispelled.

Dispersal through Insomnia: If sleep is dispersed due to powerful anticipation, and you become diffused as your consciousness simply does not go to sleep, counteract this by imagining a black bindu in the center of your heart. Bring forth the anticipation without force and just for an instant, and by releasing your awareness, without meditating on sleep, you will fall asleep and apprehend the dream-state.

Dispersal through Indolence: First, due to disillusionment [with the cycle of existence] and a spirit of emergence, you may do a little practice in retreat and so on. You may also apprehend the dream-state; but afterwards, as you have not severed your craving for sensual gratification, you become caught up in idle amusements. With a weak disposition, you become completely ordinary, and out of indolence you wreck your spiritual practice. Having no pure vision of any of the Dharmas and practices performed by others, you judge them by your own standards, and your mind slips into ruminating, "I've done that too and I'm like this now. Others are just like me."

This type of attitude was very common in Tibet, and it is also prevalent in the West. At the beginning of the practice, people enthusiastically listen to teachings and get excited about the practice. Disgusted with saṃsāra, they are motivated to attain enlightenment, spend time in retreat, and they may actually have some realizations. As a result, some people come to feel they are quite special, thinking they have become real practitioners. Whether you're a Tibetan or a Westerner, it's very easy to fall into this trap.

These problems arise because people are still very much involved in the eight mundane concerns, and this causes them to get caught up in idle amusements as before. The antidote for this is to meditate on the Four Noble Truths and the Four Thoughts that Turn the Mind. The above problem occurs especially when people acquire a little bit of fame, when they get a name for themselves as experienced meditators. It's especially important for teachers to be careful in this regard, for this is a pit into which they can easily fall.

The reference to having a weak disposition and becoming completely ordinary means that you regress in your spiritual practice. Tibetans may say, "I've spent so many years in a monastic college, and then in a practice center, and I have had such and such experiences, but I'm just like this." Then they may judge everyone else by their own standards, thinking, "These other people have done no more practice than I, so they must not be any more advanced than I am." There's a pomposity and a shamelessness in this type of attitude, and the antidote for it is to go back to the preliminaries.

> For that, meditate on the difficulty of obtaining a human life of leisure and endowment and on death and impermanence. It is most important that you meditate on the faults of the cycle of existence and mentally renounce this life. By applying yourself to solitary, single-pointed practice in retreat and so on, your earlier experiential realization will be restored, and you will again apprehend the dream-state.

When you earnestly embark on your practice a second time, make sure you don't fall into the same traps as before. This can happen very easily, as illustrated in one episode in the life of

Milarepa. Milarepa, a great realized being, requested lodging at the home of a monk, who agreed to take him in for the night. The monk housed Milarepa in the lower floor of his house, while he stayed in the upper floor. That night as the monk was falling asleep, he was thinking, "Tomorrow I think I'll have my cow slaughtered. Once it's butchered, I'll do this and this with its flesh, its bones, its hide, and its head." The monk planned every detail, except what he would do with the cow's tail. That slipped his mind. This monk had quite a reputation, and he dressed in all the finery of a high clergyman, the teacher of many disciples.

When the monk awoke in the morning, he washed himself and said his morning prayers. He looked at Milarepa, and saw that he appeared to be still asleep. The monk arrogantly chastised Milarepa, saying, "Hey, you, why are you still sleeping? Why don't you get up and practice?" Milarepa opened his eyes a little bit and replied groggily, "My problem is last night I was dreaming that I was going to kill a cow, and I dreamed of the things that I was going to do with every part of the cow. But it never occurred to me what I should do with its tail. That's why I've slept in." This is an example of a person whose lifestyle seemed to be that of a Dharma practitioner, while inwardly he was completely enmeshed in the eight mundane concerns.

> If reverence for the spiritual mentor is absent, the dream-state will not be apprehended; if the tantric pledges have degenerated, it will not be apprehended; if there is little familiarization, it will not be apprehended; and if the critical points of the practical instructions are absent, it will not be apprehended. So know how to remedy those problems.

> It is said that by training in this transitional process of dreaming, since the transitional processes of reality-itself and of becoming are like the dream-state, those transitional processes will be apprehended. Moreover, it is said that if the dream-state is apprehended seven times, the transitional process (following death) will be recognized.

These are the instructions on the transitional process of dreaming called "the natural liberation of confusion." Samaya.

The reference to recognizing the dream-state seven times implies that one can recognize the dream-state on a regular basis. If you maintain that ability throughout the rest of your life, then the chances are very good that you will be able to recognize the transitional process following death. On the other hand, if someone recognized the dream-state seven times, or even on a regular basis, and then stopped the practice, it is unlikely that he or she would be able to recognize the transitional process following death.

STABILIZING THE TRANSITIONAL PROCESS OF DREAMING AND INSTRUCTIONS ON TRANSFORMING THE DREAM-STATE INTO THE CLEAR LIGHT: TRAINING IN THE NATURAL LIBERATION OF CONFUSION

> For one month stay in strict retreat and remain in the shade. Eat light and nutritious food, and have massages and so on. Then until the fifteenth day of the month, burn an oil lamp that lasts the whole night. Make gaṇacakra offerings to your spiritual mentors, chosen deity, and the ḍākinīs, and set out a *torma* ritual offering marked with flesh. Have an experienced companion with you.

Nutritious food here refers to quite rich food, but it is not to be eaten in large quantities. This phase of the practice is for those who are advanced in this training, who have already accomplished quiescence and are adept in recognizing the dream-state as such.

> Then for the main practice, at the beginning cultivate the spirit of awakening, thinking, "May all sentient beings throughout space achieve perfect buddhahood. For that purpose, I shall meditate on the clear light, the

natural liberation of delusion. Pray, "For the sake of all sentient beings throughout space, bless me that delusion may arise as the clear light. Bless me that I may apprehend the clear light." Lie down in the sleeping-lion posture, with your head pointing to the north. Slightly hold your breath, curve your neck, and steadily cast your gaze upwards. Focus your attention clearly and vividly on a bindu having the aspect of white light at your heart. With clear, vivid awareness in the nature of light, fall asleep; and in the dream-state the clear light will appear like the essence of limpid space, clear and empty, free of the intellect.

If you have already accomplished quiescence and insight you may now be able to apprehend the clear light through such practice. However, if you lack that basis of experience in quiescence and insight, then success in this practice is doubtful.

A person of superior faculties is the individual who now nakedly identifies awareness. The present realization in limpid deep sleep is called the "clear light." The clear light of the initial transitional process occurring at the verge of death appears to all sentient beings from aphids on up. At that time it will be identified like a child crawling onto its mother's lap, and there is no doubt that in a single instant the contemplation of the Dharmakāya will manifest. Hence, this alone is the most crucial of the six transitional processes. To identify this, it is extremely important that you identify the awareness of the transitional process of living, for that realization is crucial for this apprehension of the clear light in the transitional process of dreaming.

"A person of superior faculties" is a person who immediately realizes the nature of awareness as soon as it is pointed out by one's mentor. Such people have gradually cultivated the practice over many lifetimes, so they are now spiritually mature. Your spiritual mentor acts as a catalyst to open up this realization, like someone opening the curtains on a window to let the sunlight immediately come flooding in.

The clear light does not occur in the dying process only for Buddhists, but for every sentient being. While all sentient beings get some glimpse of the clear light on the verge of death, whether they recognize it or not is another matter. The clear light of sleep occurs, I believe, as you're falling asleep. It manifests during the interval after all of the daytime appearances have vanished and just before any dream appearances arise. Similarly, the clear light momentarily manifests when you're on the verge of waking up after the appearances of the dream-state have passed and just before the appearances of the waking state arise—when some of the power of the daytime appearances is beginning to arise but the actual appearances have not yet arisen.

There are three analogous experiences. First, as the lamas of the past have frequently said, during the interval following the cessation of one thought and prior to the arising of the next thought the clear light manifests, but may or may not be recognized. Secondly, in the interval following the cessation of daytime appearances and prior to the arising of dream appearances, the clear light manifests and may be recognized. Third, during the interval after the appearances of this life have vanished and before the appearances of the transitional process have arisen, the clear light manifests. All three of these are opportunities to realize the clear light; if it is realized on any of those occasions, this is likened to a child crawling onto its mother's lap.

It is important to distinguish between the basis and that which depends upon the basis. The basis is the training during the transitional process of living, namely, the waking practice in which the lama points out to you the nature of awareness. You practice this, you cultivate it, you gain competence and realization in it; and, upon that basis, you can enter into the training pertaining to the transitional process of dreaming. In that context, this is the realization of the clear light. Therefore, the prior training in the transitional process of living is crucial for this later, more advanced training in the transitional process of dreaming.

To apprehend the clear light in the nature of reality-itself, you who nakedly identify awareness should position your body as before, subdue your awareness, and in vivid clarity and emptiness focus your awareness at your heart, and fall asleep. When your sleep is agitated, do not lose the sense of indivisible clarity and emptiness. When you are fast asleep, if the vivid, indivisibly clear and empty light of deep sleep is recognized, the clear light is apprehended. One who remains without losing the experience of meditation all the time while asleep, without the advent of dreams or latent predispositions, is one who dwells in the nature of the clear light of sleep. That is one session.

Again, this type of practice is for a person of superior faculties. In this practice, there is not likely to be any experiential distinction between you as the meditator (the person who is directing your awareness), the object of awareness, and the awareness that is so directed. That type of demarcation between the agent, the object of action, and the instrument of the action has most likely vanished altogether.

Those who can remain in meditation while in dreamless sleep have the potential to abide in the realization of the nature of the clear light of sleep. For an ordinary person, the many dreams that occur during the course of the night are produced by latent predispositions, or mental imprints. These come from the activation of the three poisons, which, in turn, stem from a lack of realization of the two types of identitylessness.

When we've had some bad dream, as soon as we wake up, we tend to be unhappy and grouchy. The reason for our bad mood is that we grasp onto the contents of that bad dream as being real, and this allows its influence to continue throughout the day. Similarly, we feel cheerful upon waking up from a pleasant dream, and due to grasping onto that dream, we may remain in a good mood for the rest of the day. Whether the dreams are good or bad, there's no essence or reality to them.

During the entire dreaming process, even the subjects—we who are dreaming—have no real existence. If we dreamers have no real existence, it goes without saying that the objects experienced in the dream are also not real. This pertains closely to the previous practice of gazing into a mirror and first praising and then reviling the reflection of yourself in the mirror, seeing how you respond in both cases. Then in your ordinary daily lives, see how you respond when you are praised or abused. If you respond as before, with gladness and indignation, this is simply due to grasping; and that is exactly what perpetuates your own existence in saṃsāra. It's imperative that our spiritual practice acts as an antidote for the three poisons, for only then will it benefit us. If we don't apply these teachings as remedies to the afflictions of our own mind, even if we study a hundred volumes of the Buddhist teachings, there will be no benefit. Even if we met with ten thousand or one hundred thousand spiritual teachers and received that many spiritual teachings, there would be no benefit. Even if we met with Padmasambhava or Buddha Śākyamuni, there would still be no benefit. How many countless manifestations of buddhas have already appeared? But here we are; we're still in delusion, still suffering from our afflictions because of not putting the teachings into practice effectively. The fact that we're still suffering and still subject to the poisons of the mind is not due to some limitation or fault on the side of the buddhas, but rather due to our own limitations. It's as though the buddhas say, "Now go east," and we turn our backs to the east and start walking west. Then what do you expect? As soon as you have the orientation of putting into practice whatever you hear, then all the practices of hearing the teachings, thinking, and meditation will be to your benefit.

> Integration with the clear light of the elements: At first, when you fall asleep with your forehead covered with warmth, earth is dissolving into water. At that time, train in the vivid sense of clarity and emptiness, and focus your interest at the heart. Then when consciousness sinks, water is dissolving into fire; and at that time do

not lose the vivid sense of clarity and emptiness. When the mind becomes agitated, fire is dissolving into air; and at that time, too, train in the vivid sense of clarity and emptiness. Falling fast asleep corresponds to air dissolving into consciousness, and at that time, too, clearly and vividly focus on your heart, without losing the earlier sense of clarity and emptiness. Then the state of dreamless lucidity corresponds to the consciousness dissolving into the clear light, and at that time your sleep will lucidly remain in the clarity and emptiness that is unborn and devoid of recollection. If you recognize the clarity and emptiness of that occasion, which is free of the intellect, this is called "recognizing the clear light." That is similar to the dissolution of consciousness into the clear light at the time of death, so this is training for the intermediate state between death and rebirth. The present recognition of the dream-state is the real training for the intermediate state. That is the second session.

When you enter the state that is unborn and devoid of recollection, you do not remember anything and you are without thoughts of any kind. This training of realizing the clear light during the sleeping process is a preparation for being able to recognize the clear light during the dying process. This is like boot camp, in which soldiers are very thoroughly exercised and trained for the occasion when they actually meet with the enemy.

Train in that repeatedly. A little while after you have gone to sleep, have a companion gently arouse you and ask, "Have you apprehended the clear light?" If not, you will by repeating this many times. This is called the "clear light of realization," and it is the foremost among all the kinds of clear light.

If you do not apprehend it by any means, train in the visionary clear light of experience. Position your body as before, present a target by focusing on the clear, vivid, nondual nature of your primary spiritual mentor and Orgyen Padma in the center of a four-petaled lotus inside your heart. Fall asleep as before, with your awareness clear and vivid, and do not lose that sense until your consciousness dissolves into the clear light. First, at the time of deep sleep, vividly remain in clarity and emptiness, without recollection; and thereafter, instead of dreaming, let the form of Orgyen Padma clearly appear at your heart. Then a clear vision of your entire body, then your bed, your meditation hut, and the surrounding environment will arise as if you were seeing it in daylight. As this vision is greatly purified, Mount Meru together with the four quadrants of the world will appear clearly. Such a vision is called the "visionary clear light." By unifying that with the clear light of realization, the basic clear light is identified, and there is no doubt that in the first transitional process you will become a buddha. That is the third session.

If you still do not apprehend it in that way, visualize your body as your chosen deity, and in the immaculately limpid center of your abdomen, which is like an inflated balloon, imagine the central, limpid channel in the aspect of light, appearing and yet without an inherent nature. At your heart, imagine the purified essence of a bindu, having a red sheen and imbued with a clear radiance, inside the central channel, which passes straight through from the crown of your head to beneath the navel. Originating from the purified essence of the vital energies, it is visualized in the aspect of glimmering light; and imagine that due to its radiance, the whole interior of your torso is of the nature of clear, resplendent light. By maintaining that with clear, empty, vivid awareness, without losing it from the time that you fall asleep until you are in deep sleep, the clear light will be apprehended. Even if it is not apprehended on the first try, with your companion, visualize that meditative object repeatedly; and by alternating among those meditative objects, one of the kinds of clear light will be apprehended.

The nature of the clear light, even after the stream of thoughts has ceased and you have gone to sleep, is a clear and empty phenomenon of the dream-state, which is like the center of limpid space, remaining nakedly, without an object. When you are about to wake up, it turns into continuous samādhi. The visionary clear light entails visual appearances being present as if you were perceiving them during the daytime, even though you are asleep. The countryside and so forth are clearly seen. You may think you have not fallen asleep, but you can be awakened. You may think you have fallen asleep, but you will clearly see the things inside your house. If that is unified with the clear light of realization, this is the best, and you will certainly be liberated in the transitional process. In the important instructions on the six transitional processes, this is called the "clear light natural liberation of delusion." Samaya.

In this practice your awareness comes out of your body, so to speak, and you look down and vividly see your own body, your room, and the surrounding environment just as if you were seeing it in daylight. This experience, which occurs while you are asleep, is analogous to the experience during the transitional process following death, in which the consciousness leaves the body and is able to perceive the surrounding environment. In this nighttime practice, you are able to see the entire environment very clearly, so you might very easily think you're not asleep at all. But you can be awakened, and upon awakening you can confirm retrospectively that you were asleep. We have now concluded the explanation of both the transitional process of living and the transitional process of dreaming.

5

The Natural Liberation of Awareness: Experiential Instructions on the Transitional Process of Meditative Stabilization

In the third general topic, the transitional process of meditative stabilization—called the "natural liberation of awareness," with practical instructions comparable to a lovely young woman gazing into a mirror and seeing clearly what had been unclear—is the subject to be taught. Previously, awareness was pointed out and was shown to be "just this," resulting in the mind being tenaciously apprehended as clarity and awareness. By grasping onto it as just that, you cannot be liberated. So here are instructions for enhancing meditative stabilization through identifying awareness by way of practice that is without grasping and that transcends the intellect. Maintaining awareness through careful examination is liberating, so these are called "the instructions on the natural liberation of awareness."

The fundamental obstacle to achieving liberation is grasping. For example, in Hīnayāna practice, there is still grasping onto personal identityness, which hinders one's attainment of spiritual awakening. The type of grasping addressed in these teachings is the subtle grasping onto awareness itself, and the natural liberation of awareness takes place when such grasping ceases. As for the analogy, imagine a lovely young woman who looks into the mirror, puts on her make-up, and makes herself as beautiful as she can. She wants other people to think she's very lovely. By looking into the mirror she can detect any flaws in her appearance, and then she can correct them. Likewise, these teachings show us how to look into the mirror of awareness and perceive that which had previously been unclear.

Prior to this stage of practice, your spiritual mentor should have pointed out to you the salient characteristics of awareness. But then those very qualities can become objects of grasping, since even if you have identified the nature of awareness, you may still be grasping onto it. Now this phase of the practice is intended to lead you beyond that grasping in a way that transcends the intellect. Among Buddhists, it is not only Hīnayāna practitioners who succumb to grasping. Even in the practice of Vajrayāna, the tendency of grasping may be perpetuated in many ways, as, for example, in the stage of generation.

Once there was a lama in Tibet by the name of Kushok Abu, who some people regarded as an incarnation of Khyentse Yeshe Dorje. He was a great lama with extraordinarily profound realization. This lama commented that if people practice the stage of generation with grasping, imagining themselves as wrathful deities with their mouths gaping wide, fangs bared, and so on, this just leads to rebirth as a king of demons. Likewise, if people meditate on their Dharma protectors with grasping, that could also lead to rebirth as a demon. The problem here is not in the visualization, but in the grasping. The stage of completion can act as an antidote for the grasping that likely occurs on the stage of generation. Conversely, the stage of generation is the antidote for the extreme of nihilism, which may arise on the stage of completion.

Similarly, there are different techniques, with signs and without signs, for developing quiescence. By moving from the methods with signs to those without signs, grasping is diminished. In that process you must make sure you don't end up in a kind of daze or trance, because there is no benefit in that whatsoever. In all these different practices, the essential problem is grasping, the major impediment to our own natural liberation. Some of you may be wondering, "Isn't it worthwhile to yearn for liberation and enlightenment? Isn't it worthwhile to have a thought of altruism, wishing to be of service to others, having a thought of compassion? And isn't grasping a part of those mental processes?" I don't have any answer to that. You'll find that out slowly.

The phrase "maintaining awareness through careful examination" means maintaining a constant awareness of awareness itself through careful observation and examination. To quote Dudjom Lingpa, "Never let your awareness leave space." In other words, always keep your awareness in the space in front of you. So these are called the instructions on the natural liberation of awareness.

MEDITATIVE EQUIPOISE OF THE THREEFOLD SPACE

Merely having awareness pointed out as before and knowing your own nature is not enough. As an analogy, due to letting one's wild stallion roam freely for many years, its owner will not recognize it; and it is not enough for the owner to recognize the horse once it is pointed out to him by a herdsman. Methods must be used to capture the wild stallion, then subdue it and put it to work. Likewise, it is not enough simply to identify this wild mind. It is said, "Oh, at this time, when the transitional process of meditative stabilization is appearing to me, the confusing multitudes of distractions have been cast off, and without wavering and without grasping, I enter into the domain that is free of extremes."

You may have the nature of your own awareness pointed out to you by your spiritual mentor, as was described earlier, but simply having it pointed out and having some glimpse of it is not enough. In the history of Tibetan Buddhism in the West, the first person to feed many of the wild stallions of the West was Chögyam Trungpa Rinpoche. Not only did he give people grass, he gave some of them cigarettes and alcohol. To the men who wanted women, he gave women, and to the women who wanted men, he gave men. As he did so, he also appeared to follow in their tracks. He appeared to like cigarettes, women, alcohol, and so forth. By so doing, he revealed to these people their own nature, and he opened the way for other great lamas—including Gyalwa Karmapa, His Holiness the Dalai Lama, and many other great lamas—to round up these wild stallions here in the West. The opportunity for me to teach now is not due to my own power, but due to the preparation accomplished by Chögyam Trungpa Rinpoche and the other great lamas who have already taught here in the West.

To understand the strategy of Chögyam Trungpa Rinpoche, imagine a region in which a peculiar rain has fallen so that whenever people drink any of the water from that rain, they go crazy. Now a king comes who has not drunk the water, and is not crazy; but since everyone else is crazy and he's not, they don't follow him. Because he seems alien, they feel no connection with him. The king then recognizes this, knows he needs to lead these people, and knows he can't do so as long as he appears to be sane and they're all crazy. So he drinks the water, appears to be as crazy as they are, and then they follow him. They say, "Oh, he's just like us." That was Chögyam Trungpa Rinpoche's strategy; he appeared to be as crazy as all of us so that he could effectively lead us, and people would think, "Oh, he's one of the guys. He's just like us."

Just as a sword cannot cut itself, and the eye cannot see itself, we have been unable to recognize our own nature. Here in the West and elsewhere, Buddhist teachers have engaged in a wide variety of activities, some of which have elicited a lot of criticism. From one perspective, a great deal of that criticism is perfectly valid; but from another perspective, those who speak of the faults of others, who become judgmental, contemptuous, and abusive, can also be said to be superficial. That is, they're only seeing the external appearances of behavior, but they're not seeing what's going on inside. They're not seeing the source from which such behavior arises, and they don't see the inner reasons for the behavior that they hold in contempt. They don't see how this type of behavior relates to the present scene here in the West, specifically in the United States. They also have inadequate insight into the application of method and wisdom on the part of bodhisattvas; for bodhisattvas may engage in a wide variety of activities in order to be of effective service to sentient beings in a variety of circumstances.

The core issue here really is your individual karma, the history of your actions, and your own individual merit. What you see and how you judge are chiefly determined by these factors: your own karma and your own merit. If you lack pure karma or merit, you will not be able to see what's really going on, for the long-term consequences of others' actions may turn out differently than what you expect. This is like trying to block the sun with your hand: you can only block a very small space under the sun, but you can't block the sun itself. It is impossible even for the whole world united to raise up a person who is lacking pure karma and merit. Slowly, slowly, as we progress in our practice, these things will become clearer and clearer. The only things that can hold us back are the obscurations we inflict upon ourselves.

In terms of finding faults, do not find fault in earlier teachers who've passed away or in those under whom you have already trained. If you want to find fault in a teacher, I suggest you find fault in me. For those of you who are merciless, you can talk about the faults of others and abuse them. If you have some mercy, you can say, "Oh, the poor thing," and feel some compassion for others for having all their faults. On the other hand, you may cultivate a pure vision of others, but this is very difficult, perhaps so difficult that it is out of the question altogether.

What about those people who spend their time finding fault in others, abusing others, and showing contempt and disdain for others? Are they buddhas? Definitely not. Are they bodhisattvas? Forget it! Buddhas and bodhisattvas are very compassionate beings, and they don't indulge in abusing, slandering, and showing contempt for other people. That's impossible. Do these people who find fault in others have their own obscurations? Definitely! And, since they are subject to their own obscurations and delusions, they not only see the impure as impure, they also see the pure as impure. They see everything as impure because of their own obscurations. This is due to their own ignorance, which is an obscuration arising from delusion. This is how they see the world, and they respond to the world as such.

Remember, buddhas don't go around abusing people. They don't go around slandering or disdaining people. That's simply not in their nature. When any of us are in the process of abusing, slandering or putting down another person, regardless of that other person's qualities, in that very act of abusing the other person, we are thereby revealing our own faults. The very acts of abuse, disdain, slander, and so forth are ways of revealing our own faults. If you squeeze a snake, it's limbs, which otherwise remain hidden, will protrude. Likewise, as soon as we abusively put the squeeze on someone else, our own faults will protrude. As followers of the Buddha, it is inapproapriate for us to continue with this tendency of abuse and slander. When we send out the arrows of contempt, the first person they strike is ourselves. Sharp words are like a two-edged sword. Thinking, "I have a really good sword," you may raise up the saber of your speech, but as you're drawing it back to strike somebody else, its backside is cutting you in half.

> Beginners must practice and meditate with unwavering mindfulness. When the wild stallion is not subdued, it must be trained with unwavering enthusiasm. If you waver, you will lose control of the horse, fall down, and hurt yourself. Likewise, if beginners pursue ordinary thoughts, they will descend to miserable states of existence and will be hurt; so sustain your meditation with unwavering mindfulness.

By having the nature of awareness pointed out to you by your spiritual mentor, you get some understanding, but that alone is not sufficient. Understanding is said to be like a patch: you sew it on, but it very easily falls right off. This initial understanding must be sustained. This natural liberation of awareness is the very understanding of your own awareness. Insofar as we understand our own present awareness, we do not look with hope to other beings. It is our own awareness that is liberating; we do not look with hope to other beings for our liberation.

Especially here in the West, when people think of meditation, they think of something that's very special. When you practice meditation, you expect to see, hold, feel, smell or taste something special. You hope to get something or to be able to bring about something special in your meditation. All such notions are misguided. In the actual practice of meditation you set aside all of your samsaric trips, and letting them be, you do nothing special. Since the very nature of awareness itself is beyond birth, abiding, and cessation, how could meditation actually be doing anything? There is nothing to meditate on, and there is no basis of meditation either. The essence of this is the fruition. Spiritual fruition itself is transformed into the path. Is there a fruition or a culmination of spiritual practice? To transform the fruit into the path, you practice without hope of accomplishing anything and without fear of not accomplishing anything. You can ask, "Well, won't I become a buddha? If I practice, won't this lead to my achievement of buddhahood?" You transform the fruition—which is buddhahood—into the path. A lot of people clap their hands in debate on this point, and the end result is that their hands get very, very red. Again, someone can ask, "Don't you become a buddha as a result of practicing this path? Isn't there, in fact, a result that comes from following the practice?" My response to this is, "Can't you be satisfied with transforming the fruit into the path?"

Take the analogy of parents. Parents nurture their children by feeding them and taking care of them in all ways. By this gradual process, the children grow up. As the parents are nurturing the children, is there anyone who comes to the parent and says, "This isn't your child"? Or does anything happen if somebody outside the family comes and says, "This is your child"? That the children are theirs is already true. Likewise, our own nature is the fruition; but in the course of our practice, we are bringing our own nature to maturity, just like parents bringing their children to maturity by caring for them. It is already our nature, and somebody else telling us it is or isn't so doesn't change anything at all. That's just the way it is.

"Meditation" is another name for not meditating on anything; and in terms of the meaning, the meditative equipoise in the meditative stabilization of the threefold space is taught in the *Tantra of the Three Phrases of Liberation by Observation*:

> O Lord of Mysteries, these are the instructions for actualizing the Dharmakāya: external space is this empty intervening space; internal space is the empty, hollow channel that connects the eyes and the heart; and secret space is the precious palace of your own heart. Direct your awareness to your eyes; direct your eyes to the intervening space, and by leaving your gaze there, primordial wisdom freely arises. When consciousness is directed to your eyes, nonconceptual awareness alone will appear, without being obscured by any compulsive ideation.

The main practice of the meditation, called the "meditation of the threefold space" is to be practiced while the body is in the posture of Vairocana with its seven attributes. Inwardly focus this empty mind-itself on the interconnecting pathway of the empty, hollow channel. Identifying the aperture called the "fluid lasso lamp" entails directing your awareness to the eyes. Let the eyes gaze fixedly at this fresh, external space, and also focus your awareness into the space in front of you. Without meditating on anything, simply without wavering, let it be steady, luminous, and even.

This practice is quite similar to the Leap-over practice. You can learn the significance of this practice only by experiencing it for yourself. Just as you must feed your children for them to grow up, you need to feed yourself through practice. By initially reading these teachings, you may get some understanding; but that alone does not suffice.

First practice in short sessions, and as you become accustomed to it, practice in longer and longer sessions. When you bring the session to an end, do not get up abruptly, but rise slowly without losing the sense of meditating; and proceed without losing the sense of awareness, without wavering, and without grasping. As you eat, drink, speak, and engage in every activity, do so without losing the sentry of unwavering mindfulness. If this happens in meditative equipoise but not afterwards, by integrating this with your spiritual practice and all activities of moving, walking, lying down, and sitting, whatever you do will appear as meditation.

Realization from such practice is not something you can demonstrate to other people, like material wealth. However, if a person claims to have realization and is carefully observed, after a while, it will become evident whether or not that person does in fact have realization.

It's important to be extremely careful here because the nature of karma is very subtle. When we achieve buddhahood, we can say we've gone beyond the distinction between meditation and nonmeditation, for it will be true. Until then, it's important to be very careful about making any such claims about ourselves, commenting, "Oh, I'm meditating all the time. For me there's no difference between meditation and postmeditation." Even a fool can say that with ease, and if you prematurely make such claims about your own spiritual accomplishments and realizations, you simply disgrace yourself.

There are different phases of the practice. For example, you may be able to meditate well during the daytime, but not at night. That is, when you fall into sleep, you fall into ordinary sleep and into the ordinary dream-state, so you are not practicing. That is like being an adolescent. Or in normal circumstances you may be able to practice quite well, but when problems arise, your practice falls apart. That is like being a weak child. The child walks around and seems fine, but as soon as it runs into a problem, its weakness becomes apparent. Regarding this progression, first of all, gain control of the mind so you can acquire some genuine experience during your formal practice of meditation. If you can establish a basis there, you may be able to carry this experience over into the postmeditative state. If you can maintain this meditative state both during and following formal meditation throughout the day, this, in turn, will help you to transform your sleep into a meditative state. If you gain some realization, this will help you to sustain your practice even in the face of major problems, adversities, and obstacles. That, in turn, will empower you to transform your transitional process following death. That is the purpose of this current practice. This is a gradual path; and by establishing a foundation and developing it gradually, the practice expands throughout your entire life, day and night, and even beyond this life. Likewise, of the Zen tradition, it's said that once a teacher takes on a disciple, that student is nurtured from childhood onward. This is really admirable. Likewise, this practice needs to be sustained through all of the above phases.

> There is a treatise that states: "When meditating, do not meditate on anything at all, for in the absolute nature of reality there is nothing on which to meditate." *The All-Accomplishing Sovereign* states:

>> Oh, this is the revelation of myself, the empty, all-accomplishing one: the human body is unborn, and ideation is samādhi. Meditation and nonmeditation do not depend on conditions. The object of meditation is all phenomena just as they appear. Without any manner of placing awareness anywhere, letting it be in its own state, without modification, is meditation.

> And:

>> O heroic Vajra, become acquainted with reality. If the contemplated reality, the mysterious

awareness, does not appear, those who grasp onto and become habituated with words and sounds will not encounter the oral transmission of myself, the All-accomplishing One.

And:

> Do not apply your mind to anything and do not meditate. Do not modify your body, speech, or mind, but let them loose. Without regard for the planets, constellations, lunar date, or time,[45] do not engage your mind, and be free of mantras and mudrās.

THE SELF-LIBERATION OF EVERYTHING THAT APPEARS FOLLOWING MEDITATION

Following such meditation of equipoise, it is important to be guided. After meditating, practice without losing the sense of meditative equipoise; and in particular, whatever thoughts arise, repeatedly let them appear and be released. Each one dissolves in a state of natural liberation. Evenly release each one in the state of nongrasping. Moreover, the natural character of thought is to dwell primordially in natural liberation. When a former thought arises as hatred, and a later one arises as compassion, the earlier hatred did not go anywhere. It is released in natural liberation, without being liberated by anyone. Hatred has never remained immutably. Moreover, the birth of hatred is self-arisen and is a natural appearance of the creative power of primordial wisdom. Thus, since it cannot be said that "it arises from this," the nature of hatred is unborn. In the meantime, this hatred has no location. If it did, and if all the hatred that has arisen from beginningless eons until now were to be put together and measured, it would be impossible for it to fit into the universe with its many thousands of galaxies. Hatred is unborn and has no location, so however it arises, it has never been grounded in reality. Therefore, where has the hatred that arose until yesterday gone today? Where will the hatred that arises tomorrow come from today and where will it exist? Where is the hatred that arises today present now? When love arises, where has hatred gone?

They all appear from the creative power of self-arisen primordial wisdom, so they are not additional, and they are not eliminated even if they are rejected. They are present in the natural liberation of their own character, so they are not destroyed or released by other antidotes. Hatred, nakedly seen, is primordially present as self-liberating, and it is effortlessly liberated in its own state. Right now there is no additional basis of liberation; by identifying hatred as self-arisen primordial wisdom, and by transforming hatred itself into the path of actual meditation, all appearances arise as meditation. Then, with no need to seek elsewhere for meditation, the knot of the mental grasping that occurs in quiescence will unravel right where it is.

Thus, just as hatred is ascertained as unborn and self-liberating, know that whatever mental signs arise, including the eighty-four thousand mental afflictions, they all are unborn and self-liberating. So there is no point to getting rid of thoughts and cultivating nonconceptuality. If one bamboo stalk is hollow inside, all bamboo stalks are hollow inside; if one bamboo joint is closed off, all bamboo joints are closed off; if you know that one waterdrop is wet, you know that all waterdrops are wet. Likewise, by knowing that an instant of thought is unborn and self-liberating, you know that every thought is unborn and self-liberating. Ascertaining an instant of mental consciousness as unborn and self-liberating is called "ascertaining on the basis of a single instance." If one rejects that instant of consciousness, then looks for something else, there is nothing to be identified; so it is called "identifying on the basis of oneself." Since its character is revealed as self-liberating, it is called "establishing confidence on the basis of liberation."

In establishing confidence on the basis of liberation, there are four great ways of liberation. Whatever thoughts arise, their character remains primordially liberated, self-liberated, instantly liberated, and completely liberated. When a thought of attachment suddenly arises, its character remains primordially liberated, so there is now no additional basis of liberation. It liberates itself, without being liberated by anyone else, so there are no other antidotes to liberate it. As a thought instantly observes itself, it is without an inherent nature, and there is nothing to see; since it is instantly released, it is not immutable. Since the arisen thought occurs by itself, its release is also complete; so now there is no need to exert effort to release it.

If one arises, it is primordially liberated; if two arise, they are self-liberated, instantly liberated, and completely liberated. Since this critical point of the manner of their liberation has not been fathomed until now, thoughts are grasped in the usual way; and as a result, you wander in the cycle of existence, and there is no time when you are liberated. Now, with the four types of liberation, know the problem. Once your spiritual mentor has pointed it out and the certainty of liberation has arisen, now what do you have to do with meditations that entail wielding the spike of mental grasping? Whatever appears, let it go as self-liberating. Do not meditate; let awareness roam freely. Settle your awareness evenly.

These four types of liberation did not originate from the profound instructions of the spiritual mentor. You did not discover them by being fine, courageous people. You did not happen to discover them by being very lucky. The character of all sentient beings primordially remains as those four great types, but they do not know they are liberated. Bound by the ungraspable, they remain wandering about in the cycle of existence. While they roam in the cycle of existence, they have never been parted from the four great ways of liberation. It is impossible for them to part from them, and they will not. While their character is liberated, due to grasping they are subject to confusion and they continue to experience suffering.

For example, even when they painfully experience the suffering of the Avīci hell, they suffer without recognizing that their character remains in the four great types of liberation. If they were to know that the innate character of the thoughts of suffering is liberated, there would never be any suffering. Due to being obscured by the three kinds of ignorance, they do not know the manner of their liberation.

Whether you receive these teachings orally or study the written text, it's most important to put these teachings into practice. As these are Atiyoga teachings, it is useless to try to practice them without first devoting yourselves to the preliminary practices. Emphasize your own practice, rather than thinking of how you can broadcast these teachings to other people. There is no benefit in telling other people about these teachings or in taking on the role of a spiritual mentor if you have only a conceptual understanding; and you may actually be sowing seeds for your own lower rebirth. Put the teachings into practice, gain experience in them; and thereafter you can teach from your own realization. If you are not qualified to teach this, even if you think you are acting out of altruism or compassion, you are making a mistake. Be careful of attributing such lofty motivations to yourself. If you think you can serve the Dharma more effectively than the great lamas—such as His Holiness the Dalai Lama, His Holiness Dudjom Rinpoche, Gyalwa Karmapa, and so forth—you might want to think again. On the other hand, if you engage in this practice purely for the sake of sentient beings, that's fine. But bear in mind that it is very difficult to have a motivation free of the eight mundane concerns and free of all trace of self-centeredness.

Between the two types of the Spirit of Awakening—the spirit of aspiring for awakening and the spirit of venturing toward awakening—for now we should really focus on the former. The spirit of venturing toward awakening requires a firm foundation in hearing, thinking, and meditation, as well as a thorough training in the six perfections. It's not so easy. Raise yourself as a parent raises a child. Nurture yourself, feed yourself with practice; and eventually, when you come to spiritual adulthood, you will be able to do whatever is needed. If you would really like to serve the Dharma and sentient beings, use what you already have to fulfill those lofty and noble ideals. Namely, use your body, speech, and mind. For example, with your body, you can offer prostrations and engage in various devotional practices. In terms of serving other sentient beings, practice the first perfection, the perfection of generosity. Make gifts, and be of service in ways that you can, whether it's with material things or in other ways. Then proceed gradually through the other five perfections. Cultivate and practice the perfections of ethical discipline, patience, zeal, meditation, and wisdom. Grow through training in those perfections gradually, accumulate merit, and purify your mind-stream. These are very practical ways of serving sentient beings by means of your body, speech, and mind. However, without having any real experience of the Great Perfection, difficulties will arise from trying to teach it. On the other hand, if you put these teachings into practice, realization will gradually arise, and you will be in a position to share these teachings with others.

A scriptural source for the four great types of liberation is the *Primary Tantra on the Penetration of Sound*:

> Your own awareness is free of conceptualization, so it is endowed with the four great types of liberation. As it is primordially liberated (which is the point of not modifying anything), there is no additional basis. As it is liberated by itself

(which is the point of not investigating), there
are no antidotes. As it is instantly liberated
(which is the point of leaving it in its own
state), it vanishes right where it is seen. As it is
completely liberated, there is no exertion.

Being primordially liberated means there's nothing extra to do
and nothing in need of modification, because awareness is primordially liberated, just as sunlight is primordially present, even
though it may be temporarily obscured by clouds. Because awareness is self-liberating, there is no need for any other antidote,
such a meditation. However, insofar as we are still proceeding
along the path, techniques of meditation are necessary; pragmati-
cally speaking, we need to use them.

In terms of the instant liberation of awareness, it's not that
awareness vanishes "right where it is seen" but rather in the very
moment of recognizing the nature of awareness, all impurities
and obscurations instantly vanish. This is like the analogy of the
rope that is mistaken for a snake. As soon as you see that it is
indeed a rope, the whole appearance of a snake instantly vanishes. Thus, there is nothing to apply to the mind to counteract its
impurities and make them vanish. There's nothing that helps
them vanish or anything that prevents them from vanishing.
Awareness is "completely liberated," because of its absolute, total
liberation in terms of its center and its periphery, and in terms of
the three times—past, present, and future. Therefore, there is no
need to exert physical, verbal, or mental effort to liberate it.

The Pearl Rosary states:

As it is primordially liberated, it is eternally exalted. As it is self-liberated, objective conditions are
exhausted. As it is instantly liberated, appearances
are pure. As it is liberated from extremes, the four
alternatives are purified. As it is liberated from
singularity, it is empty of multiplicity.

In the self-liberation of awareness, causes and conditions have totally vanished. In the instant liberation of awareness, appearances are primordially pure. Such purity does not occur after some time, nor does it come from anywhere else than the very nature of awareness. Awareness is liberated from all the extremes of nihilism, eternalism, and so on. The "four alternatives" are to be existent, nonexistent, both existent and nonexistent, and neither existent nor nonexitsent. Awareness is liberated from being any of these four alternatives. Since it is of the single nature of the entirety of saṃsāra and nirvāṇa, awareness is "empty of multiplicity."

> Thus, since all appearances and sounds remain in the four types of liberation, they are not bound by anything, and they are not liberated by anything. Everything self-arises from its own state and is self-liberated. Whatever appears is free of the three extremes of birth, cessation, and abiding, so reality-itself is self-appearing. Therefore, due to the spiritual mentor's simply pointing this out, once you know reality-itself to be self-appearing, you will realize appearances and consciousness as reality-itself.

In the four types of liberation, nothing is bound by anything, but in the cycle of existence, we are bound by self-grasping: grasping onto a personal self and grasping onto phenomena. However, in terms of their own nature with reference to these four types of liberation, all appearances and sound are not bound by anything, nor are they liberated by anything; so no antidotes are necessary.

I've observed that when many of you meditate, you are like an archer straining to find the target and to direct your arrow toward the target. Your mind is full of tension, and you're trying to hold steady. On the one hand, such earnestness and diligence are good. You become entranced with your meditation object, like a deer that has been mesmerized by the sound of a guitar. On the other hand, too much effort and tension in your practice can create problems. You're straining hard, trying to hold onto the object, which appears to be unstable. To counteract such excessive tension, lighten up. Ease up a bit in the meditation. Let your mind be more spacious.

Bear in mind the previous analogy of taming a wild stallion. If you aggressively hold onto a rope tied to the stallion's bridle, and yank on it, while grimacing and trying to hold the stallion down, the stallion will also respond aggressively. And this will tire you both out. A more skillful approach is to tame the stallion gently. Then the horse will also respond with gentleness. I think there's wisdom in this approach, because the very nature of that which is doing the disciplining and that which is being disciplined is awareness. Consequently, if you take this more gentle and easy approach, I suspect there will be fewer problems.

Whatever appears is liberated in its own state, so appearances are free of negation and affirmation, as is stated in the *Primary Tantra on the Penetration of Sound*:

Thus, everything is reality-itself, and apart from this there is nothing to be accepted and not the slightest thing to be left aside. Whatever appears is reality-itself, and apart from this there is no contrived reality-itself. Whatever is done, non-conceptuality arises. Without rejecting or accepting, it is self-appearing.

The Jewel-Studded Gem states:

When penetrating consciousness shines on objects, appearances are self-appearing. At that time, let consciousness be uninhibited.

Self-Arising Awareness states:

The meaning of having nothing on which to meditate is to not reject anything. If you have no grasping or attachment, you discover the unsurpassable. Without rejection and free of an object that is rejected, there is no objectified rejecter, so how could there be anything rejected?

The Mound of Jewels states:

> O Speech Vajra, with your empty consciousness observe the primordial wisdom of all appearances. All appearances of every kind arise to assist it—amazing!

Your consciousness is empty consciousness, because it lacks any kind of substantiality, essence, or core. Appearances, being creative expressions of awareness, do not hinder or in any way harm awareness, but rather they arise to assist awareness. This is like the relationship between mud and a flower. Mud does not hinder the flower, but rather helps it to blossom.

> Whatever appears, it does not budge from its own basis—ha ha! With your empty awareness observe fully liberated appearances. They are great as their own antidotes—amazing! Mental afflictions are self-liberating on their own—ha ha! With your empty awareness observe the imaginary nature[46] that is primordially liberated. Effortlessly, the result is obtained—amazing! By apprehending one thing, all of saṃsāra and nirvāṇa are purified in nonduality—ha ha!

Self-Arising Awareness again states:

> Do not cling to appearances. Do not affirm nonexistence. Do not reject existence. Do not accomplish buddhahood. Do not practice meditation. Do not cultivate the view. Do not put a stop to deceptive appearances. Do not experience pure appearances.

The earlier treatise also states:

> For the view, observe self-arisen primordial wisdom. It is beyond virtue and vice, meditation and view—amazing! Without moving the basis, whatever physical actions are performed, they are free of virtue and vice, benefit and harm—ha ha!

In this mode of experience, whatever physical actions you perform, the basis does not move. This can be understood in terms of the ocean. Even though the surface of the ocean may be moving with the waves, its depths do not move. Likewise, physical actions are like the waves on the ocean's surface, while the nature of awareness is like the depths of the ocean.

> Observe the type of presence of the character of things. These appearances do not turn their coats or change their coloration—amazing! Whatever joys and sorrows you enact, in reality there is no change—ha ha! Observe the great emptiness, the primordial wisdom that is the source of everything. Various recalled and imagined activities appear—amazing! Whatever is done is liberated, without birth, in the unceasing expanse—ha ha!

This "type of presence" simply refers to the nature of phenomena. Appearances do not change in any way in terms of their actual nature. This entire citation refers to the nature of awareness. Of course, on a conventional or relative level, there are joys, sorrows, and a lot of change; but the nature of awareness is beyond any such change. Activities naturally appear; they self-arise.

The All-Accomplishing Sovereign states:

> Be not distracted from the view of thoughts being liberated in their own state; leave them in

their nature without making effort. Everything
is self-arisen and is liberated in its own state.

Thus, all phenomena of appearances and consciousness
are bound by no one and liberated by no one. When you
realize how they appear from a state that is primordially
free of bondage and liberation, there is nothing to accept
or reject anywhere. Due to knowing that whatever appears
is of the nature of reality-itself, apart from that there is no
fine meditation to be practiced. A bad thought is not to
be cast away. Whatever happens, it is free from bondage
and liberation. The *Perfection of Wisdom* states, "Form is
unbound and unliberated...omniscience is unbound and
unliberated." Realize that and be liberated. As a result, like
going to an island of jewels and gold, everything is liberated in the great emptiness of reality-itself, the grasped
meditative object is liberated in its own state, and you will
become a buddha with no transitional process.

Please bear in mind that this all pertains to the nature of awareness. From that perspective, all these statements hold true.
There's no excellent meditation to be practiced in order to smell,
see, or hold onto something special. Once you've attained perfect
enlightenment, it is like being on an island composed only of
jewels and gold, where everything you see is of the same nature.
Here, in that realization of enlightenment, everything you see
appears as reality-itself, so there are no ordinary appearances.

There are three ways of becoming a buddha. The best is
by realizing the meaning of the four great types of liberation and becoming a buddha in this very life, such that
your aggregates, together with their contaminants, disappear. Middling is to become a buddha while dying by
means of the instructions on transference, or else to
become a buddha in the transitional process of reality-
itself by the power of truth becoming manifest. The least

is to become a buddha by being released in a Nirmāṇakāya pure realm in the transitional process of becoming, or else to choose a fine birthplace, take birth, encounter this Dharma, and become a buddha. Here are the instructions on the best way to be free of the craving of samādhi in the transitional process of meditative stabilization, on identifying the four great types of liberation, and becoming a buddha. These are the instructions on the transitional process of meditative stabilization called the "natural liberation of awareness." Samaya.

Sealed, sealed, sealed.

To accomplish buddhahood in "the best way" is to accomplish it by achieving the rainbow body, specifically the "great transference rainbow body," in which you are totally transformed, so that you do not leave even your fingernails behind at death. The power of truth becomes manifest by means of the two stages of generation and completion. The key to being free of the craving of samādhi is to release grasping. The best student is an "instantaneous person" who gains realization as soon as the nature of awareness is pointed out. What type of person is an instantaneous individual or one who will achieve the great transference rainbow body? It is a person who has, over the course of many lifetimes, already trained first in the sūtras, then in the tantras, and finally in the Great Perfection. By means of this long training from lifetime to lifetime, such a person is spiritually mature and ready to come to perfect awakening.

This person can be likened to a garuḍa, which is immediately ready to fly as soon as it hatches from its egg, in contrast to other birds who must develop and exercise their wings before they can leave the nest. Thus, the instantaneous person is like a garuḍa, while the rest of us ordinary people are like the ordinary birds who have to practice more gradually. This is done by training in the six perfections of generosity, ethical discipline, and so forth. If one follows this route the whole way through three countless eons, this finally culminates in the achievement of perfect enlightenment. All of us here have to train gradually; we need to engage in the training and practice with body, speech, and mind. In this way, we will gradually ripen our mind-streams.

There are wonderful treatises with profound teachings on the Great Perfection, such as *The Seven Treasures of Longchen Rabjampa*, and there are wonderful lamas who have come here to offer such teachings. By receiving such teachings, by reading books from the growing body of literature on the Great Perfection translated into Western languages, and by meditating gradually, the view of the Great Perfection will be realized.

What are the tangible benefits of purifying our minds of afflictions such as attachment, hatred, and delusion? The first benefit is that we will never return to this cycle of existence. Our liberation will be irreversible. It is said that we are presently subject to the māra, the demon, of the psychophysical aggregates of form, feeling, and so on. When our minds are purified, the māra of the aggregates is conquered. We become free of suffering and free of the aggregates. As a result of purifying the mind of afflictions, we will see all the teachings and our own mentor as being utterly pure. Our faith in the Dharma will grow enormously. We will actually see our own spiritual mentor as a buddha. This pure vision is not something contrived or arduous. Another result is that as we engage with sentient beings throughout the world— observing how they strive for happiness but do not find it, how they wish to be free of suffering and do not find it, and how in the midst of this they continue to sow the seeds of suffering and harvest the result of grief—we will experience immeasurable compassion for all sentient beings. These are some of the indications that will manifest as a result of purifying our own mind-streams of mental afflictions.

In contrast, now, when our own minds are still very much subject to the mental afflictions, we oscillate between attachment and hatred, aggressiveness, competitiveness, and so forth. Genuine compassion does not arise, and we continue to engage repeatedly in nonvirtuous activities. Insofar as we pursue these nonvirtuous tendencies, we are like Aṅgulimālā, who made a rosary of the fingers of all the people he killed. If we continue in our nonvirtuous tendencies, the Great Perfection teachings will be of no benefit to us.

People with little background in Buddhism may receive these teachings, as long as they do so with the intention to practice. If your motivation is simply one of curiosity, these teachings will turn into poison for you. To illustrate this, there were two people who once went to a lama for spiritual instruction. The lama gave them teachings on the Great Perfection. One of the two gained a sound understanding of the teachings, and he went into retreat to put them into practice. He gained confidence in the teachings, and he gained realization. The other person, having heard these teachings on the Great Perfection, came away with the impression that the lama had said there is no difference between virtue and vice. Thinking that he did not have to abandon anything or follow anything, that he could be totally uninhibited, his behavior became uninhibitedly nonvirtuous. His mistake was to think there is no difference at all between virtue and nonvirtue. The fact that he had such a profound misconception of the teachings was his own karma; and as a result of that, he engaged in all the ten nonvirtues and so forth. Eventually these two people met again and compared notes as to what they had been doing in regard to what they thought was the implementation of the lama's instructions. They found that their views were not at all compatible and decided to go back to the lama to find out the truth. They went to him and explained the situation. The lama said that the one who had gone into retreat was right and the one who had acted without inhibition was incorrect. At that point the person who was told that he was completely wrong got very angry. He defended himself saying that he had received the same teachings as the other person, that he had been diligent, but that now he was being told he had done everything wrong; and then he went away. Eventually, he was reborn as an animal. The other practitioner became a buddha.

The moral of the story and my own counsel is that you do practice, and that you practice bearing in mind that your actions do have karmic consequences. It's important to be extremely conscientious about the nature of our activities. Like the first person in the story, we need to be conscientious about our actions. It's important that we do practice; it's important that we do cultivate compassion; and it's very important that we do not make a mistake. The fact that I continue to come back to these subjects is not because I think you so stupid that I have to repeat myself. In fact, I'm making these points again with the hope that your practice will go very well. The reason for re-emphasizing these points is from my own experience. Long ago when I was teaching in Berkeley, I was teaching about the nature of karma, the disadvantages of the cycle of existence, and so on. After a while, the students ordered me to stop teaching those kinds of subjects because they didn't want to hear any more about saṃsāra. I thought, "Well, this is a free country. If they don't want to hear it, that's that." However, as I continue to watch, some students still don't understand. Don't try to cover up unpleasant subjects, face them. That's the best response.

6

The Natural Liberation of Mindfulness of Transference: Experiential Instructions on the Transitional Process of Dying

In the fourth general topic, the transitional process of dying (practical instructions that are like dispatching the sealed commands of the king), the natural liberation of mindfulness of transference is taught. These are the practical instructions for becoming a buddha at death for those who will die with an ordinary mind, for those who are not trained in the previous cycle of Breakthrough or in the illusory body, dreaming, and the clear light, who have not realized the meaning of the four great types of liberation, and especially for those who have received those instructions but have not had time to meditate. These are for government officials, householders, and distracted people who have received profound practical instructions, but, not putting them into practice, have left these instructions on paper and have only heard the Dharma. This natural liberation of mindfulness of transference is an important, forceful method for becoming a buddha without needing to meditate.

We don't need to look elsewhere for "householders" and "distracted people." These teachings are for us. We are distracted because we are so caught up in the eight mundane concerns and have only a conceptual understanding of the Dharma. We leave the teachings on paper or tape, and then we forget about them. Traditionally in Tibet, teachings were certainly not recorded, and, by and large, people would not take notes either. It is good to record teachings in order to facilitate our practice; but if we don't get around to putting the teachings into practice, then such records simply become storage. Consequently, these current teachings on the mindfulness of transference are very important.

> Everyone who is born will certainly die, and there is no telling when death will occur; but since it will happen soon, at all times take heed of death.

As soon as you're born, you're marked for death. There's no question about it. Is there any certainty at all as to when death will occur? The reality is that we will certainly die, and we have absolutely no certainty as to when we will die. By and large, we live as though we had thousands of years to go, as if death were a very, very distant prospect. In the meantime, we may even have confidence that, if we do die, we will be born in a pure land or that death will be something quite casual like moving next door or like moving from California up to Oregon. It's not like that.

> Examine the distant signs of death, the proximate signs of death, the uncertain signs of death, and the certain signs of death in accordance with the *Natural Liberation of Signs: Signs of Death*.

In terms of these "signs of death"—distant, proximate, and so forth—we don't really need a soothsayer or a person who is especially well-versed in the various signs of death. There's no need for that. We can merely look at the very process of aging. If we note the process of aging, that's a sign of death. As we get old, we should know that death is coming soon; that's a proximate sign of death. Illness is a sign of death. Particularly, as we get old, we can know that one foot has already gone over the threshold of death. We don't need professionals here; all we need to be is honest.

> Earnestly apply the means of cheating death in accordance with the signs of death. If you perform the transference when the signs of death are not complete or

without applying the means of cheating death, this entails the misdeed of killing a deity, and you incur the nonvirtue of committing suicide. Since this is an even greater misdeed than the acts of immediate retribution, by all means perform either the general or specific means of cheating death three times or more in accordance with the *Natural Liberation of Fear: Cheating Death.* If the means of cheating death are performed three times but the signs of death do not change, death is certain, so then initiate the preparations for transference.

"Cheating death" means doing something to avert the danger of imminent death, so it means saving a life. Steps should be taken for cheating death when you see proximate or distant signs of death. The way you cheat death is by engaging in Dharma practices to increase your life span. Such practices include saving the lives of fish or other animals that are to be killed, and there are also other Dharma practices performed for longevity.

It is said that even if you are a person who has committed the five deeds of immediate retribution, with the transference at the appropriate time you will achieve either rebirth in a favorable state of existence or liberation, so its benefits are very great. For transference there are two parts: training and application.

If you faithfully practice these teachings on transference, together with the four remedial powers and the Vajrasattva purification practice, then even if you have committed horrendous crimes, these can be purified; and you'll either take a favorable rebirth or achieve liberation.

TRAINING

As an analogy, a man who suspects his external enemy is coming puts on his armor, prepares his arrows, and exercises before his enemy is present, so that whenever the enemy appears, he is ready to strike. Likewise, here you train before the signs of death occur. Since you do not know when you will die, start training now, for it is crucial that at the time of your death, you are ready to put these instructions into action.

The practice of transference may be done at the time of the teaching, or you may engage in it when you are specifically guided in the transference. As in the preliminaries to the instructions, ponder the difficulty of obtaining a human life of leisure and endowment and the sufferings of the cycle of existence. By so doing, become disillusioned with the cycle of existence and bring forth the attitude of wishing to emerge from it. On that basis, earnestly recall that, although you have obtained something that is difficult to acquire, it will not remain long, for you will die.

Then sit cross-legged in the bodhisattva posture upon a comfortable cushion and block the apertures of the cycle of existence. Straighten your body, cover both your knees with your hands in the mudrā of touching the earth, and extend your shoulders. Then imagine a luminous, dark blue syllable HŪM at your heart, and a replica of it going to your anal tract and completely blocking the aperture of hell. Another replica emerges and by going to the aperture of becoming,[47] it blocks the preta aperture. Likewise, imagine one HŪM blocking the animal aperture in the urinary tract, and luminous HŪMs at the navel, the mouth, the two nostrils, then both eyes, and then the two apertures of the ears completely blocking each one. Imagine that an upside-down white HAM is displayed at the Brahma aperture on the crown of your head and blocks it.

In the center of your body imagine a straight, erect central channel, like an inflated intestine of a lean sheep, with its lower tip reaching down below the navel and its upper tip reaching to the Brahmā aperture. White with a yellow sheen, it goes straight through the middle of the body. At the lower end, beneath the navel where the three channels converge, is a white, radiant bindu of the nature of awareness. It is clear and limpid, pulsing with the breath, and fluttering as if it is just about to rise up. In the space above the crown of your head imagine your spiritual mentor being present, bearing the smiling countenance of Vajradhara. Draw your physical power upwards and concentrate it, forcefully close off your anal tract, roll your eyes upward, press your tongue against your palate, and hold a tight fist with your thumbs pressed against the base of your ring fingers. Forcefully draw upwards from beneath your navel, and for the verbal part say "HIG KA, HIG KA" while drawing upward with your inner power. Due to the strength of the lower vital energies, the bindu cannot help but be drawn automatically up through the central channel. So with seven HIG KAs it is drawn to the navel, then with seven HIG KAs to the heart, then with seven to the throat, then with seven to the point between the eyebrows, and then with a HIG KA it reaches the HAṂ at the Brahmā aperture. Imagine the bindu descending again, spinning down beneath the navel, where it comes to rest. Relax a bit with that sense.[48]

Signs of succeeding in the transference by doing that several times include the occurrence of oily warmth at the Brahmā aperture, prickliness, itchiness, numbness, swelling, and softness on the crown of the head, and the emergence of lymph and blood at the Brahmā aperture. At that time, the spiritual mentor should carefully check the Brahmā aperture. When prodded with a peacock quill or a stalk of grass, it sinks down fully. That indicates that you are trained in the transference. However, if you do not stop there, but continue in the practice, this will decrease your life span; so stop the visualization and adhisāra. Massage the crown of your head with butter or grain oil.

If the signs do not occur in that way, they will if you draw up the bindu with intense effort many times. If it does not reach the Brahmā aperture even though the crown of your head becomes swollen, headaches and so forth will occur. Therefore, imagine the HAM at the Brahmā aperture opening, and the bindu unimpededly emerging from the Brahmā aperture and touching the feet of your spiritual mentor. Then imagine it returning back down the Brahmā aperture and coming to rest beneath the navel. By doing that several times, the Brahmā aperture will open. Blood or lymph will certainly emerge and a stalk of grass will be able to be inserted into it. Then if the Brahmā aperture is not blocked with the HAM, your life span will be diminished, so it is important to cover it. From then on, it is important that you do not recite the HIG KA or perform the adhisāra, but practice moving the bindu through the central channel and block the Brahmā aperture with HAM. That is the training in transference.

As HIG KA is the mantra for gathering in life,[49] draw up the bindu until you succeed in the transference, but after you succeed, do not draw it up with the HIG KA. If with intense effort you perform the transference too much, you will always be virtually comatose, consciousness will be forced upwards, and you will experience dizziness and so forth. If that happens, pound the soles of both your feet with your fists, massage the crown of your head, and forcefully imagine very heavy gold *stūpas* on each of your feet. By making it come down many times, those symptoms will be pacified. For the most part, the critical points are to be observed in practice.

The preceding discussion has been concerned with the "transference of training," and this is to be well practiced when you are free of illness and before signs of death occur. Samaya.

In Tibet if people had a sense that they were going to die soon, it was very common for them to give everything away. Those who were rich would start distributing all their wealth to others, and even those who were poor would offer everything up to the Three Jewels. Whatever land, houses, livestock, and other possessions people had, they would offer them away in the final weeks and months prior to their death. Even monks would commonly have their own dwelling within their monastery, and they would offer that away prior to death. If they were going to die soon, their possessions were not going to do them any good.

When the Tibetans came as refugees down to India, most of us were impoverished. Many of the monastic refugees were temporarily settled in Buxa in eastern India, and when they saw that death was imminent, they would offer what little they had to make a big tea offering for the other monks. The purpose of this is to overcome all attachment for material possessions. Dying monks wouldn't generally offer gifts to relatives but generally to other monks, the Three Jewels, their spiritual mentor, and so forth. Giving everything away decreases one's attachment, making it easier to become liberated from the cycle of existence.

There is tangible benefit in virtuous acts of generosity just before your own death. However, if that's not been done, then after your death, other people may perform virtue on your behalf; but it is very difficult for that to be of real benefit. The reason is that the stream of consciousness of the person who has died is wandering around in saṃsāra and the mind-streams of those who are practicing devotions are probably distracted. Consequently, there are two wanderers, and it's difficult for one to benefit the other. Moreover, the consciousness of the person who has passed away and is wandering around is also clairvoyant. It can see the minds of those who are reciting the liturgies for the dead person's benefit. If the consciousness sees that these people are reciting the devotions while their minds are wandering all over the place, that consciousness may respond negatively. The person who has died may lose faith; and, as a result of that, he or she may go to a lower realm.

It is beneficial to engage in virtue just prior to your death. There are no disadvantages whatsoever, and it can only help. It is possible that a very great lama might benefit a person who has already passed away, but it's still difficult. Look for yourself and examine this experientially. Do you get benefit from your spiritual mentor when you're dreaming? If not, then it will be all the harder after you've died and are in the transitional process. So it's a good idea to devote yourself earnestly to virtue, especially the virtue of generosity, just before your death. If you can do that, it is excellent.

APPLICATION

First of all, the motivation is very important. Cultivate the Mahāyāna motivation, the Spirit of Awakening. Don't think that these teachings on the transference of consciousness are something to ignore. On the contrary, this practice can act as a cause for the omniscient state of enlightenment both for yourself and for others.

> If the signs of death are complete and they do not disappear even when the means of cheating death are performed three times, at that time consciousness is to be transferred. This has four parts: the Dharmakāya transference, the Sambhogakāya transference, the Nirmāṇakāya transference, and ordinary transference.

This entails looking at the signs of approaching death; and, if you engage in the methods for sustaining your life and they don't work even after you've tried them three times, then you're on the verge of death. It's now time to put these teachings into action. In traditional Tibet there were no life-support systems, and there were no special hospital procedures for sustaining the lives of people on the verge of death. When people saw that they were near death, they would apply these practices.

The Dharmakāya Transference

> Alas, now when the transitional process of dying is happening to me, I shall rid myself of attachment, craving, and grasping for anything, and I shall unwaveringly engage in the clear experience of the practical instructions. My own unborn awareness will be transferred over to the domain of space.

Until now, we haven't even accomplished our own self-interests, let alone the interests of others, because we have fallen into attachment, craving, and grasping for all manner of things. We may have received the quintessential instructions of the Dharma, but we have taken them lightly. Although we may have taken refuge, it may not be very real or meaningful for us. On the verge of death, it is imperative to rid ourselves of attachment and to enter into the clear experience of the practical instructions on transference.

> Being struck by a fatal illness or finding that the signs of death are complete are indications of the transitional process of dying. These practical instructions on the transitional process of dying are like a lovely maiden looking into a mirror so that that which was not clear becomes clear. Here there are two parts: having someone else induce the visualization and inducing the visualization yourself.

If you know the highway system in a certain area, and your enemy suddenly shows up, you will know how to get away. Likewise, here that which was not clear earlier becomes clear through these teachings. It's best if you can induce the visualization for this practice yourself; but, if can't, you can have someone else help you in the visualization.

> *Having someone else induce the visualization.* You yourself may know that the signs of death are complete, or even

if you do not, your physician and nurses may know this due to your symptoms. If your mindfulness is clear, you, too, may examine the proximate signs of death; and if you are dying and if your spiritual mentor lives nearby, invite him to join you.

In Tibet, lamas would sometimes intuit that a person would die within a certain period of time. With that knowledge, the person could prepare accordingly. It was also common in Tibet to invite one's spiritual mentor to aid one through the transition of dying.

Offer whatever things you have to your primary spiritual mentor, and be without even a moment of attachment. If there is attachment to even the tiniest thing, this will cast you into the miserable states of existence, as stated in *The Account of the Monk's Three Conflagrations.* Even if you do not get the authority to offer it in actuality, mentally release it by offering it with your mind. In particular, do not leave near you even one thing that arouses attachment or hatred. That is the meaning of the phrase, "I shall rid myself of attachment, craving, and grasping for anything." At that time bring forth clean renunciation, as stated in the *Tantra of the Union of the Sun and Moon*, "With gifts and festivities, please your spiritual mentor, the sangha, and the special objects for accumulating merit."[50]

The crucial point here is to be without even a moment of attachment because attachment and grasping are the primary elements that perpetuate our ongoing existence in saṃsāra. Not only is attachment itself detrimental at the time of death, but if you have attachment, then you are also primed for anger. For example, as you're dying, if you find out that someone you don't like is getting your possessions, you could find that very irritating and frustrating, because there would be nothing you could do about it. And that could lead to anger. To die with an angry state of mind is very harmful, so it's important to be free of both attachment and anger. At least at the moment of death itself, be detached, even if you haven't been able to totally eradicate attachment until then. At least be temporarily free from it during the dying process. If you can eradicate attachment altogether, that is excellent, for it will lead to your own liberation.

For example, if you've been in an automobile accident and you see that you've been mortally injured, you can't write a new will or distribute your goods with your dying breath. What you can do is to mentally offer everything that you have, including not only your material possessions, but also your relatives and everyone around you. Release attachment for everything. Such a sudden death might also occur if you're in the armed forces and are killed in action. If you die overseas, it may be totally impractical to offer away all of your belongings in reality. Nevertheless, you can offer them mentally, and that is what should be done.

When you're dying, it is important not to have anything in your field of vision that will ignite your own attachment. For example, if there are people for whom you have a lot of attachment, don't have them around when you die. If there are people whom you really don't like or for whom you have resentment and so on, they should stay away at that time. Friends or others for whom you don't have a lot of attachment or aversion should help you out here. If they see items to which you may be attached, they can remove those items to create a very neutral environment which does not incite either your attachment or your hatred. Actually, it is not so good to have so little control of your mind that you can't even be in the same room as these objects, but this is a safeguard.

> Then, once your spiritual mentor has arrived, if your earlier pledges have been broken, confess them, and restore whatever downfalls have occurred. If you have precepts, restore them. If you do not have precepts, establish a foundation by going for refuge, and take precepts.

If you have broken any of your tantric pledges regarding your spiritual mentor or anyone else, now is the time to confess and restore them. Also, if you have taken any other precepts or pledges—be they novice monastic precepts, full monastic precepts, bodhisattva precepts, or the tantric precepts and pledges—you should confess any infractions of those and restore them.

> Then if you have previously trained in transference, position your body in the meditative posture, and have your spiritual mentor lead you many times in the previous visualizations for transference. Indications of success are that as soon as your breath stops, the crown of your head becomes swollen, or there will certainly be indications of success such as blood or lymph.

Indications of success in transference include not only a swelling of the head, but a stinging sensation on the crown of the head, blood or lymph emerging from the crown of the head; and the hairs on the crown of the head may easily be plucked out without any force, or they may simply fall out. If you show any of these signs, nothing more needs to be done, for the transference has been successful.

> If these indications occur, there is no need to perform the visualizations for the transitional process; but if they do not, your spiritual mentor should put his lips to your ear, or else point a bamboo or a rolled up piece of paper at your ear. Then he should guide you in the visualization in accordance with the *Liberation Through Hearing in the Transitional Process*, by slowly reciting in your ear the words beginning with the transitional process of the clear light of reality-itself in sequence up through the transitional process. By so doing, it is impossible not to have success.

The spiritual mentor may use anything, be it a rolled up piece of paper or a pipe, to channel his voice as he speaks into the ear of the dying person. At this time it is common to recite the

Liberation Through Hearing in the Transitional Process, also known as the *Tibetan Book of the Dead*. It's very important that the person reading the text speaks slowly and distinctly so that the dying person can hear him. If you speak too quickly, it can confuse and agitate the dying person. Actually, something like a pipe may be unnecessary as long as the dying person can hear your voice clearly. On the other hand, you might speak in a louder voice than usual, so that the dying person can hear your words distinctly.

> As an analogy, if a king were to dispatch a message with a reliable person, it would be impossible for that person to forget about it; and if he were to do so, the king's punishment would follow. So out of fear, he would make sure the message is received. Likewise, in this case, out of fear of the precipice of the miserable states of existence, make sure to bear in mind the practical instructions, and you will surely discover the transitional process of reality-itself.
>
> If your spiritual mentor is not present, let yourself be guided in the visualization by a spiritual friend of the same spiritual lineage, or one of your vajra brothers or sisters whose pledges are unbroken and whose view and conduct are compatible with your own.

The term "spiritual friend" is synonymous with "lama," or "spiritual mentor." Even if your own spiritual mentor is not present, and if there is another one from the same lineage, then you may invite that person to help you in this transitional process. You may also call on one of your Dharma friends, vajra brothers or sisters, to help you, especially those whose ethical discipline is of high quality. If none of these people are available and you have no Dharma friends around, you can simply bring in another person to read the text and help you through. This, too, would help; it would certainly be better than nothing. It would be better if that person had pure ethics; but, even if not, the most important thing is that, as you're dying, you hear the words clearly. Therefore, have a person who can read clearly.

The *Tantra of the Union of the Sun and Moon* states:

> At that time, merge the practical instructions of the spiritual mentor with your own mind-stream. Repeatedly perform the visualization with these points. Have your spiritual mentor, a Dharma sibling, or a vajra brother induce the conscious visualization.

That is having the visualization induced by someone else.

> *Inducing the visualization yourself.* If your spiritual mentor, Dharma sibling or friend cannot join you, or if you die alone in retreat, and you are a person with fine experience who does not need to have the visualization induced by someone else, you may induce the visualization of the previous practice by yourself. If you are an individual who has apprehended the clear light, has trained in the view of emptiness, and has fully identified awareness, the Dharmakāya transference is best. Thus, like before, be without even a single item that arouses attachment or hatred. If you are physically able, sit in the posture with the seven attributes, or sit upright. If you are not, lie down on your right side, with your head pointing north; and several times sincerely bring forth the Spirit of Awakening, thinking, "Now I am dying. So in general in the three realms of the cycle of existence and in particular in this degenerate era, I rejoice that I can transfer my consciousness while having the companionship of such profound instructions as these. Now I shall recognize the clear light of death as the Dharmakāya, I shall send out immeasurable

emanations to train others according to their
needs, and I must serve the needs of sentient
beings until the cycle of existence is empty."

The posture of lying down on the right side is the posture of
the Buddha when he passed into parinirvāṇa. This Dharmakāya
transference is for a person who has experience in all the advanced
stages of practice. This person then dies with the companionship
of the instructions both in theory and in practice. In this way one
accomplishes both one's own interest and the interests of others.
The fulfillment of your own interest is to actually realize the nature
of the Dharmakāya. To fulfill the interests of others, one antici-
pates sending out countless emanations to serve the needs of sentient beings until the entire cycle of existence is empty.

In Tibet, when old Dharma practitioners were on the verge of
death, they would commonly be especially happy when they
would see that death was very near. Of course, the reason why they
were so content was that they were well prepared for this transitional process. About such people, it was said, "Death is not death;
it's a little buddha passing over." That's just a way of saying that,
for this kind of person death is an enlightening experience. On the
other hand, most of us are not so well prepared; and, if we're not
well prepared, then it's a very different situation altogether. Many
of us live as though our own deaths are thousands of years away
without any real regard for our actions and their consequences.
The type of death following that lifestyle is very different.

When I was young I witnessed quite a number of times these
old Dharma practitioners who experienced glee as they realized
that they were facing death. They had prepared for death
throughout the course of their lives by meditating on impermanence, the suffering that is the nature of the cycle of existence,
the reality of emptiness, and so forth. Many lamas and old
Dharma practitioners died in that way. Sometimes other people
who heard about those who were cheerful at death would try to
mimic them, even though they weren't prepared themselves.
However, when they were actually dying, then they would

become distraught, and they would suffer more than ordinary people. Consequently, death is something to prepare for. All of our Dharma training, hearing, thinking, and meditation should prepare us for this transitional process.

> Then be without distraction, thinking, "The fact that I have devoted myself to my spiritual mentor and have sought profound instructions is for that purpose," and unwaveringly enter into the clear experience of the practical instructions.
>
> Then with no mental modification, free of a basis of anything that is transferred and anything that transfers it, leave your awareness for a long time without fabrication, vivid, unwaveringly steady, nakedly clear and empty, and stable. If your breath stops while you are in that experience, the basic clear light and the clear light of the path, which is being cultivated now, meet like the strands of a bridge arching over a river. This is the "meeting of the mother and child" clear light.

This is also like the convergence of two rivers. In the analogy of strands of a bridge arching over a river, all of the nine vehicles of the Dharma are like the river, and the Great Perfection is like the bridge that arches over. Therefore, the Great Perfection is called the sole bindu, the very nature of awareness, the essence.

The defining characteristics of the basis, the path, and the fruition are as follows. The nature of the basis is one of transition, of change, and of fluctuation. The nature of the path is to be free of all forms of grasping, craving, and clinging. The nature of the fruition is universally pervasive and transcendent. It is the quintessential nature of saṃsāra and nirvāṇa, and in it there are no ten bodhisattva grounds or five paths.

These are the defining characteristics of the view, meditation, and conduct. The view is the single nature of the nondual nature of saṃsāra and nirvāṇa. The defining characteristic of meditation is that all of our joys and sorrows, hopes and fears are thoroughly equalized in one taste. The nature of the conduct is naked aware-ness, with nothing to be rejected or accepted. This naked, or unmediated, awareness is our own awareness, our own nature, and not something to be sought elsewhere. It's not even to be sought in other buddhas. Moreover, in realizing the nature of your own awareness, you recognize that the mind of all the bud-dhas of the three times and ten directions and your own mind are indivisible. To realize this is to realize the intention of all the buddhas; and with this realization, you achieve a state of utter fearlessness, never returning to the cycle of existence.

Upon hearing about this irreversible release from the cycle of existence, some people may feel some consternation, thinking, "Once I'm totally out of the cycle of existence, what then? Maybe I'll be lost!" Don't worry, you will not be lost. This realization is the fulfillment of your own interest and the natural fulfillment of others' interests. You are now able to serve the needs of sentient beings immeasurably, like the rays of the sun shining out in all directions. The sun doesn't have the intention to send out rays in order to do something; it is simply in the nature of the sun that these rays spontaneously flow out. Similarly, once you have become a buddha, you don't need to bring some special intention forth in order to serve the needs of sentient beings; rather, your service flows out unimpededly and spontaneously. Consequently, please don't worry about being lost, for that is simply slipping into nihilism. There's nothing to be sad about in such a realization. There are no grounds for consternation. In addition, it's difficult to get there anyway.

> The unborn Dharmakāya, the unimpeded summit, is achieved, and in an instant you will be liberated. Those with fine experiential realization should repeat this alone again and again. Thus, this is called the "pristine Dharmakāya transference," and it is the best of all transferences.
>
> For those who have not identified it and who lack expe-riential realization, even if they apply the Dharmakāya

transference, it would be like showing an object to a blind person, or pointing out a star to a dog. It is important that the transference and visualization be adjusted to the individual's mental capacity.

If there is success in the Dharmakāya transference, the outer sign is that the sky becomes immaculate; the inner sign is that the luster of the body does not vanish for a long time, and it has a clear complexion; and the secret signs include the appearance of a white AḤ and a dark blue HŪṂ. That is the Dharmakāya transference. Samaya.

In the event of a successful transference, the sky becomes very serene. Another sign that has occurred many times with old Dharma practitioners is that the corpse has no bad odor, and it retains a lifelike complexion for a long time after the death. Such signs have occurred many times in the past, both in Tibet and India. For example, in 1958, both the speech and the body emanations of Dudjom Lingpa were alive. They met on one occasion, and they died together, even though they had no illnesses. Immediately following their deaths, which occurred in the winter, there was thunder, which is very unusual in that season. Also, there was an earthquake, and people saw strange snowflakes like flowers falling from the sky. For days after that, the sky became utterly serene and clear. These are definitely signs of great beings entering into nirvāṇa.

More recently in Buxa, India, where there was a refugee settlement of many of the monks, there was one lama—whose current incarnation is fairly young—named Drugpa Kyabgön. In 1961 or 1962 when he passed away, he remained sitting upright in the meditative posture in deep meditative concentration for two weeks following his death; and there was no odor whatsoever. Also, when His Holiness Dudjom Rinpoche passed away, for two weeks there were signs such as the appearance of rainbows and bindus, witnessed by thousands of people from various countries.

The Sambhogakāya Transference

If you have chiefly practiced the stage of generation, and especially if you have little comprehension of emptiness, the Sambhogakāya transference is preferable. If you can, sit upright in the previous posture, and perform the transference visualization done earlier at the time of training. In particular, at the crown of your head, clearly visualize upon a lotus, sun, and moon seat your spiritual mentor in the Sambhogakāya appearance, such as the great Vajradhara, Vajrasattva, or Avalokiteśvara. Specifically, imagine him in the aspect of your own chosen deity whom you have revered in the stage of generation. Inside your body, clearly visualize a white bindu or the seed syllable of your chosen deity—such as a white AH, a dark blue HŪM, or a red HRĪH—at the lower end of the limpid, immaculate, central channel beneath your navel. It is best if you clearly imagine that the apertures are blocked with HŪM.

When you visualize the white bindu or seed syllable of your chosen deity, be sure to visualize it inside your body, not the body of your spiritual mentor. It is best if you can block all the apertures to the various states of cyclic existence with the syllable HŪM, but it's all right if you can't do that full visualization.

If they are not clearly visualized, do not pay attention to the apertures, but focus your consciousness single-pointedly inside the central channel. Thrust your physical power upwards; forcefully close off your lower aperture; roll your eyes upwards; press your tongue against the palate; draw the lower vital energies upwards; and focus your consciousness inside the central channel. Calling out "HIG KA, HIG KA," gradually draw it upwards; and when it reaches the Brahmā aperture, imagine the Brahmā aperture, which was covered with the HAM, opening up. From its white, immaculate interior, imagine your consciousness shooting up like an arrow and being absorbed into the heart of your chosen deity. Focus your awareness right at the heart of your chosen deity. Without letting it descend, repeatedly draw it up and merge it. Then also leave your chosen deity in the nature of nonobjectivity. If your breath passes away during that experience, you will achieve the state of a Vidyādhara, indivisible from your chosen deity; and you will become a buddha as a Sambhogakāya.

In the above visualization you send the white bindu, which is of the nature of your own consciousness, up into the heart of your chosen deity. In the training period prior to the time of implementation, you say HIG as your consciousness ascends; and then, with the KA, you would allow your consciousness to come back down again. When you're actually dying, it's best not to say the KA. Just say HIG because you're only shooting the consciousness up like an arrow, without drawing it back down again. This is a one-way trip. You send it up, and it merges into the heart of your chosen deity or spiritual mentor, where it dissolves, without coming back.

In that way, if you succeed in the Sambhogakāya transference, the outer sign is that the sky becomes filled with rainbows and light; the inner signs include the emergence of blood or lymph, and the appearance of dew drops or swelling at the Brahmā aperture on the crown of the head; and the secret signs include the occurrence of one or more of the five kinds of relics, and the appearance of forms of deities, their hand symbols and so on. That is the Sambhogakāya transference. Samaya.

The above practice is especially for people who trained well in the stage of generation. In such practice, you regard your entire environment as being a pure land, casting off ordinary appearances and grasping. You also see inner appearances and all sentient beings as pure, appearing and yet not inherently existent. This pure vision is a central feature of the stage of generation, and it is essential to apply this practice in the dying process for the Sambhogakāya transference. These teachings are to be applied either during the dying process itself or, if you are not successful at that time, during the subsequent experiences after death when the peaceful and wrathful appearances arise. This practice is not just for the sake of drama.

The Nirmāṇakāya Transference

In terms of the physical posture, by lying on your right side the vital energies will move from the left nostril. At that time, pray that a Nirmāṇakāya may be present in front of you, such as the great Śākyamuni, the Medicine Buddha, Maitreya, or the body of Orgyen Padma, your spiritual mentor and friend, or a painting or statue of one of them. Lay out plentiful offerings to that being. If there is no actual form, clearly visualize it, and mentally make emanated offerings. You and others should then pray, "Now in dependence upon my death, may I take birth as a Nirmāṇakāya for the sake of all sentient beings, and may this be of great service to the world. May that very Nirmāṇakāya be endowed with the physical signs and symbols of enlightenment, and may there be no obstacles to my life and enlightened deeds."

As you pray that a Nirmāṇakāya may be in front of you, this can be any of the various representations of the body, speech, and mind of the buddhas. It is suitable to place representations of any of those in front of you. If you find yourself dying in a hospital, for example, it may not be practical to have even a single physical representation of the buddhas' body, speech, or mind there with you; and it may be simply impossible to lay out any offerings. In that case, don't worry or be upset. If you have nothing physical to offer or no altar to put it on, this is no problem. Offer your body, speech, and mind and don't be upset. That's fine. This option of simply offering your body, speech, and mind is a good one. For countless lifetimes in the past, we have grasped tenaciously to our body, speech, and mind as being "mine." As long as there's that strong identification with, or sense of possessiveness to, "my body, my speech, my mind," the prospect of offering them up is out of the question. During the dying process in one lifetime, if you can genuinely offer up your body, speech, and mind, wouldn't there be great merit in that?

> "May I take birth as a great Vidyādhara, serving as a representative of the victors of the three times." Mentally bring forth such a sincere yearning. Beneath the navel, imagine the three-cornered Dharma-source, and inside the limpid, immaculate, central channel imagine a white and red bindu, glistening, on the verge of rising up. Close the lower aperture by contracting it, and draw upwards. The lower vital energies inexorably push the bindu upwards, and by saying "HIG KA, HIG KA," as many times as you can, draw it up. It reaches the aperture of the left nostril, with awareness accompanying the vital energies, and in an instant, like an arrow, they merge into the heart of the Nirmāṇakāya in front of you. Let the vital energies and awareness be as they are without collecting them back. Repeating this again and again until the departure of your consciousness will result in certain success. After your consciousness departs while in that experience, it is certain that you will later be born as a Nirmāṇakāya who will serve the needs of sentient beings.

The Dharma-source is shaped like a tetrahedron. The pink bindu is the color of cherry blossoms. Imagine your awareness merging into the heart of the Nirmāṇakāya in front of you or into that of your spiritual mentor. The reference to "expelling from the left nostril" is unusual. Some teachings on the transference of consciousness speak only of directing the awareness up through the crown of the head. If you can get it through the crown of your head, that's fine. However, this text presents another option, and it is not in conflict with other methods in terms of the final result of the practices.

> In that way if there is success in the Nirmāṇakāya trans-
> ference, the outer signs include the appearance in the sky
> of clouds and rainbows like a wish-fulfilling tree and like
> an open parasol, and a rain of flowers from the sky; the
> inner signs include the emergence of blood, lymph,
> regenerative fluid, or dewdrops from the left nostril; and
> the secret signs include the appearance of many tiny
> relics, the skull does not break but remains whole [even
> when the body is cremated], and hand symbols of deities
> appear. This is the Nirmāṇakāya transference. Samaya.

The regenerative fluids are the red and white *bodhicitta* described in the tantras. On a number of occasions in Tibet these red and white fluids emerged from the nostrils of dying practitioners. Also, when the body of such a person is cremated, the skull remains unburned and unbroken, and there may be symbols like the hand symbols of the deities actually appearing in the skull itself.

Forceful Transference

> The preceding instructions apply to gradual death, but
> in the case of sudden death, there is no time to practice
> such meditation; therefore, "instant transference" is
> important. Moreover, since you do not know what the
> circumstances of your death will be, starting now you
> should alternate between practicing the training transfer-
> ence and the instant transference.

Thus far, in this chapter entitled "The Natural Liberation of Mindfulness of Transference: Experiential Instructions on the Transitional Process of Dying," the Dharmakāya transference, the

Saṃghogakāya transference, and the Nirmāṇakāya transference have been taught. All of these enable the dying person to master the dying process. But you may die a sudden death, as in an accident, in which case there is nothing you can do with your body or your possessions at the time of death. So it's very important to prepare for this possibility right now. All of us will certainly die, and death will separate us from everything with which we identify: our bodies, our possessions, and so forth. Therefore, it is helpful to release our attachment and to offer up everything right now. Completely release your own body, possessions, and everything else so that you have the sense that they are no longer yours. Without anticipation of any reward, gratitude, or affection—an "I love you," a hug, a kiss, a little present, or anything else—offer them without any strings attached. There is no one to receive this offering. Buddha Śākyamuni is not going to come out of the clouds and say, "Thank you" or "Where's my stuff?" and take it away. The point of this offering is to release the grasping towards all of these things with which you identify. This grasping is like the lord of death, who is depicted with his mouth gaping open, his fangs showing, and his hands holding on to the cycle of existence. Whether such a being as the lord of death really exists is another question. But it is true that grasping is well depicted with its mouth open and its hands holding onto the desire, form, and formless realms. Moreover, grasping has a voracious appetite; it clings to all types of phenomena. Consequently, even if we can't totally eradicate our own grasping, it's important starting right now to do all we can to decrease it.

We can question whether we really have any power or mastery over our own bodies, let alone possessions or external things with which we don't have a direct connection. Not only do we lack true mastery over our own bodies, we don't even have control over our own consciousness. Observe your own mind and see for yourself. Is this mind something that's totally under your control, or does it operate under the power of its own influences? During the course of your life, events arise not simply according to your own will, but in dependence upon your previous actions, or karma. For example, you may have had the intention to graduate from high school or college, but did you? If not, you may have had the intention, but the consequences of your own actions intervened, and these determine many of the events of our lives. The type of work we get, the type of work we lose, where we go, where we stay—all of these are influenced by the actions we've committed in the past. Therefore, since there's no autonomous control during the course of our lives, how could we ever find such autonomous control after death?

For these reasons, it's important to prepare now for the dying process and to do all that we can to decrease our grasping onto any type of phenomenon. We should be able to see for ourselves whether grasping onto our own bodies, speech, and minds helps us in any way. All of us here are educated; we've all been to school to varying degrees. We've all learned how to think, so we should be able to investigate this topic for ourselves. We should be able to identify our own grasping, and see on the basis of our own experience and with our own intelligence whether or not there is any benefit in grasping. Grasping is the root cause of our continuing rebirth in this cycle of existence known as saṃsāra. It is the true handcuffs; whether they're gold handcuffs or iron handcuffs, they bind us.

There are people who are known as practitioners utterly committed to the Buddhadharma. Such people, however, commonly have a great deal of attachment to their own Dharma tradition, lineage, or sect and have aversion, contempt, or hostility towards other lineages. This is not the way the Buddha presented his own Dharma, and this is not the purpose of his having taught the Dharma. I also sometimes hear people comment, "Oh, such and such is a good lama, but he really doesn't know the real world." Look to the greatest lamas of the past, such as Milarepa, Guru Rinpoche, and Tsongkhapa. Many of them were mendicants who lived on alms. Do they fall into this category of being good lamas but not knowing the world? This judgment is often simply a veil covering the conceit of thinking oneself smarter or more knowledgeable than the buddhas themselves.

There are many circumstances that may lead to our own deaths, but we have no idea which one will actually strike home. Therefore, it's important to alternate practicing the preceding types of training in transference and the present practice, which is simply called "instant transference."

It is like this: vividly bear in mind, "If I am to die suddenly, I must focus on the crown of my head." This resolve is of essential importance. For instance, on the evening of the twenty-second day of the lunar month, if you have a sincere resolve, thinking that you must get up as soon as the moon rises, when the moon rises in the middle of the night, you will get up. It is like that. Moreoever, right now resolve to practice focusing your attention immediately on the crown of your head whenever great terror arises. Then in the case of "sudden death," such as falling off a high, rocky precipice, the thought will arise, "I'm going to die!" As soon as this happens, it is best if you recall your spiritual mentor or chosen deity on the crown of your head. If you do not have time to do that, it is critically important that you direct your attention at the crown of your head. The reason why our attention becomes focused at that time is that now, when we are experiencing great terror, we suddenly call out "Father mentor!" So at that time, too, we shall surely recall our spiritual mentor or direct our awareness at the crown of our head. Thus, this point is very profound.

In this practice you focus on the crown of your head; and even if you can't visualize clearly, imagine as well as you can any emanation of the Buddha, be it Amitābha, your own spiritual mentor, or anyone else. This resolve is of essential importance.

On the twenty-second day of the lunar month, one week after the full moon, the moon rises quite late at night. This text was written in Tibet when there were no wristwatches, so the author couldn't simply say, "If you want to get up at two o'clock in the morning, you anticipate that, and then you wake up at that time."

In the course of your life, as soon as you think your death may be imminent, focus your attention at the crown of your head. If you can do that just before you are to die, that will contribute to your liberation. Or even after you realize you've just died, if you direct your awareness up to the crown of your head to your spiritual mentor or some other emanation of the Buddha, that too will lead to your liberation. Therefore, it is important to remember this focus either just before or just after death. Resolve that, if you find yourself in danger of imminent death, you will direct your awareness to the crown of your head. If you fail to do so and if you recall no Dharma practice during the dying process, you will most likely experience fear, hope, and confusion at death. Even now, when people's lives are not going badly and they are experiencing little suffering, a lot of people comment that they feel confused. If you're confused when you're not facing death and when you're not experiencing great suffering, how do you expect to feel when you're actually dying? It's going to be worse. People in the West have been spoiled rotten, indulging in this confusion rather than doing something to counteract it.

When you realize you're about to die, it is helpful to imagine on the crown of your head your spiritual mentor or any other being who is an object of your faith, such as Avalokiteśvara, Buddha Śākyamuni, or any emanation of the Buddha. Moreover, this is also the time to recall the practical teachings you've received concerning the dying process. When your own death is imminent, it is most important that you think of the being in whom you have the most faith.

In Tibet when disaster struck it was very common for people to call out in their distress, "*lama kyeno!*" meaning "the spiritual mentor knows!" This is calling upon the presence of these enlightened beings. In times of crisis call out to any enlightened being in whom you have faith. On the other hand, in the West, if people call out in distress to the "the three jewels," they might be referring to their car, their girlfriend, and their house.

There's no point in calling out "Oh, God!" or "Oh, Lama!" or "Oh, Three Jewels!" if these are empty words for you. It's important to know the meaning of the object of your reverence and to be familiar with the excellent qualities of the objects of refuge. Insofar as you're aware of these qualities and call upon these objects of your refuge in times of crisis or the time of your own death, there are real blessings from that. If you've grown accustomed to this practice during the course of your life, this will surely be your natural response at the time of death.

> Likewise, when, for instance, you are completely engulfed in a great fire, or you are roughly swept along in a great river, or you are struck on the head by lightning, or your heart is pierced by an arrow, immediately and earnestly recall your spiritual mentor on the crown of your head or direct your awareness straight at the crown of your head. That is also called "momentary transference" and "forceful transference." As this is very profound, mentally train in this well.

In the earlier section on the Nirmāṇakāya transference, the dying person is encouraged to lie down on the right side and to expel the vital energies, or breath, from the left nostril. However, it is even more important to focus the awareness at the crown of the head. You may recall other aspects of the more complex practice of blocking all of the apertures with seed syllables, which is also designed to help the consciousness emerge from the crown. If you do all the more complicated practices, that's fine; but it's most important to focus the awareness on the crown of the head.

> It is said that when ordinary great terror arises there are also many advantages to calling out the names of buddhas, saying, "Father mentor!" or "Orgyen!" This being the case, there are unimaginable advantages to focusing your attention on your spiritual mentor at the crown of your head.

Then there are great differences in terms of the pathways of the transference of consciousness; namely, there is a ninefold classification pertaining to individuals of superior, middling, and inferior faculties. The Brahma aperture on the crown of the head is the pathway for going to the pure land of the ḍākinīs, so if your awareness leaves from there, you will achieve liberation. That is the supreme pathway, so it is important to train in focusing your attention there. If your consciousness leaves from your eyes, you will be born as a world monarch; and if it leaves from your left nostril, you will obtain a pure human body. Those are the three superior apertures.

If it leaves from the right nostril, you will be born as a *yakṣa*;[51] if it leaves from both ears, you will be born as a deity of the form realm; and if it leaves from the navel, you will be born as a deity of the desire realm. Those are the three middling apertures.

If it leaves from the urinary tract, you will be born as an animal; if from the aperture of becoming, which is the pathway in which the regenerative fluids and white and red bindus move, you will be born as a preta; and if it leaves from the anal tract, you will be born as a being in hell. Those are the three inferior apertures.

Thus, there are very great differences in the pathways of the transference of consciousness, so at death there are immeasurable advantages to directing your awareness at the crown of your head. That is the forceful transference. Samaya.

Ordinary Transference

Those of you who have not realized the meaning of emptiness and who do not know the meaning of the stages of generation and of completion should lie down on your right side, with your head pointing north. Your spiritual mentor, a spiritual sibling, or a friend should guide your awareness in the visualization; and if you are

physically able, they should have you go for refuge, cultivate the spirit of awakening, and confess your sins. Then
take the lay vows, and if there is time, take a tantric initiation. By dying with the excellent karmic momentum of
having just those fresh, untarnished pledges, you are
freed from the miserable states of existence, and there are
incalculable advantages.

If you have not gained realization of the reality of emptiness and if
you're not well versed in the practice of the stages of generation and
completion, then you should practice this ordinary transference. The
essence of the stage of generation is to look upon all appearances as
being the body of the Buddha, all sounds as being the speech of the
Buddha, and all mental events as being the mind of the Buddha.
The essence of the stage of completion is to realize the nature of reality-itself. If you have not gained any such experience, realization, or
understanding, you should lie down on the right side with your head
pointing north. Then take the refuge vows, the bodhisattva vows,
and disclose any nonvirtuous actions you've committed.

In Tibet when people saw that they were going to die soon,
they would commonly take a cycle of initiations pertaining to the
peaceful and wrathful emanations of the Buddha. This can have
tangible benefit for the dying person. If you have made no preparations for death, either when it is distant or imminent, but other
people recite prayers on your behalf after your death, it's very difficult for this to be of practical benefit to you. If this is done by a
highly realized lama there may be some benefit, but there is little
benefit if such prayers are made by an ordinary person. If you can
take the tantric pledges and precepts just before death, there is
virtually no possibility of breaking them before you die. That
gives you excellent karmic momentum as you die, and it's a good
way to bring your life to a close.

A major problem among American Buddhists is that they just
don't get around to engaging in the practices they've been taught.
On the whole, American Buddhists in the Tibetan Buddhist tradition have already received teachings on refuge and taken the

vows of refuge, and they have received the bodhisattva precepts. Many of you have also received a lot of initiations, so at death you wouldn't be taking an initiation for the first time. But during the course of your lives you seem to find little time for implementing these teachings. Therefore, when you're facing your own death, you shouldn't try to do something very special. If you can simply direct your faith to the objects of refuge of the Buddha, Dharma, and Sangha, and recall the spirit with which you entered into the practice—to strive for spiritual awakening for sake of all sentient beings—that's enough.

In the case of a person who cannot do even that, gently call out the person's name and say, "On the crown of your head is the Lord of Great Compassion.[52] Revere him!" and stroke the crown of the person's head. Tug slightly at the hair at the Brahmā aperture. That will cause the consciousness to leave from the Brahmā aperture.

In the case of a person who is no different than an animal and is incapable even of that, have the person point his head north and say many times, "Homage to Buddha Ratnaśikhin." That will definitely free the person from the miserable states of existence, for previously this buddha prayed, "May all those who hear my name be freed from the miserable states of existence." Moreover, it is said that if one utters the name of the Buddha, the Sovereign Healer, King of Lapis Lazuli Light, simply by hearing this name, one is protected from the suffering of the miserable states of existence. Similarly, utter out loud all the names of the buddhas that you know; recite whatever blessed essences that you know, such as the six-syllable mantra. In particular, if you have a mantra of protection worn on the neck, read it. Recite the *Liberation Through Hearing*, and offer whatever prayers you know. By so doing, it is possible to establish an excellent karmic momentum, so this has very great advantages. It is said that at the very least, just by dying while lying on your

right side, with your head pointing north, you will not
go to the miserable states of existence.

If you can't remember Buddha Ratnaśikhin, remember
Amitābha. You may also recite the six-syllable mantra of OM
MAṆI PADME HŪṂ or the one-hundred-syllable mantra of
Vajrasattva.

> Thus, all the benefits of practicing Dharma should come
> at the verge of death, so it is important to be skilled at
> dying. These are the instructions on the transitional
> process of dying, called the "natural liberation of mind-
> fulness of transference." Samaya.

> Sealed, sealed, sealed.

Whatever practice you're doing, it should relate to your death
and help you in the dying process. If it doesn't give you any tangible benefit when you die, you've missed the point. As an analogy,
if you make a soup out of pieces of dried lung, the pieces of lung
all go to the surface of the soup. Similarly, if you put puffed popcorn in water, it floats right to the top. Don't let your practice be
like dried lung soup or popcorn floating in water. Your practice
should have some substance of enduring value and tangible benefit to you as you die. This is very important whether you're a
scholar, a practitioner, or a meditator.

On the one hand, there is certainly benefit in whatever
Dharma practice we engage in, including hearing, thinking,
meditation, devotions, and so forth. On the other hand, in
America it is common for people never to be satisfied. There are
two types of dissatisfaction. The first is not being satisfied as you
are engaging in hearing, thinking or meditation, until you actually
accomplish liberation. That kind of dissatisfaction suggests a lack
of complacency, which is a good thing. With the second type of
dissatisfaction you may receive Dharma teachings that have the
power to bring you to liberation and enlightenment in this very

lifetime. But out of dissatisfaction you set them aside and don't put them into practice. Rather, you wait for teachings that are said to be even more exalted, secret, esoteric, and you go running after them in the hope that they will be especially effective. For example, you may first receive fine teachings on the madhyamaka view and gain some intellectual understanding but not get around to implementing this view in meditation. Then you may hear about Mahāmudrā and go running after that. Without practicing that either, you may then hear about Atiyoga, the Great Perfection, and we think that's even higher. But a bad habit has already been established, and now you're accustomed to looking for more and more esoteric teachings. In the process, you have not laid a foundation for anything. This is a problem in this country. Beginners don't know any better, so they are not to blame.

Another common tendency is to adopt a frivolous attitude toward Dharma, a kind of smorgasbord mentality of nibbling at one teaching after another without ever really chewing and digesting the teachings that you receive. That's a problem, and the solution is to commit yourself firmly to a spiritual discipline and proceed in the practice stage by stage. Establish a foundation in the practice and build upon that. As we review our own lives from our childhood to the present, we can ask ourselves, "What foundation have we, in fact, established thus far?" Many of us really haven't even finished our education, which indicates the same type of attitude of not carrying through with good intentions. We've had many chances to further our education, but we have not taken advantage of them and let them slip by. Therefore, focus on your practice and digest what you have already been taught.

Some people cling very tenaciously to a particular sect or tradition of Buddhism. For example, some Hīnayāna practitioners think that theirs is the only true Buddhist teaching and that Mahāyāna teachings are fraudulent. Some people might follow the Mahāyāna tradition and think that the Hīnayāna is fraudulent or inferior. This type of sectarian attitude, of course, is of no benefit whatsoever. On the contrary it is counterproductive. If you're following Hīnayāna, you're focusing on the foundations of the whole of Buddhist practice. This entails meditating on the Four Noble Truths, the twelve links of dependent origination, and cultivating the attitude of turning away from the cycle of existence. Upon that foundation you may proceed to the Mahāyāna and cultivate the spirit of awakening, cultivating first of all the spirit of aspiring for enlightenment. To facilitate this, you may cultivate the four immeasurables of loving-kindness and so forth. On that basis, you can proceed to cultivate the spirit of venturing toward enlightenment, with which you cultivate the six perfections of generosity and so on. Upon that basis, then you may enter the Vajrayāna. There are many avenues of practice, but if you focus upon the stage of generation practice, for example, and gain realization of the peaceful and wrathful emanations of enlightened beings, that would lead you to liberation. Upon the basis of such practice, you may enter into the Atiyoga, or the Great Perfection. However, it is by establishing the foundation that you can carry through with the above sequence of practice. If you fail to establish that foundation and simply move on to something else and then give up on that, too, there's no benefit. All expressions of a sectarian mentality are more expressions of the same old problems of attachment and aversion. It's fine to say "I'm a Nyingmapa" or "I'm a Gelugpa" with the attitude of being committed to a particular path until you reach its culmination. But if you don't come to the fruition of the path and instead just remain attached to it, there's no benefit. If you're following a Buddhist path, the cutting edge of your practice should be subduing the three poisons of your own mind: attachment, hostility, ignorance. Your Dharma practice should act as an antidote for these three poisons.

If your Dharma practice doesn't counteract and subdue the afflictions of your own mind, it's questionable whether you are actually a Buddhist. To be a Buddhist means to subdue the poisons of your own mind, to cultivate the spirit of awakening, and to turn your mind away from the cycle of existence. If, in the course of your practice, none of that is happening, what does it mean to call yourself a Buddhist?

Some of you may want to practice Atiyoga, the Great Perfection. Why is it called "Great?" Why is it called "Perfection?" It's called Perfection because all the qualities of enlightenment are perfected in this practice. It's called "Great" because there's nothing greater than this. However, if you adopt a sectarian attitude of grasping onto yourself as a practitioner of the Great Perfection, you do not know what the Great Perfection is. The teachings on the Great Perfection state that the whole of saṃsāra and nirvāṇa are of one nature. If that is the case and, in the meantime, you're grasping onto this notion of being a practitioner of the Great Perfection, then where are you in saṃsāra and nirvāṇa? If you don't even know the meaning of the term "Great Perfection," I suggest you stop making any such claims about yourself. All phenomena are of one taste, and all Dharmas are of one taste. For example, in the Gelugpa tradition, there is a common practice known as Lama Chöpa, the worship of or devotion to the spiritual mentor. In this practice you recite, "you are the spiritual mentor," "you are the chosen deity," "you are the ḍākinī," "you are the Dharma protector," and so forth. The practice of focusing on the spiritual mentor is for the sake of experiencing the enlightened qualities of the spiritual mentor. Such practice is found in all traditions of Tibetan Buddhism, not only the Gelugpa. There is one taste in all these traditions.

Among the wide variety of practices that are accessible to us, if we were to focus on guru yoga alone and if we were to do this very well, we would find that the entire significance of the stage of generation and the stage of completion is included in that. The entire Hīnayāna path and the entire Mahāyāna path are included in that. The whole of tantra and the whole of Atiyoga are included in that. If you can practice guru yoga well, that would be sufficient. You don't need to make a big deal out of your practice; just practice and do it well. If you don't do that and you go around with the arrogant sense that you're following the highest of all practices and that you're an Atiyoga practitioner, you're simply bringing disgrace upon yourself.

Some of you may at times take on the role of a Dharma teacher. Generally speaking, the thought can easily arise that the teacher is somehow higher than the students and that's why the teacher is teaching and the other people are being taught. If you are at times taking on the role of a spiritual teacher, counselor, or guide, it's important first of all to examine your own mind. As you approach the Dharma throne, from a vantage point of emptiness see that it's empty. As you mount the throne to give Dharma teachings, it is important to recall first the excellent qualities of the Buddha, Dharma, and Sangha and the qualities of your own spiritual mentor. Ask for their blessings. Recall their kindness. Mentally make offerings. With an attitude of reverence, think of these things as you are about to give teachings yourself. As you are then looking out on those who have come to you for teachings, respond to their request and their interest with a spirit of generosity. This is your gift to them. Offer the teaching with the motivation of being of benefit to others. In fact with such a motivation, there is benefit for others; and there is also benefit for yourself. The very act of offering teachings to others purifies the defilements and nonvirtuous karma you have accumulated for yourself and helps you to accumulate merit for yourself. In these two ways, this is of benefit to you. Also, as you're giving teachings, you hear the teachings you're giving, and so you're teaching yourself as well. You may even learn from the words being uttered from your own mouth. As you're teaching, it is also very helpful to visualize on the crown of your head your own spiritual mentor or other object of refuge. Whatever tradition you belong to—be it the Gelug, Kagyü, Sakya, or Nyingma— bring to mind the being in whom you have the greatest faith. Even if you have faith in many beings, you can still visualize just one being, but imagine this one as being of the same nature as all these other objects of refuge. They are all included in one.

You do have faith, and you do have compassion, so this should be brought to bear as you take on the role of teacher. In contrast, if you mount the Dharma throne with the sense of being special, while the other people are ordinary, that's not even a

Buddhist attitude. Look to the examples of others. When His Holiness the Dalai Lama is about to offer teachings, he first goes to the Dharma throne and makes three prostrations. Why is he doing this? He's recalling the qualities of the Buddha, the Dharma, the Sangha, and his spiritual mentors; and he's doing this with a worshipful and reverent attitude. He's not prostrating to the throne thinking, "That's where I'm going to sit; and since I'm such a holy man, I'll bow to this throne on which I'm going to sit."

If you teach Dharma, do it with this worshipful and reverent attitude, and you will not need anything else fancy. Just do it in this simple way. On the other hand, if your motivation and the Dharma are incompatible, there's no benefit in your teaching. It will not be of benefit to you when you die, but will rather have a detrimental effect. The result will be a fraudulent Dharma teaching, and this will simply serve as a cause for your own rebirth in one of the lower states of existence.

That is the type of attitude a teacher should have for teaching Dharma. Now, what about students? I've traveled around this country a lot, I've been to schools, and I've seen the deportment of students in American schools. Students commonly have their feet up, pointed toward the teacher; they are perched back in their chairs, with their backsides facing into the teacher's face. While in that posture, they ask questions of the teacher, and the teacher answers while having to look at their backsides. That may be okay for American schools, but it's not okay for Dharma. It's not that that type of posture hurts the teacher—whether it's in a Dharma context or in a more mundane context—but it does impair the student. In a way, this country is lawless; there are no rules about the type of posture students should have in a classroom. However, this kind of casual or perhaps even arrogant posture is actually detrimental for the students themselves. It's of no benefit or harm to the teachers, but it's harmful to the students. If you wish to learn the proper, or most beneficial, deportment on the part of students in the context of Dharma, you can find a detailed discussion of this in the text called *The Fifty Verses of Guru Devotion*, which has been translated into English. Bear in mind that those fifty verses on how the student is to relate to the teacher are all for the benefit of the student. They are not for the sake of the teacher. Behaving in the proper way is of benefit to the student, purifying nonvirtuous tendencies and imprints, accumulating merit, and cultivating excellent qualities on the part of the student.

Among the four spiritual orders of Tibetan Buddhism—Gelug, Sakya, Nyingma, and Kagyü—the Gelugpas tend to be the most outstanding examples when it comes to the manner in which the disciples devote themselves to the teacher. They are really exemplary. Although I'm not a Gelugpa, I lived seven or eight years with members of this order, so I saw how they behave. On the other hand, I'm not a Nyingmapa either, nor am I a Kagyüpa or Sakyapa. I'm a Buddhist, and I have faith in all of these traditions. I am not claiming to have knowledge or understanding of all of them, but I do have faith in all of them. By making the above claim about the Gelugpas, I'm not implying the other orders are not any good. Their conduct may also be excellent, but I find the Gelugpas especially outstanding in that particular facet of practice. And, of course, the other three do know how disciples should relate to their spiritual mentors. However, perhaps under the influence of the different regions of Tibet in which each of these traditions tended to be more dominant, you'll find some differences among the four spiritual traditions. For example, the Gelugpa tradition has flourished very strongly in the area of Lhasa, the capital of Tibet. Lhasa society is one in which courtesy, and good manners are very well cultivated. The denizens of Lhasa tend to be very sophisticated people, and this has influenced the spiritual tradition that is most dominant there, which is Gelugpa. If you go to other parts of Tibet, like Golok, Kham or Amdo in the northeast of Tibet, there is not such cultural refinement of courtesy and etiquette. Those regions are where the Nyingma and Kagyüpa traditions have flourished most strongly. Therefore, perhaps these traditions were affected due to those societal influences. I myself am from Gyalrong, in the Kham-Amdo region, so I was not raised in a very culturally refined environment. I didn't learn much etiquette. If you can behave courteously toward your spiritual mentor, that's a very good thing. At the same time, it's important that your outer deportment toward the spiritual mentor is not artificial or contrived. Honesty, purity, and respect are what I consider to be important.

7

The Natural Liberation of Seeing: Experiential Instructions on the Transitional Process of Reality–itself

In the fifth general topic, the transitional process of reality-itself (practical instructions, like a child crawling onto its mother's lap, on belief concerning self-appearances), the natural liberation of seeing is taught. The instructions on the transitional process of living, entailing the natural liberation of the foundation, the instructions on the transitional process of meditative stabilization, entailing the natural liberation of awareness, and so forth entail coming to certainty through investigating the nature of the existence of the originally pure reality-itself, then practicing. They are called the "cycle of the Breakthrough to the ground." By identifying awareness that directly perceives reality-itself and becoming accustomed to it, you now determine the appearances of the transitional process of reality-itself; and that is called the "liberating path of the Leap-over." In this there are four topics: (1) striking the critical points of the body, speech, and mind, (2) the alighting of direct perception upon oneself due to the three kinds of critical points, (3) the ways in which the four visions arise due to practice, and (4) final, concluding advice.

The practices of the first and second transitional processes and so on are for the sake of realizing the transitional process of reality-itself. Likewise, in the Pāramitāyāna the first five of the perfections are cultivated for the sake of the sixth perfection, wisdom.

STRIKING THE CRITICAL POINTS OF THE BODY, SPEECH, AND MIND

In striking the critical points there are three parts: (a) the critical points of the body, (b) the critical points of the speech, and (c) the critical points of the mind.

The Critical Points of the Body

In the critical points of the body there are also three parts: (i) the Nirmāṇakāya posture, squatting like a *ṛṣi*, (ii) the Sambhogakāya posture, like a reposing elephant, and (iii) the Dharmakāya posture, like a lion in the form of a dog. The *Primary Tantra on the Penetration of Sound* states:

> With the lion posture of the Dharmakāya, one is freed from all deceptive fears, and one sees with vajra eyes. In dependence upon the Sambhogakāya posture of a resposing elephant, one emanates forms of reality-itself and sees with the eyes of Dharma.

The Pearl Rosary states:

> There are three kinds of critical points of the body: the manner of a lion, of an elephant, and like a ṛṣi.

With no more than seven pupils, when the sky is limpid and there is no wind, lead your pupils to a solitary place. First, the Dharmakāya posture like a lion in the form of a dog entails positioning the body in the shape of a dog. Place the soles of both your feet on the ground; make your hands into vajra fists; plant your big toes a little way into the ground; extend the upper part of your body like a lion, throwing yourself erect; cast your strength into your throat; and direct your senses at their objects.

The preceding training needs to be taught when the sky is perfectly clear with no rain, no clouds, and no haze. You will probably have to leave the city to perfect this training. When you "cast your strength into your throat," you arch your neck a little bit. While putting your chin down, you straighten out the back of the neck. When you "direct your senses at their objects," the sense you are directing is your visual sense, or your gaze.

This phase of practice, which concerns the Leap-over stage of Great Perfection practice, is traditionally taught to only a few students at a time who are well prepared for this practice. They would have already completed all the preliminary practices; they would be trained in practices involving the channels and vital energies; and they would have already been trained in the stage of generation and completion. They would also be trained in the Breakthrough practice, which requires experience in the cultivation of both quiescence and insight. Students with such a basis in practice are suitable vessels for the cultivation of this advanced phase of the Leap-over.

These advanced Great Perfection teachings were not designed for people who don't even have any sense of refuge. So why am I offering this as a public teaching? There are a number of great, contemporary lamas who say the time has now come to make these teachings public. Yangthang Tulku Rinpoche, His Holiness Jigmey Phüntsok, and His Holiness Orgyen Kusum Lingpa have stated that now is the time when the teachings on the six transitional processes should be taught openly. Karma Lingpa himself, the lama who revealed these teachings initially, also wrote a prayer that these teachings may flourish in the final era of degeneration and people's behavior is incompatible with Dharma. Thus, the time for these teachings to become public is now.

However, if you study these teachings in a frivolous manner or out of idle curiosity, this will lead to your own lower rebirth in a miserable state of existence. But if you listen to and study these teachings with faith, even without practicing them, you will receive a seed of liberation, which is of great benefit. So no one should refute the points, and no one should advise their Dharma friends not to receive these teachings on the Great

Perfection, because they are too esoteric, or advanced, for them. Please do not countermand the advice of these great lamas.

For example, the teachings on "liberation through hearing" state that simply hearing such teachings with faith places a seed of enlightenment upon one's mind-stream. Thus do not let skeptics prevent others from having the opportunity to receive these teachings. Such skeptics do not have wisdom beyond that of Karma Lingpa, who revealed these teachings in the first place. Remember that he was the one who said that at the appropriate time, these should be made public. The teachings are very precious, and they may be of great benefit to you at death. Come what may, do not hinder each other in your practice.

Second, the Sambhogakāya posture like a reposing elephant entails lying face down like an elephant; press your knees against your chest; point your toes outwards; press your elbows on the ground; and lift your throat up a little bit.

Third, the Nirmāṇakāya posture like a squatting ṛṣi entails putting your body in a squatting position; place your ankles together; plant the soles of your feet on the ground; completely straighten your body; press your knees against your chest; cross both your wrists and hug your knees; and make your spine straight and erect.

By striking the three kinds of critical points of the body, you strike the critical point of the presence of the primordial wisdom of awareness in the body so that it is directly perceived. This is like the fact that although a snake has limbs, if the snake is not squeezed, the limbs remain hidden.

The Critical Points of the Speech

In the critical points of the speech there are also three parts: (i) training in speech, (ii) being still, and (iii) being firm. First, training in speech entails talking no more than three or four times in one day and talking less and less. Second, being still entails completely silencing your speech, with no verbalization whatsoever. Third, being firm entails remaining firm as if you were mute, without saying anything at all.

The Critical Points of the Mind

Without letting your awareness be distracted elsewhere, do not let it veer away from your focused target.

THE ALIGHTING OF DIRECT PERCEPTION UPON ONESELF IN DEPENDENCE UPON THE CRITICAL POINTS

Here there are three parts: (a) the critical points of the apertures, (b) the critical points of the object, and (c) the critical points of the vital energies.

The Critical Points of the Apertures

The critical point of the apertures is the eyes. The *Primary Tantra on the Penetration of Sound* states:

> In terms of the apertures,[53] look with the eyes of the three *kāyas*.

No Letters states:

> In terms of the eyes, gaze at the domain of space.

The Pearl Rosary states:

> In terms of the apertures, do not move from just that.

Nirvāṇa Traces states:

The critical points of the apertures are gazing upward, downward, and sideways.

Here there are three parts: The purpose of the Dharmakāya gaze, in which you roll your gaze upwards, is to stop deceptive appearances at once; the purpose of the Sambhogakāya gaze, in which you look sideways, is to see the pure visions of primordial wisdom; and the purpose of the Nirmāṇakāya gaze, which is dropped downwards, is to gain control over the vital energies and the mind. Therefore, do not be separated from the three gazes, which are the critical points of the apertures.

In the Dharmakāya gaze, you slightly roll your eyes upwards, but not so much that you look like you're dead. Some lamas teach that after one adopts any of the above postures, one lets the gaze rest in whatever way that is comfortable. However, according to tradition, there is a correspondence between these postures and gazes. That is, the Dharmakāya gaze corresponds to the Dharmakāya posture, and so on.

The Critical Points of the Object

Here there are two parts: the outer absolute nature and the inner absolute nature. The *Primary Tantra on the Penetration of Sound* states:

The absolute nature is outer and inner. The outer is apprehended as the cloudless sky, and the inner is the pathway of the lamp.

The Blazing Lamp states:

By placing your awareness in the outer absolute nature, your own awareness is purified in its own state, and it appears.

Self-Arising Awareness states:

> The absolute nature is a natural halo.

Nirvāṇa Traces states:

> The critical point of the object is space that is
> free of conditions.

The outer absolute nature is space that is free of conditions, and the inner absolute nature is the lamp of the utterly pure absolute nature. Since empty space is the object that appears to empty awareness, by focusing on the critical point of the object, primordial wisdom freely arises.

The Critical Points of the Vital Energies

Here there are three parts: holding, expelling, and gentle stability. The *Primary Tantra on the Penetration of Sound* states:

> By all means be gentle with the vital energies.
> This occurs by fully expelling them.

Nirvāṇa Traces states:

> The critical point of the vital energies is to be
> very gentle.

First, gently hold them, then expel them far out like an arrow, and afterwards very gently let the vital energies naturally settle. In terms of the critical point of the awareness, imprison the strands. *No Letters* states:

> The essence arises like strands, subtle, flickering,
> and darting.

Self-Arising Awareness states:

> The body of light bearing the five primordial
> wisdoms radiantly appears as strands, going and
> coming, darting and covering.

The Lion's Perfect Strength states:

> The reality of self-appearing awareness is present
> as the strand of primordial wisdom.

One imprisons the strands by holding them in. To know the meaning of the word "strand," you must engage in the Leap-over practice for at least several months. In this practice, currents of transparent light, imagery, and designs appear in your field of vision. Flickering, subtle, darting, and transparent, these strands are outer manifestations of the primordial wisdom of awareness. Following the appearance of these strands, various bindus also appear, in which rainbow lights and visions of your chosen deity may be seen. Sequences of concentric spheres also appear within these bindus. These visions of bindus are creative expressions of primordial wisdom, while the strands are awareness-itself, which is to say, the primordial wisdom of awareness. Once again, you must put the teachings into practice and see for yourself what they mean.

To get some intimation of this experience, squint your eyes a little bit while gazing at an electric light. You will likely see patterns of light, which are precursors of the strands that will appear in authentic Leap-over practice. In such practice, you may gaze at a source of light, such as the moon. The Leap-over teachings say, "When the sun is rising in the east, you should face to the west. When it's in the west, you should look to the east." This is to prevent you from hurting your eyes. Do not practice Leap-over while looking at the sun, because you'll go blind. It's better not to even look directly at a candle. It is all right to look at a dim electric light and see some visual images, but do not mistake that for the genuine practice of the Leap-over.

Nirvāṇa Traces states:

> Imprison the strands of awareness.

Thus, by not being separated from the three critical points, observe the strands of awareness. At first, do this in many short sessions, then continue with longer and longer sessions. Then practice at special times during the day and night. You will be trained in one and a half months.

We are commonly advised to begin with short sessions and to gradually progress to longer ones. But many people do just the opposite: they start off with long sessions, and then decrease them until they quit practicing altogether. Start with many short sessions, then gradually increase the duration of each one, and decrease the number of sessions per day. You may work up to one-hour sessions, one-and-one-half-hour sessions, two-hour sessions, twelve-hour sessions, then all-day sessions. This is the strategy followed by the lamas of the past. If you practice well like that, after one and a half months, you will perfect it.

THE WAYS IN WHICH THE FOUR VISIONS ARISE DUE TO SUCH PRACTICE

Here there are four parts: the direct vision of reality-itself, the vision of progressing experience, the vision of consummate awareness, and the vision of extinction into reality-itself. *Nirvāṇa Traces* states:

> Due to the direct vision of reality-itself, the view of grasping onto cogitation dissolves. Due to the progressing experiential vision, the primordial wisdom of the transitional process is made manifest. Due to consummate awareness, you recognize the Sambhogakāya. Due to the vision of extinction into reality-itself, you obtain the

fruition of the Great Perfection, free of activity.
Once you have thus come to the culmination of
the basis and path, there is no nirvāṇa to be
sought elsewhere.

The Direct Vision of Reality-itself

The spiritual mentor teaches, "Perform the critical
points of the body like this, perform the critical points
of the speech like this, and for the critical points of the
mind, focus on this." By practicing like that, without
relying on the superimpositions due to mental analysis
and words, students directly see as their object the vision
of the awareness of reality-itself in empty space, without
its being contaminated by any compulsive ideation. So
that is called the "direct vision of reality-itself."

These visions arise directly without any superimpositions of
visualization. For example, in the stage of generation, you
superimpose a lot of visualization upon your experience. You
superimpose the palace, the deities within the palace, and so
forth. You also superimpose words, such as the words of a
sādhana, so you engender this experience through words and
visualization. There is superimposition in other types of practice as well.

However, in contrast to that, in the Leap-over phase, visions
arise without relying on any superimpositions, either of visualizations or of recitations. This occurs upon the basis of empty space.
This is where the vision is experienced, and it is no way contaminated by compulsive ideation or ordinary thinking. That is called
the direct vision of reality-itself. The reason why the Leap-over
phase of the Great Perfection is so awesome is that it is direct. It
is unmediated by compulsive ideation, and it does not depend
upon conceptual or verbal superimpositions.

The *Primary Tantra on the Penetration of Sound* states:

> The direct vision of reality-itself surely emerges
> from the apertures of the sense faculties, and it
> is radiant in the cloudless sky.

> Thus, by practicing in accordance with the critical
> points, between your eyebrows there is the so-called
> "lamp of pristine reality-itself." It appears like the colors
> of a rainbow or the eye of a peacock feather. Inside it is
> the so-called "lamp of the empty bindu," and it is like
> the concentric circles of ripples when you throw a stone
> into a pond.

In this phase of practice, you may see white or blue halos or circles. But not everyone sees the same thing. The type of visions you experience depends upon your own metabolism, so this varies from one person to another.

> Inside a form like the round plates of a shield there
> appears a bindu about the size of a mustard seed or a pea.
> Inside that is the "vajra strand of awareness," which is fine
> like a knot tied in a strand of a horse's tail, like a string of
> pearls, like an iron chain, like a lattice of flowers moving
> with the breeze, and so on. All those appear in combina-
> tions of two or three and so on, and they are called the
> "sole bindu of the strand of your own awareness."

In this phase of practice, you may see many tiny, fine bubbles of light. They are innumerable, and they may appear in different colors. They are all effervescent, shimmering, darting, and moving around. They are not "out there," existing as some independent reality in the space in front of you. Rather these lights appear due to the movements of the vital energies in your own body. As you gradually calm and subdue the vital energies in your body, then these visions also calm down.

A wide variety of visions may arise in this phase of practice. These little strings of light may be like hairs, or strands, of light across the field of your vision. Sometimes they may decrease in number while you're gazing at them. Sometimes they may become thicker. Sometimes they may be straight and sometimes they may be crooked, and they may also appear in round patterns. They may shift in all these various ways.

> The absolute nature and awareness are neither joined nor separated, but are present in the manner of the sun and its rays. The mark of the absolute nature is the halos, the indication of primordial wisdom is the bindus, and the mark of awareness and the embodiment is the strands. In terms of their location, they are present in the center of the *citta*,[54] and in terms of their pathway, they directly appear to the eyes, which are the refined essence of the sense faculties. The *Primary Tantra on the Penetration of Sound* states:

>> The direct vision of reality-itself surely emerges from the apertures of the sense faculties, and it is radiant in the cloudless sky.

> Thus, analytical views, including views entailing grasping onto cogitation, words, intellectual understanding, and so on, dissolve. *Nirvāṇa Traces* states:

>> Due to the direct vision of reality-itself, views entailing grasping onto cogitation dissolve.

The Vision of Progressing Experiential Visions

> Among visionary experiences and cognitive experiences, cognitive experiences arise in various ways such as the sense of bliss, the sense of clarity, and the sense of emptiness. Unstable and transient, they are common to the various yānas, and they are to be little emphasized. Furthermore, such traditions as Mahāmudrā also say

that cognitive experiences are like mist, and one should not place credence in the value of such experiences. Rather, one should place the strongest emphasis on the value of realizations. Here, the criteria for the value of realizations are determined by way of visionary experiences, and since visionary experiences are not transient, they should be most strongly emphasized.

Thus, as a result of engaging in visionary experiences, at times the absolute nature and awareness become clear and at times they do not. By continuing to practice, the absolute nature and awareness are separated from the point between the eyebrows, they become separated from sensory phenomena, and the lamp of the empty bindus effortlessly arises and approaches. The bindus turn into the size of peas, and awareness proceeds like a bird that is just able to fly.

As mentioned earlier, an instantaneous practitioner, one who immediately gains realization upon hearing the teachings is like a garuḍa chick: as soon as the chick hatches, it is immediately able to fly. On the other hand, ordinary people like ourselves are more like children: we need to go through the various phases of the training, hearing the teachings, understanding the view, and engaging in the practice. Then gradually realization arises.

By continuing to practice, visions of the five lights transform so that they appear in a fragmented fashion, vertically, horizontally, like spear-points, similar in aspect to a black yak-hair tent, and like the squares of a chessboard; and those lights pervade everything in front of you. Moreover, the bindus also transform so that they are like a mirror, and awareness appears in the manner of a running deer.

By continuing to practice, visions of the absolute nature appear in the aspects of a jewel lattice, lattices, full and half lattices of light, checkered, radiant, like spear-points, and a multilayered stūpa, a thousand-petaled lotus, a halo, the sun and moon, a castle, a sword, a vajra, a wheel, and like the shape of a fish's eye. Moreover, that light fills the environment in which you live. The bindus become like brass bowls, and your awareness becomes like a bee hovering over nectar.

All such visions may appear as single or multiple phenomena. It is important, however, that you don't make a big deal out of these appearances. Don't respond to them with grasping or with aversion. Simply witness them.

> By continuing to practice, the light saturates the environment, the bindus become like rhinoceros-skin shields, the light pervades everywhere you look, and the absolute nature and awareness constantly appear day and night. The body of a deity appears in each of the bindus, and individual, subtle divine embodiments arise in the midst of awareness. Awareness remains motionlessly.

Deities may appear inside the bindus that make up the strands of awareness, and in the meantime, "awareness remains motionlessly."

> When such appearances arise, the phenomena of the transitional process are established in that way, so there is no later intermediate state between death and rebirth.[55] Thus, the practice of the transitional process of reality-itself is just this main practice.

The *Primary Tantra on the Penetration of Sound* states:

> In the progression of the experiential visions, the colors of primordial wisdom come out vertically and horizontally; the bindus clearly appear as various divine embodiments, and the luminous environment appears to awareness.

Nirvāṇa Traces states:

> Due to the progression of experiential visions,
> the primordial wisdom of the transitional
> process is made manifest.

There are certainly various problems that arise in the course of earnest Dharma practice. First of all, you may be able to alleviate some of these problems by listening well to the teachings. However, if you practice solely for your own benefit, then you'll never accomplish anything. There have been countless enlightened beings in the past, and not a single one achieved spiritual realization through self-centeredness. It doesn't work. We have been in this cycle of existence since beginningless time, and it is self-centeredness that has perpetuated this cycle of existence. It's part of the problem, not part of the solution. It manifests through expressions of attachment and aversion. Living according to the principles of attachment and aversion is incompatible with Dharma, and it's even incompatible with accomplishing mundane ends. The three poisons of attachment, aversion, and delusion are to be banished, like a poisonous snake. Especially the poison of attachment is to be eliminated. Insofar as you can lead your life free of these three poisons, you will accomplish your spiritual and mundane aims.

While many people ask me how to enrich their spiritual practice, I find that much of their conversation consists of expressions of attachment and aversion. I can guarantee that as long as people continue to cultivate these mental poisons, there will be no progress in their spiritual practice. Insofar as you are still living your life according to those principles of attachment and aversion, Buddhist teachings on the Four Noble Truths become pointless. The teachings on the Four Thoughts that Turn the Mind become pointless. The teachings on the six perfections become pointless. It all gets wasted. In that case, there's no point in being a Buddhist. Buddhism is wasted on you.

The Vision of Consummate Awareness

Then by continuing to practice, five divine embodiments with consorts appear inside each of the previous bindus. They are innumerable and immutable, and they reach a consummate amount, as if by the handful and by the pound. Then you may even stop meditating. At that time, your body is liberated into clear light, its elements proceed into their natural purity; the aggregates of your material body are liberated in their own state; appearing and yet not inherently existent, you are naturally liberated as a Sambhogakāya; and as the Sambhogakāya is nakedly recognized, grasping onto the embodiment is released in its own state.

For this next phase of the experience to occur, you must continue to practice. Do not give up, as so often happens. By continuing to practice, the five divine embodiments of buddhas appear with their consorts inside each of the previous bindus. In the previous visions, there were many bindus that filled the field of your vision. Now, inside each of those bindus, you will see these five embodiments of buddhas with their consorts. If you reach this point in the meditative process, you no longer need to meditate. From this point on, the experiences will arise of their own accord.

This is like farming. Once the soil has been well tilled and the seeds have been sown, if the sun comes out, the farmer can relax. Now everything is up to the natural course of events. Likewise, once your children have grown up, they are beyond your control, so you can relax and just watch what happens. Similarly, in this phase of spiritual development, you can just sit back and relax; and the rest of your spiritual development will take care itself.

At this point, you are naturally liberated as a Sambhogakāya. Moreover, there is no notion of "I am this embodiment." All such grasping has been released, and you've been liberated in your own state.

The *Primary Tantra on the Penetration of Sound* states:

> In the vision of consummate awareness, the
> signs and symbols of the Sambhogakāya clearly
> appear, and from indeterminate colors of the
> rainbow, the deities and consorts of the five
> families appear. Then the five couples are united
> with radiant bindus; and with the appearance of
> the bodies of the deities and consorts, deceptive
> appearances dissolve into a pure realm.

Nirvāṇa Traces states:

> Due to the vision of consummate awareness, the
> Sambhogakāya is recognized.

The Vision of Extinction into Reality-itself

The progression of the preceding visions comes to an end;
and, in those experiences of visions there is no nature of
grasping onto appearance or nonappearance. At that time
there occurs what is called the "vision of extinction into
reality-itself." Experiences are extinguished, the material
body is extinguished, the grasping of the sense faculties is
extinguished, the assemblage of deceptive thoughts is
extinguished, all philosophical tenets and deceptive
appearances are extinguished, your material body disap-
pears and you become a buddha. That is called "extinction into reality-itself," for it entails the extinction of
activity, deceptive appearances, and the progression of
experiential visions. It is called the "extinction into reality-
itself," but it is not nonexistence as in the case of nihilism,
in which there is an extinction into nothing. Rather the
primordial wisdom of knowledge and excellent qualities
become manifest. In short, the power of the qualities of
the three embodiments is brought to perfection.

At this point, there is no sense of "this is an appearance" or "this is not an appearance." There is no impurity, nor is there any sense of "this is purity." All such conceptual constructs have been transcended altogether.

> The experiences that are extinguished here are the various visions that have occurred thus far. Grasping onto all of the five sense objects of visual forms, sounds, and so on is extinguished. One's material body refers to one's tainted body, that is, the body created by your own previous actions and mental afflictions; this also disappears. At this point, all of conventional reality is extinguished. Do not interpret this in a nihilistic way. It's not to say that everything has simply become nothing. Reality-itself entails the fulfillment of the qualities of spiritual awakening, including the boundless enlightened activities of the Buddha. Saying conventional reality has vanished is like saying all the clouds have dissipated in the clear blue sky, but it is not suggesting that the sun has vanished. On the other hand, you do not grasp onto the sky, saying, "That's truly existent." That kind of grasping is simply an expression of the other extreme of eternalism. Reality-itself is free of a nihilistic extreme, for it's not simply nothing. Yet, since reality-itself cannot be grasped as truly existent, it is free of the eternalistic extreme.

The primordial wisdom of knowledge is of two types: ontological and phenomenological. Ontological knowledge is knowledge of reality as it is. Phenomenological knowledge is knowledge of the full range of phenomena. In buddhahood these two modes of knowledge have come to perfection, and innumerable qualities of enlightenment, which were previously latent, now become manifest.

> Thus, upon seeing the direct vision of reality-itself, in dependence upon the vision of progressing experiential visions, in which the absolute nature and awareness

progress higher and higher, awareness is brought to its consummation; you experience the pure realm of the three embodiments. Like the moon come to fullness or a physique that has come to its full strength, when the progression of experience ceases, the intellect is consumed, phenomena are consumed, and grasping is consumed. This is simply called the "vision of the extinction into reality-itself."

You may wonder whether the extinction into reality-itself of the Great Perfection and the culminating path and qualities of the five paths of the sūtra tradition are the same. They are not at all the same. Even if one has come to the culmination of perfecting the power of the six thousand qualities of the ten bodhisattva grounds and five paths of the sūtra tradition itself, one still does not see at all the qualities and power of tantra, and they are not perfected. So there is a great difference between the extinction into reality-itself and the final path.

The *Primary Tantra on the Penetration of Sound* states:

> The vision of the extinction into reality-itself is empty of experiential visions. The body is consumed, the objects of the senses are consumed, the deceptive assemblage of thoughts is naturally liberated, and then there is a disengagement from words that are the basis of speech.

And:

> Thus, upon the cessation of the continuum of the body, the contaminated aggregates disappear, resulting in manifest buddhahood.

If you plant a seed of an apple tree, you nurture it until the tree grows up. Then you don't need to look elsewhere for apples. To begin with, you had the seed; then you nurtured it, and then you receive the fruit right there, without having to go elsewhere. Similarly, we already have the cause of buddhahood within us, and we've also obtained for the time being this precious human life of leisure and endowment. Within this context, we have the opportunity to engage in hearing, thinking, and meditation. With the conjunction of the cause, which is within us, and these conditions of the precious human life and the various stages of practice, we can harvest the fruit of perfect enlightenment.

As we know from a wide range of experiences, it's not enough simply to have the cause but no contributing conditions. The crucial, contributing condition for spiritual awakening is perseverance in the practice.

Nirvāṇa Traces states:

> Due to the vision of the extinction into reality-itself, the fruition of the Great Perfection, free of action, is achieved. In this way, upon coming to the culmination of the basis and the path, there is no nirvāṇa to be sought elsewhere.

This is the culminating path of the Great Perfection. Then there are no qualities of nirvāṇa and no other paths to be sought. This is the ultimate. Even if the culminating paths of the lower yānas are achieved, if the gateway of the qualities of tantra is not seen, then one must enter into tantra and train in hearing and thinking. Thus, even if one has come to the culmination of sūtra practice, one has not come to the culmination of the tantras. As this is the culmination of all paths, there is no ascending beyond it, so the grounds are perfected, and the paths are perfected. Since there are no other higher paths, this is called the Great Perfection. That is the teaching on the ways in which the four visions appear.

CONCLUDING ADVICE

Establish a basis in the three nonmovements, establish the criteria of the three positions, strike the nail with the three achievements, and perfect the four states of confidence. These are treated more extensively elsewhere. These are the instructions on the transitional process of reality-itself, called, the natural liberation of seeing. Samaya.

Sealed, sealed, sealed.

8

The Natural Liberation of Becoming: Experiential Instructions on the Transitional Process of Becoming

In the sixth general topic, the transitional process of becoming (practical instructions that are like completing the unfinished task of joining a broken water canal with a channel), the natural liberation of becoming is taught. These practical instructions on the practice of the transitional process of becoming are for those who have not seen the four visions and have not recognized the transitional process of reality-itself; they are like completing the unfinished task of joining a broken water canal with a channel.

CLOSING THE ENTRANCE OF THE WOMB AS A DIVINE EMBODIMENT

If you are now one who meditates on a divine embodiment, when the visions of the transitional process arise—such as snow and rain, a blizzard, and the appearance of being chased by many people—as soon as you recall the clear appearance of the deity, all those will arise as your chosen deity. To train in the power of that, remain alone in a solitary place, and meditate like this: "What is this? Regarding these present phenomena, I have died and am wandering in the transitional process; so this place, these companions, and these indistinct appearances are phenomena of the transitional process of becoming. Thus, previously I did not recognize that transitional process, and I wandered on. Now I shall arise as the embodiment of my chosen deity." With that thought, imagine that the outer environment is a pristine Buddha realm, the beings within it are assemblies of your pristine chosen deity, and all sounds are the natural sounds of your pristine chosen deity. Afterwards, evenly place your awareness in the experience of nonobjectivity. By practicing that again and again, when the transitional process of becoming arises, first you will recognize that transitional process. Then, upon recalling the stage of generation, the transitional process will arise as a divine embodiment, the entrance of the womb will be closed, and you will achieve the state of a Vidyādhara.

The visions of the transitional process occur after you've died. For example, if you apply this pure vision to snow or rain appearing during the transitional process, they turn into cascades of flowers. Your own body and everything around you arises in the form of your chosen deity. By that means, you can be liberated. However, it's not enough just to be attracted to this idea. You need to practice by hearing, thinking, and meditation.

Millions, billions, trillions of times, we've already experienced the transitional process. That is, we have died a countless number of times in the past, so we've already experienced the transitional process countless times. To train in this now, imagine your present experience as already being the transitional process. You do this to counteract your previous tendencies of grasping onto that which is truly nonexistent as being truly existent and grasping onto deceptive appearances as being real. This is the discursive meditation to be followed.

That practice corresponds to the stages of generation and completion. First of all, to counteract tendencies toward nihilism, imagine yourself and everything in your environment as being pure. Then, to counteract grasping onto the eternalism, complement the preceding practice of the stage of generation with the practice of the stage of completion.

After death, when you are on the verge of taking your next rebirth, you will recognize the transitional process for what it is.

Once you achieve the state of a Vidyādhara, you can go wherever you like, to any pure realm or anywhere else.

> If you see people or animals copulating, or you see a beautiful woman being attracted to you, as soon as passion arises for her, think, "Alas! Having wandered about in the transitional process of becoming, I am preparing to enter a womb. So now I shall close the entrance of the womb."

Blocking the Person Who Is Entering

> As soon as passion poignantly arises, with instant, total recall, vividly imagine yourself as the embodiment of your chosen deity. For one who is not trained in that, when one sees a male and female copulating during the transitional process, if you are taking birth as a male, jealousy arises toward the male, and passion arises for the female. If you are taking birth as a female, jealousy arises toward the female, and passion arises for the male. At that time, if you are accustomed to the stage of generation, instead of passion and jealousy arising, you will recall yourself as your chosen deity standing upright. That visualization, the arising of poignant passion, the closing of the entrance of the womb, and your maturation as the embodiment of the deity occur simultaneously.
>
> Therefore, also at the present time when there is a beautiful woman, romantic speech and behavior, or the arising of intense passion, let that be a catalyst for you to recall your body vividly as the clear appearance of the deity. Then, without rejecting passion, it comes to your aid. However strong your passion is, by training in the stage of generation of your chosen deity, you will have no difficulty in being liberated during the transitional process.

The reference to seeing a beautiful woman is for men, so if you are a woman, switch the gender. This teaching is appropriate for us to practice right now. In this type of training, you imagine that you are already in the transitional process; and you implement these practices. This can be a legitimate part of your Dharma practice. On the other hand, if you really don't have a Dharma practice and you simply use the Dharma to seduce people, that's not Dharma at all. It's simply a cause for your own rebirth as a preta or one of the other msiserable states of existence. So it's important to understand the proper context of this practice.

You will have no trouble being liberated in the transitional process if you are extremely careful with such practices involving passion. It's very common for people nowadays to misuse these practices. Women call themselves ḍākinīs and use this as a license for trying to seduce men. Men and women lie about their own degree of realization, claiming to be adepts in the stage of generation and so forth. This is especially common in the United States. Also, in India some Western men grow their hair long, tie it up in a bun, and pretend to be highly realized in controlling the channels and the vital energies. Such people are mistaken.

It is possible to engage in genuine practice of this kind, but it's very important that it be carefully done and totally without any such fraudulence. For the most part, we don't now have control over our minds, and if we lack control during life, there's no hope of having such control after we die. When we're wandering about in the transitional process, we will be propelled by our previous actions and habits. There are occasions in the transitional process when great fear and suffering will arise. We will have the sense of losing our bodies, and we will experience a great urge to acquire a new one. That will impel us to seek out a womb into which we can enter. We may see a variety of sentient beings, such as animals, copulating, and this craving may lead us to rebirth as an animal, a preta, or a hell being. Insofar as we succumb to that urge, liberation is out of the question. It will be difficult even to obtain a human rebirth.

Blocking the Entrance of the Womb that Is to Be Entered

If you see any man and woman in sexual union, as soon as

passion and jealousy arise, say, "I'm wandering in the transitional process. Alas, at this time when the transitional process of becoming is appearing to me, I shall maintain a single-pointed visualization in my mind, and shall earnestly conclude an excellent, but unfinished task." Upon blocking the entrance to the womb, be aware of turning away from it. This is a time for fervent, pure vision. Accustom yourself to thinking vividly of that man and woman as your chosen deity and consort, visualizing them, having reverence for them, and having a sincere sense of receiving an empowerment. Even if you do not witness the act of sexual union, bring it to mind, and by recalling the clear vision of your chosen deity, the stage of generation will thus come to your aid, and the entrance of the womb of the transitional process of becoming will be closed. Thus, this is profound. Samaya.

Both of the preceding practices of blocking the person who is to enter the womb and blocking the entrance of the womb that would otherwise be entered are for people who are already generating themselves as their chosen deity. Why would you do that visualization? It is for two purposes: such practice can lead to both the common and supreme siddhis in this lifetime. After death, this practice acts as a preparation for achieving the supreme siddhi, namely perfect enlightenment. Those are genuine purposes of engaging in the stage of generation. By accomplishing those aims, either in this lifetime or in the transitional process after death, your own interest is fulfilled. You are also in a position to then serve the needs of others, so others' interests are fulfilled; and this is also a service to the Dharma.

CLOSING THE ENTRANCE OF THE WOMB BY IMAGINING YOUR SPIRITUAL MENTOR WITH CONSORT

When you witness sexual intercourse, recall an object of passion, or when your own passion arises strongly, imagine your objects of passion as Guru Orgyen Padma and his consort Yeshe Tsogyal embraced in sexual union. Get rid of the attitude of jealousy and respond with reverence and devotion. Powerfully imagine receiving the four empowerments; and especially by recalling the meaning of the third empowerment, bring to mind the inborn reality, and you will close the entrance to the womb and be liberated during the transitional process. Again, eliminate jealousy, then meditate on the spiritual mentor with consort. This is a time for sincere, pure vision. So it is said.

In the third empowerment you put your index finger in a red powder and touch it to the center of your chest, symbolizing the union of method and wisdom. Such practices are designed to facilitate a realization of the nature of emptiness, or ultimate reality. Likewise, in some initiations one is shown an image of a naked woman, and this is for the same purpose.

CLOSING THE ENTRANCE OF THE WOMB WITH THE PRACTICE OF THE FOUR BLISSES

Become very well trained in the *Great Bliss Instructions on the Lower Orifice*, then seek out a qualified mudrā, take her to a solitary place, and meditate on the illusory body of the mudrā. Then both you and the mudrā should regard yourselves as your chosen deities. First, the practice regarding form entails exchanging brief glances of passion. The practice regarding sound entails romantic words and engaging in speech that arouses passion. The practice regarding smell entails smelling the lotus and the fragrance of the mudrā. In terms of taste, bite down and suck on rock sugar and raw sugar. In terms of touch, fondle and suck the breasts, gently embrace and tickle, and rub the center of the lotus. Disrobe and gaze at the vajra and lotus, arouse passion; and when the mudrā is intoxicated with desire, passion is aroused, and the vajra is ready, gently offer it into the lotus. After moving it up and down as far as its base, remain in the sense of emptiness for a little while without moving. By moving it gently, without losing that experience, first bliss arises and is recognized. With that sense, remain completely in bliss and emptiness. If it seems like the bliss is vanishing, by moving and thrusting more and more strongly in accord with your experience, pleasure increases and supreme bliss is recognized. Then the primordial wisdom of nondual, inborn bliss and emptiness is recognized. By practicing that, in the best case, at the time of death, once the elements have gradually withdrawn and finally dissolve, the *rakta* obtained from your mother rises up; the Spirit of Awakening obtained from your father descends from the crown of your head; the white and red bodhicittas arise as the visions of the white path and the red path, after which they meet at the heart. Together with the arising in immeasurable, inborn bliss, when consciousness is diffused and you are becoming light-headed, inwardly the breath stops. So if a person who practices the four blisses and the procedural path of bliss and emptiness at that time and who recognizes the inborn bliss on the occasion of the third empowerment ascertains this, that person will instantly be elevated to a boundless state. Thus, the profound presentation of the procedural path and messenger's path of tantra is like that.

Even if this is not recognized there, in the transitional process of reality-itself, as soon as you see the peaceful and wrathful deities and consorts embraced in union, you will recall and recognize the primordial wisdom of inborn bliss on the occasion of the third empowerment; and you will be liberated. If you do not recognize it there, during the transitional process of becoming, as soon as you see a male and female copulating, you will recognize the primordial wisdom of inborn bliss, the primordial wisdom of the bliss of the experience during the empowerment, and the entrance to the womb will be closed. Then you will surely be liberated during the transitional process and will achieve the state of a Vidyādhara.

Therefore, as this is a more profound and swift path than other tantras, right now, without worrying about what people will say, train in the *Great Bliss Instructions on the Lower Orifice*, for that is the main part of the practice of the transitional process. Thus, it is important to seek out a qualified, youthful consort and train in the profound path of bliss. The details are to be known in the *Great Bliss Instructions on the Lower Orifice*. That is closing the entrance of the womb with the path of passion, and it is a prospect for superior people[56] of good fortune. Samaya.

HOW THOSE ON THE PATH OF LIBERATION CLOSE THE ENTRANCE OF THE WOMB WITH THE ANTIDOTE OF RENUNCIATION

Now lay-precept holders, novice monks, or fully ordained monks who cherish their vows emphasize meditation on foulness or forcefully practice renunciation as soon as they witness sexual intercourse or recall an object of passion. During the transitional process when they see a male and female copulating, they will recall their training and renunciation. Either the entrance of the womb will be closed without their entering it, or else they will take birth in a perfect womb and achieve a fortunate rebirth. This path is a bit inferior to the preceding. Samaya.

The meditation on foulness entails observing or imagining the various components of the body: the blood, the fat, the tissue, and so forth. This is one type of meditation used to counteract passion. It is designed for people having such precepts, and it is an expression of their earnest intent to maintain pure ethical discipline. Such renunciates use this meditation on foulness to counteract sensual desire, which is a cause of the perpetuation of our existence in saṃsāra. However, such people should not think that those who engage in sexual intercourse are inferior, nor should they respond to them with aversion. Instead of applying the antidote directly to their own minds, such renunciates rather examine the object of sensual desire, emphasizing its foulness. In this way they alter their perception of the object as an indirect means of counteracting a tendency of their own minds.

Whatever practice you do, engage in it for the benefit of this and future lifetimes. Whatever approach you take, your practice should bring about benefit for both yourself and others. It should act as an antidote for the perpetuation of suffering in this cycle of existence. If it doesn't counteract suffering, then what good is it? By progress along this path of practice, you may achieve the common siddhis and the supreme siddhi, which is buddhahood.

By now, we should have a pretty good idea what the practices are. Our present situation is that we are wandering in saṃsāra. When we're experiencing good fortune, it's common for us to become exuberant and excited. This indicates an absence of patience in the face of joy. In times of adversity, we experience overwhelming sorrow. Both these overwhelming emotions in response to felicity and adversity stem from grasping onto a sense of personal identity and from self-centeredness. They lead to attachment and aversion.

For those of you who would really like to effectively counteract your suffering, I recommend that you study Śāntideva's treatise called *A Guide to the Bodhisattva Way of Life*. This offers practical counsel for those who are suffering. Moreover, your suffering will be alleviated by meditating on the Four Thoughts that Turn the Mind, the Four Noble Truths, and the nature of actions and their consequences. This is the medicine that relieves your suffering. Other helpful teachings are to be found in the text entitled *Transforming Felicity and Adversity into the Spiritual Path*, which is translated in the book *Ancient Wisdom*.

When tragedy strikes, it is very common, especially in the United States, for people to say, "Why did this happen?" or

"How can this have happened?" One often hears the response, "I can't believe this happened!" or "I'm just astonished that this could have happened." There's nothing good about this inability to acknowledge and accept adversity. It arises from grasping onto our own personal identity, and it stems from the five poisons of delusion, attachment, hatred, jealousy, and pride. We are dominated by these five poisons. Among those five, four are like ministers of the king. The king is delusion, and the others—attachment, hatred, pride and jealousy—are like the ministers of the king. The rest of the eighty-four thousand mental afflictions are like the subjects of the king. When we think, "I am someone special," that self-grasping leads to suffering and to lower rebirth. The path of hearing, thinking, and meditation is for the sake of liberating us from these afflictions and the suffering that ensues from them. As the obscurations of your mental afflictions dissipate and vanish, the sun of your primordial wisdom will shine forth.

For those of you who are teachers, it is important not to be puffed up and proud. Rather, we need compassionate teachers. The first thing that is important is the motivation. Whether for hearing, thinking, or meditation, the motivation is paramount. There are different types of motivation. There are honorable motivations and dishonorable motivations; there are virtuous motivations and nonvirtuous motivations. Of course, among those, we need to bring forth an honorable and virtuous motivation, a Mahāyāna motivation, specifially the motivation of the Spirit of Awakening. This motivation counteracts self-centeredness, replacing it with a motivation focused on the well-being of others. In contrast, if we teach, write, or debate with a sense that we're someone special, that would be disgraceful. Therefore, it is most important, first of all, to bring forth a suitable motivation.

CLOSING THE ENTRANCE TO THE WOMB WITH THE CLEAR LIGHT

> By training in that way in the instructions on the Breakthrough and integrating that with the meaning of emptiness, the superior individual will recognize the

basic clear light during the transitional process of dying and, with no transitional process, will proceed to the boundless Dharmakāya. Even for the least of individuals, the reality of emptiness and the clear light will vividly arise in their mind-streams when they witness sexual intercourse during the transitional process of becoming, and they will be liberated. Samaya.

To understand the comments, you must review the transitional process of dreaming and the practices pertaining to the natural liberation of delusion. If you train in the practice of your chosen deity when you're in the transitional process after death and you see a couple engaging in the act of sexual intercourse, that is the time to generate yourself as your chosen deity with consort. By recalling and implementing here your practice of the stage of generation, you will be liberated. If you have gained a fine experience in the stage of completion or in the Great Perfection, by bringing forth your realization of emptiness at this point, you will achieve liberation during this transitional process of becoming.

CLOSING THE ENTRANCE TO THE WOMB WITH THE ILLUSORY BODY

Now, once you have trained in the natural liberation of the appearance of the illusory body, when the fears of the transitional process arise and the entrance of the womb appears, illusion-like samādhi will arise in your mind-stream, and you will be liberated.

This pertains to the preceding practices of the transitional process of dreaming and the illusory body. Recall that there are two types of illusory body, the pure and the impure, and that these are to be cultivated in the practice of dream yoga. The point of all this is to see your body, speech, and mind and everything else as being of the nature of illusion.

To synthesize the primary points of all those practices, a practitioner of the stage of generation trains in seeing all the appearances of the transitional process of living as being of the nature of gods and goddesses. And a practitioner of the stage of completion trains in distinctly seeing everything that appears as self-arisen, primordial wisdom and emptiness. Moreover, by training in regarding all appearances as being like reflections in a mirror, appearing and yet devoid of an inherent nature, such that appearances and emptiness are indivisible, the deceptive appearances of the daytime will arise as pure visions. Due to that, one is free from clinging onto the true existence of dreams, and one either recognizes the dream-state as the dream-state, or it arises as the clear light. Due to that, the deceptive appearances of the transitional process arise as pure visions, and one is liberated during the transitional process.

This practice begins in the daytime by cultivating a pure vision and training in the illusory nature of everything you experience. Becoming accustomed to that during the daytime places imprints upon your mind-stream; and these carry over into the dream-state, so this pure vision also occurs at night. Familiarization with that in the dream-state carries over to the transitional process after dying. In that way, it is possible to recognize the nature of the transitional process for what it is, thereby liberating yourself from it. The point of this is to gain liberation from the suffering of the cycle of existence for oneself as well as for others.

During the daytime, we naturally see all appearances as impure. This tendency carries over into the night, so dreams, too, are seen as impure. Because of this habituation, the appearances in the transitional process following death are also seen as impure. All this occurs due to the habituations of our own minds.

That practice entails constantly, evenly resting your awareness in the unmodified, originally pure experience of the fresh appearance of the present. If thoughts issue forth, apprehend them with the confidence of the four great types of liberation. Cultivate the sense that whatever appears is self-arising and self-liberating. In addition, reflect that, "All these present appearing objects are objects appearing after I've died and am wandering in the transitional process. They are unstable and chaotic. These objects are also present as the objects appearing in the transitional process of becoming, and sentient beings who are born and move about are also sentient beings of the transitional process. This roaring sound of the vital energies, thunder, lightning, rain, hail, darkness, uproarious human voices and barking of dogs, song and dance, games, wars, conversations in different languages, the performance of various actions, and this cacophony of random and varied chaos are certainly the transitional process. These companions I meet today and this evening, relatives, and fellow travelers have also died and are wandering with me in the transitional process. They are not truly existent, and like a dream and an illusion, they have no objective existence, or true existence."

It is not easy to recognize the unmodified, originally pure nature of appearances because we stubbornly discriminate between good and bad, classifying reality, and structuring things according to our own self-centered ideas. As a result, when some people try to rest in this unstructured, uncontaminated state of awareness, they make themselves tense by sitting up too straight and straining their breathing. That's not an unstructured state; it's just one more structured state. On the other hand, some people think that resting in unstructured awareness means to lounge around in a completely casual way. That's also another extreme.

Resting the mind in its unstructured, originally pure state means that you do not follow after any thoughts that arise, be they virtuous or nonvirtuous. Thus, whatever comes up in the mind, you let it come up and let it be without reacting to it, without classifying it, and without responding to it or trying to modify it. This is like observing the wind, whether it comes from the north, the south, the east, or the west; whichever way the wind blows, there it is. That is the quality of unstructured awareness. This is very hard to do in practice. One reason for that is even though we may do it for a short time, we're not satisfied. We don't trust it.

When you cultivate the sense that whatever appears is self-arising and self-liberating, you just let it come and let it go. See all mental events simply in their own nature. When thoughts arise, they are not stored someplace, as if in a mental bank. If we had such a bank, we would all be filthy rich. Rather, mental events naturally arise, and they naturally disappear.

In this practice here, it's important not to lose the awareness of the nature of the mind or the nature of mental events. Whatever comes up, don't block it. As soon as you try to block it, you've lost the nature of it; and you're no longer doing this practice. If you feel that you must do something to make the thoughts go away, you're not doing the practice. If you feel you need to sustain these mental events, again you're not doing the practice. The practice here is to allow awareness to rest in its own natural state, originally pure.

Recall that in the earlier practice of the transitional process of dreaming, even during the waking state you look at daytime appearances and think, "This is a dream. This is really a dream. Right now, I'm dreaming." Similarly, in this practice of the transitional process of becoming, during the day and night, you regard everything as the indistinct, chaotic appearances after you've died and you're wandering in the transitional process. They are unstable, fleeting, and evanescent. These objects are those of the transitional process of becoming. Sentient beings who are born and move about are also sentient beings of the transitional process. In other words, when you see other beings, the environment, and so forth during the daytime, think that these are beings moving around in the transitional process following death.

For example, during the entire course of a conversation, think of it as taking place during the transitional process. The purpose of this meditation is to cultivate the constant awareness, day and night, of the lack of true existence of phenomena. In this way, we recognize the manner in which we are normally confused by our grasping onto the true existence of phenomena.

Again place your awareness evenly in the experiences beginning with going for refuge up to the stage of generation, the stage of completion, emptiness, and Mahāmudrā. By growing accustomed to such propensities, you should constantly think, "This is the transitional process," and even say out loud, "This is the transitional process. This is the transitional process. O dear! I'm wandering around in the transitional process. Mentor! Mentor!" At times, repeatedly utter the "Prayer of Calling for Help," the "Primary Words of the Transitional Process," "Liberation through a Narrow Passage," and prayers for protection from fear. Again and again look at the *Liberation through Hearing* and the entire cycle of teachings on the transitional process.

In short, train your mind in the Dharmas of the transitional process; there is no meditation superior to those visualizations. Constantly practice the visualizations of the transitional process. Afterward, evenly rest in the unmodified experience of the mind-itself. Upon arousing your mind-stream with the visualizations of the transitional process, apply yourself diligently to spiritual practice. Carefully read the *Liberation through Hearing of the Transitional Process of Reality-itself* and *Liberation through Hearing of the Transitional Process of Becoming.* Train your mind well in all the six lamps, the supplementary Dharmas of the transitional process, and in identifying the transitional process. By so doing, there is no doubt that superior people will be liberated in this life, middling people at death, inferior people in the

transitional process of reality-itself; and even the most inferior people will be liberated by concluding their unfinished
task during the transitional process of becoming. These are
the instructions on the transitional process of becoming,
called, the natural liberation of becoming. Samaya.

At times you may be aghast at the nonvirtuous thoughts arising
in your mind. They may even seem stronger than ever before. In
reality, such thoughts have been present all along; you just did
not recognize them. It's good to notice them and be concerned
about them. First of all, recognize nonvirtue when it arises, then
gradually abandon it. For example, it is good to abandon the
nonvirtue of killing and to go out of your way to protect the lives
of others. Even having the motivation to protect the lives of others is part of the practice. Likewise, avoid all kinds of stealing,
including cheating, double-crossing, and so forth, and cultivate
the opposite of stealing, which is generosity.

You can experience the clarity or purity of the mind for yourself through the practice of the Great Perfection and specifically
through the cultivation of meditative quiescence. It's important to
join such practice with prayers to your spiritual mentor. You can
make prayers to your spiritual mentor as being indivisible from
Padmasambhava, Vajrasattva, Buddha Śākyamuni, Mañjuśrī, and
so on. The reason for viewing them as being indivisible is that it
offers protection from ordinary appearances. Once we have recognized our own spiritual mentor as being the Buddha,
Padmsambhava, or Vajrasattva, we don't need to do any other special meditation on our chosen deity. For now we've recognized the
Buddha as the Buddha.

Many people who have a strong desire to engage in spiritual
practice yearn to go into retreat. That's fine. But until you leave
for retreat, it's important to practice right now. It is certainly
worthwhile to go into retreat, but it's not absolutely necessary.
Moreover, simply being in retreat does not lead to instant awakening. It's not so easy. The most practical avenue is to implement
these teachings as much as you can right now in your daily life.

Let your practice flow into the present, rather than anticipating some future situation that you consider more ideal. To reach liberation, you must recognize the great value and rarity of your present life of leisure and endowment, and practice diligently throughout the course of your life and during the transitional process following this life.

Amazing! This natural liberation, essential teaching on
the six transitional processes
Is the synthesis of all the contemplations of the victors;
It is the quintessence of all the profound Dharmas of the
yānas;
It is the experiential teaching that leads beings on the
path of liberation.
In the final era of a future eon,
When all beings behave contrary to the Dharma,
May this profound path liberate beings!
May each one without exception achieve perfect buddha-
hood!
May the profound Dharma of this great teaching on the
six transitional processes
Called the *Natural Liberation through Contemplating:
Experiential Instructions*
Continue to be taught until the cycle of existence is empty!
Samaya.
The treasure is sealed.
The secret is sealed.
The profundity is sealed.

Colophon

The siddha Karma Lingpa unearthed this from Gampo Dar Mountain. He created a single lineage and appointed Guru Nyida Özer to be the master of this profound Dharma. May there be virtue!

PART THREE

SUPPLEMENTAL PRAYERS

9

Three Prayers Concerning the Transitional Processes

PRAYER OF SUPPLICATION

Homage to the victors, the peaceful and wrathful deities.

These are the primary words of the six kinds of transitional processes:

Alas! At this time when the transitional process of living is appearing to me,

I shall abandon spiritual sloth, for there is no time to waste in this life.

I shall unwaveringly enter the path of hearing, thinking, and meditation,

And I shall train so that appearances and the mind arise as the path, and the three embodiments become manifest.

On this occasion when human life is obtained but once,

This is no time for remaining in the ways of distractions!

This precious human life is extremely short in its duration, so there is no time to waste in this life. Life is wasted when we indulge in the eight mundane concerns, and it is spent fruitfully by applying ourselves to hearing, thinking, and meditation on the Dharma. In our present situation, phenomena arise as impure appearances and we grasp onto them as such. This is a prayer that appearances arise as the path. Through such training, the three embodiments—the Dharmakāya, Sambhogakāya, and Nirmāṇakāya—become manifest. In the process, your own primary spiritual mentor also becomes manifest.

Recall the extraordinary rarity of obtaining a human life of leisure and endowment in terms of some analogies. For example, imagine throwing peas at a pin with its tip pointing upwards.

The likelihood of one of the peas landing on top of the pin and sticking there is similar to the likelihood of achieving a human life in the whole of cyclic existence. To take another well-known analogy, if you had a bucketful of peas and threw them against the wall, the chance of one of those peas sticking on the wall is like the chance of obtaining a human life.

It is important to meditate thoroughly on the nature and value of a human life of leisure and endowment. Ponder carefully the eight types of leisure and the ten types of endowment, and consider the great difficulty of obtaining such a human life endowed with all of those qualities. This precious human life imbued with leisure and endowment is something we have obtained now, but it will soon be destroyed, for it is impermanent. It would be such a tragedy if, after having this extraordinary opportunity, we allowed it to be wasted. If we lose just a dollar or two, we get all upset and think, "Oh, too bad! I've lost that money!" Imagine wasting a human life of leisure and endowment with which it is possible to accomplish the omniscient state of enlightenment. If it's too bad to waste a dollar or two, then what about the situation of wasting such a life?

As human beings, we are endowed with a certain degree of intelligence, but it is important that we use it. Having obtained this precious opportunity, if we continue in a life of spiritual sloth, applying ourselves vigorously only to the eight mundane concerns, this is not smart; it is dumb. One may be ambitious, energetic, and hard-working in a worldly sense; but, from a Dharma perspective, that person who is working eighteen hours a day is said to be lazy. We are just part of the crowd if we show such stupidity as to waste this opportunity. This pertains to all of us; we are all in the same situation. It's important to ponder well what our opportunities are. For example, many of us here strived very diligently to receive Buddhist teachings in the past. Now that we've received teachings, isn't it time to put them into practice? It's not that I'm saying you have to do this for me. Quite to the contrary, each of us here is suffering from our own mental afflictions. We are carrying them with us at all times. If we go into retreat, we carry our mental afflictions with us into retreat. If we live at a monastery, we carry our afflictions into the monastery. If we're practicing Dharma, we carry our mental afflictions into Dharma practice. We are the ones suffering from mental afflictions, so we need to put these teachings into practice, and we have the opportunity to do so.

For example, when people hear teachings on practices involving a consort, they become absolutely riveted to the teacher's speech, as if their ears are growing bigger and bigger. On the other hand, when the teachings turn to the nature of suffering and the cycle of existence, their ears and eyes seem to retract back into their heads. Even their bodies seem to shrivel up. Likewise, when people are introduced to teachings on the Great Perfection, their eyes start to expand, the ears come poking out. On the one hand, the Great Perfection is profoundly simple. On the other hand, the Great Perfection is the peak of the nine yānas, the ultimate teaching of the eighty-four thousand collections of the teachings of the Buddha. It's good to listen to these, but it's difficult to chew these teachings if you don't have teeth. For Buddhists genuinely striving for liberation, I encourage you to focus on the Four Thoughts that Turn the Mind. To engage effectively in the practice of the Great Perfection, look first to this foundation.

Life is impermanent. In order to gain insight into this reality, you should attend to the elderly, the sick, people with very serious illnesses such as cancer and AIDS. As we learn about these people and encounter them, it's important to recognize that death is not something faced only by the old and the sick. They will die, but we too are subject to death. Everyone in the world is subject to death. In fact, if people hadn't been dying all along, where would we have any place to put them? Death is simply in the natural order of things. This has been true in the past, it is true in the present, and it will be true in the future. In the midst of this universal reality, if we should still persist in the notion that death is for other people and not ourselves, this is truly stupid. Lord Buddha said, "All composite phenomena are impermanent," and we can see this from our own experience. In the course of our own lives from the very moment we are conceived, with each passing second, there is impermanence and change. We used to be very tiny as infants, then very small. We grow up big, and then we will die. This is simply the natural course of things. This is true of all sentient beings. Impermanence is true of the animate universe, and it's also true of the inanimate universe. All this is subject to decay and destruction. Ponder this well. If you would like to have a richer and fuller understanding of this topic, then it would be of benefit to you to go back to the teachings on the Four Noble Truths and the Four Thoughts that Turn the Mind. Look at those teachings; doing so will be of benefit to you.

These teachings on the human life of leisure and endowment come in the context of the first of the six transitional processes, namely the transitional process of living. If you establish a good foundation here and gain genuine insight, there will be good results as you go on to the practices pertaining to the other transitional processes. On the other hand, if you overlook these teachings in the transitional process of living pertaining to human life and so on, then it will be very difficult to succeed in the later practices pertaining to the transitional process of reality-itself and so on. A sign that one has not yet established a sufficient foundation in these fundamental practices is that one finds oneself too busy to receive teachings, for one is too busy with other priorities. Likewise, because of our other priorities, we are too busy to meditate, behaving as if we're immortal and that death does not pertain to us. It's for other people. With this attitude, we just don't have time to hear teachings, to think about the teachings; and we don't have time to meditate. The reason for this is that we don't have a foundation for practice. See for yourself whether this is true. If you have that kind of attitude at times, take a look at it. For those of you going to school, for example, you may find that getting an education keeps you very busy. It's very demanding, you're extremely busy, and it's easy to procrastinate in terms of spiritual practice. If you think you're busy now, what do you expect is going to happen after you graduate? You will be even busier. In the course of going to school and getting employment, life slips by. Opportunities slip by. Opportunities that were accessible and practical while we're young may not come again when we're old. For example, if you don't go to school when you're young, it's difficult in middle age or later to go back to school and try to get an education. If you had a good opportunity when you were young and didn't take it, then it's difficult to do it when you're older. If that's the case for school, bear in mind that it's even more difficult when it comes to Dharma.

> Alas! At this time when the transitional process of dream-
>   ing is appearing to me,
> I shall abandon negligence and the cemetery of delusion.
> With unwavering mindfulness, I shall enter the experience
>   of the nature of being.
> Apprehending the dream-state, I shall train in emanation,
>   transformation, and the clear light.
> Do not sleep like an animal,
> But practice integrating sleep and direct perception!

The first of the transitional processes, namely the transitional process of living, provides us with a great opportunity to find happiness both in this lifetime and in future lifetimes. Another such opportunity arises in the transitional process of dreaming. First of all, apprehend the dream; then engage in the practices of transforming and emanation, and eventually gain a realization of the clear light in the context of this dream yoga practice.

We sleep, and while we're sleeping, we dream. We've had the teachings on this, and we have the opportunity to practice. Now, what's missing? We don't get around to it, and we don't try. The great thing about this practice is that you can sleep and practice at the same time, and in that way gain realization of the clear light. During the daytime, we have the opportunity to engage in hearing, thinking, and meditation and to experience the fruition of the path. And at nighttime, we have the opportunity to hear teachings, ponder them, and put them into practice through the night to gain the fruition of the practice while we're sleeping. By engaging in this process throughout the day and night, we have the freedom to achieve buddhahood. Isn't that astonishing!

Some of us may have the excuse that, during the daytime, we are extremely busy, having many demands on our time. It is so difficult to find time to sit down, hear teachings, ponder them, and meditate. But how many people can say that, during the nighttime when they're are sleeping, they're too busy to practice? Some people have big screen TVs linked up with VCRs, and they have so much diligence that they watch until two o'clock in the morning regularly. If those people were to apply that kind of enthusiasm to Dharma practice, the results they would achieve would be amazing.

> Alas! At this time when the transitional process of medi-
> tative stabilization is appearing to me,
> I shall abandon the confusing masses of distractions.
> Without wavering and without grasping, I shall enter the
> state that is free of extremes.
> I shall attain stability in the stages of generation and
> completion.
> Abandoning activity, as you meditate single-pointedly,
> Do not let yourself fall under the influence of delusive
> mental afflictions.

The phrase "without wavering and without grasping" is the crucial point of this practice. The reason for this is that we wander around in saṃsāra due to distraction. As the mind is pulled in all different directions, grasping naturally takes place. We grasp onto that which is not truly existent as being truly existent. We grasp onto the division of self and others. We grasp onto good versus bad. All of these are expressions of grasping and, as a result, we fail to achieve liberation; and we succeed in bringing a great deal of suffering upon ourselves. The importance of nongrasping does not imply that reality is empty like an empty cave, which would imply the extreme of nihilism. To enter into the experience that is free of extremes, we must be free of the extremes of nihilism and eternalism.

These verses address the first three of the transitional processes, those of living, dreaming, and of meditative stabilization. If you are well trained in those, you don't need to fear the transitional process of dying. Even if you have not brought those practices to their culmination but have trained in them seriously, the transitional process of dying is easy.

> Alas! At this time when the transitional process of dying
>   is appearing to me,
> I shall abandon attachment, craving, and grasping onto
>   anything.
> Without wavering, I shall enter the experience of the
>   clear, practical instructions.
> I shall transfer my own unborn awareness to the absolute
>   nature of space.
> I am about to be separated from the composite of my
>   body of flesh and blood.
> Know that it is impermanent and illusory!
> Alas! At this time when the transitional process of reality-
>   itself is appearing to me,
> I shall abandon fear and terror toward anything.
> I shall recognize that whatever appears is the natural
>   appearance of awareness.
> Know that it is the manner of appearance of the transi-
>   tional process!
> There will come a time to meet that crucial threshold.
> Do not be afraid of the peaceful and wrathful assemblies,
>   which are your own appearances!

During the transitional process of reality-itself, various sounds and forms arise, and it is crucial to recognize these as being of your own nature, and therefore not to be feared. Many people seem to be courageous with regard to such things as the consequences of their own nonvirtuous actions. We engage in nonvirtuous actions with great courage and fortitude and with no sense of shame. Unfortunately, at death it will be hard to maintain that kind of heroism. Right now we are holding the reins of our own future, of our own destiny. Following this life, will we go to a pure land? Will we go to a fortunate state of existence? Will we go down to a miserable state of existence? Where are we bound?

Holding the reins of our own destiny, right now we have the opportunity to determine where we will go following death. If we neglect this present opportunity and wait until death is right at our door, it will be very difficult to have the same kind of control that we have now. Don't think that you have to listen to me, for you will face this situation yourself. As the text says, "One day you will come to this tight place." This phrase is so significant, because you will be in that situation. It will be up to you.

Is this account of the transitional process of reality-itself true? There are some people who think that this whole discussion of seeing peaceful and wrathful emanations is Buddhist dogma and that it is relevant only for Buddhists. Absolutely not! All sentient beings have these experiences. It is also a mistake to believe that only Buddhists witness terrifying phenomena after death, while others will have only pleasant experiences of light and so on. Let's look at that hypothesis. Is it true that only Buddhists have horrible dreams and everyone else just has wonderful dreams? Do Buddhists have worse dreams than other people? There doesn't seem to be a shred of evidence for that. If that's not true, then because of the close parallel between the transitional process following death and the dream-state, evidence from one can be used for drawing inferences about the other. Therefore, this teaching is not just for Buddhists. It's not just for human beings. It seems many kinds of animals also have dreams. Have you never seen a dog sleeping and heard it bark due to a bad dream? Therefore, they have the same problem that we do. Now is the time that we have the opportunity to put these teachings into practice. If we waste this time to practice, we will end up meeting "this tight place," and we will have a big problem.

Next we go on to the sixth of the transitional processes: the transitional process of becoming. If you have trained well in the first five transitional processes, you will have the control and the freedom to practice in the sixth transitional process, in which you can have the freedom of going wherever you wish—for example, to a pure realm. That will be your choice. Without having any such training in any of the preceding five transitional processes, you will find yourself in a tight place. If you're wondering how you will do, look at how you behave while dreaming. If you have no control in the dream-state, how do you expect to have any kind of control, choice, or freedom when you are in the transitional process following death? Moreover, that transitional process after death will entail a lot of suffering and a lot of confusion, so how's it going to be? On the other hand, if you've trained well in those first five, then you will go from one good state to another. It will be like joining two pipes together.

Alas! At this time when the transitional process of becoming is appearing to me,
I shall hold the single-pointed visualization in mind,
And earnestly complete a fine, unfinished task.
Block the entrance of the womb, and recall the causes of turning back.
This is a time in which sincere, pure vision is needed.
Abandon jealousy, and visualize the spiritual mentor with consort!

You should see appearances as the male deity and emptiness as the consort. If you are able to practice at this time, you visualize your mother-and-father-to-be as your spiritual mentor with consort in the midst of the maṇḍala. You enter into that union with a spirit of altruism in order to be of service to others, and it is in that way that you can take birth as Nirmāṇakāya. In the transitional process of becoming you generate yourself in a pure form, for example, as Padmasambhava or Vajrasattva. Generating yourself in that form, you also look upon the mother and father as your spiritual mentor in this divine form, and you enter into that union. It's crucial that the motivation be an altruistic one.

"With a casual attitude that takes no heed of dying,
You engage in pointless activities of this life.
To return now empty-handed is to have confused desires.
Recognize that what is needed is the sublime, divine
  Dharma.
Will you not practice the divine Dharma right now?"
Thus speaks the kind spiritual mentor.
If the spiritual mentor's advice is not taken to heart,
Will you not be cheating yourself?

Then recall the practical instructions of the spiritual
  mentor.
Samaya.

THE NATURAL LIBERATION OF ALL ATTAINMENTS: A PRAYER CONCERNING THE TRANSITIONAL PROCESSES

The Prayer for Liberation through the Narrow Passage of the Transitional Process

Homage to the spiritual mentors, chosen deities, and
  ḍākinīs.
Please lead us to the path of great mercy.
When I am wandering in the cycle of existence due to
  confusion,
May the spiritual mentors of the oral lineage lead me
To the radiant path of unwavering hearing, thinking, and
  meditation.
May the assembly of supreme consorts, the ḍākinīs, sup-
  port me.
Please liberate me from the terrifying narrow passage of
  the transitional process.

Bring me to the state of truly perfect buddhahood.

When I am wandering in the cycle of existence due to strong hatred,

May Lord Vajrasattva lead me

To the clear, radiant path of mirrorlike primordial wisdom.

May the supreme consort Buddhalocanā support me.

Please liberate me from the terrifying narrow passage of the transitional process.

Bring me to the state of truly perfect buddhahood.

When I am wandering in the cycle of existence due to strong pride,

May Lord Ratnasambhava lead me

To the clear, radiant path of the primordial wisdom of equality.

May the supreme consort Māmaki support me.

Please liberate me from the terrifying narrow passage of the transitional process.

Bring me to the state of truly perfect buddhahood.

When I am wandering in the cycle of existence due to strong attachment,

May Lord Amitābha lead me

To the clear, radiant path of the primordial wisdom of discernment.

May the supreme consort Pāṇḍaravāsinī support me.

Please liberate me from the terrifying narrow passage of the transitional process.

Bring me to the state of truly perfect buddhahood.

When I am wandering in the cycle of existence due to strong jealousy,

May Lord Amoghasiddhi lead me

To the clear, radiant path of the primordial wisdom of accomplishment.

May the supreme consort Samayatārā support me.

Please liberate me from the terrifying narrow passage of the transitional process.

Bring me to the state of truly perfect buddhahood.

When we actually enter into the transitional process following death, the five buddha families and the five primordial wisdoms will arise and manifest to us. We will experience what is called the Path of Light. We will hear certain sounds, we will see rays of light, and we will experience these five classes of buddhas with their consorts. If we practice now and become familiar with this, then following our death, when we enter into the transitional process, it will be possible for us to recognize these five buddhas, the five primordial wisdoms and so on.

What's the point of that recognition? To achieve liberation. Your own five poisons are, in reality, the five buddhas. Recognizing this, when these various manifestations of the five buddhas and their retinues arise to you, recognize them as being indivisible from yourself; they are self-appearances. Through that recognition, liberation is gained.

> When I am wandering in the cycle of existence due to strong delusion,
> May Lord Vairocana lead me
> To the clear, radiant path of the primordial wisdom of the absolute nature of reality.
> May the supreme consort Ākāśadhātvīśvarī support me.
> Please liberate me from the terrifying narrow passage of the transitional process.
> Bring me to the state of truly perfect buddhahood.
> Alas! When I am wandering in the cycle of existence due to the five strong poisons,
> May the victors of the five families lead me
> To the clear, radiant path of union with the four primordial wisdoms.
> May the five great consorts of the absolute nature support me.
> Please liberate me on the radiant path that transcends the six impure states of existence.
> Please lead me to the five supreme pure realms.

The union of the four primordial wisdoms is the primordial wisdom of the absolute nature of reality, because that is the source of the other four. When we're actually in the transitional process, various rays of light will appear: those corresponding to the six impure realms of existence, as well as rays of pure light. Between those two, the rays of pure light that are associated with the pure realms and so forth will be more radiant, whereas the ones pertaining to impure states are dimmer. Being dimmer, they're easier to look at. Consequently, people who don't have any latent propensitites for the purity may just find it easier to follow the dimmer ones. Whereas if, through practice, we acquire latent propensities for the pure rays of light, it will be much easier to follow those. Thus, the point of the practice is to be able to recognize them when they arise.

> When I am wandering in the cycle of existence due to
>   strong latent propensities,
> May the heroic Vidyādharas lead me
> To the clear, radiant path of innate, primordial wisdom.
> May the assembly of supreme consorts, the ḍākinīs, support me.
> Please liberate me from the terrifying narrow passage of
>   the transitional process.
> Bring me to the state of truly perfect buddhahood.
> When I am wandering in the cycle of existence due to
>   strong, confusing appearances,
> May the assembly of blood-drinking wrathful deities lead me
> To the clear, radiant path that eliminates fear and terror.
> May the assembly of wrathful Ākāśadhātvīśvarīs support me.
> Please liberate me from the terrifying narrow passage of
>   the transitional process.
> Bring me to the state of truly perfect buddhahood.

We should have some idea already of the significance of these verses based on the previous accounts of the six transitional processes. These verses pertain particularly to the transitional process of dying. At that time, we'll hear various sounds; and it's important that we be able to recognize these as sounds of our own nature. If you already have some background and familiarity in the stage of generation practice, this will enable you to recognize those sounds as your own nature and to recognize the various wrathful deities, ḍākinīs, and so forth as being your own nature. Through such recognition, liberation is won. If we are unable to recognize these appearances in that transitional process as being our own nature and we see them as something other than ourselves, it will be a bit difficult because we'll want to look to someone for support, to back us up and to help us escape. Because we're not dealing with the actual reality, we're responding to something that is not true and then asking for help to get out of that which isn't real in the first place.

For example, if you're out wandering in the forest and come across a rope that you mistake for a snake, but then you recognize the rope for what it is, you don't need anyone to save you from the rope. Whereas, if you fail to recognize the rope as a rope and still think that it's a snake, you may look for someone to protect you from this terrible snake-like object. That's a problem. It is best to recognize your own nature. Then you will not need somebody else to liberate you from fictitious problems.

> May the element of space not arise as my adversary,
> And may I see the deep blue realm of the Buddha.
> May the element of water not arise as my adversary,
> And may I see the white realm of the Buddha.
> May the element of earth not arise as my adversary,
> And may I see the yellow realm of the Buddha.
> May the element of fire not arise as my adversary,
> And may I see the red realm of the Buddha.
> May the element of air not arise as my adversary,
> And may I see the green realm of the Buddha.
> May sounds, light, and rays not arise as my adversaries,
> And may I see the realm of the multitude of peaceful and
>   wrathful deities.

May the elements of the colors of the rainbow not arise
   as my adversaries,
And may I see the realms of various buddhas.
May I recognize all sounds as my own sounds.
May I recognize all light as my own light.
May I recognize all rays as my own rays.
May I recognize the transitional process as my own nature.
May the realms of the three embodiments become manifest.
Samaya.

The Prayer for Protection from Fear in the Transitional Process

Homage to the victorious peaceful and wrathful deities!
Alas! When the course of my life has run out,
Beyond this world my relatives will be of no use.
When I wander alone into the transitional process,
May the might of the compassion of the Great
   Compassionate One arise,
And may the darkness of the gloom of ignorance be dis-
   pelled.
Parted from by beloved companions, I shall wander
   alone.

Our lives are like butter lamps: they have only so much oil in
them and when all the oil has burned up, our lives are extinguished. When the course of our lives has run out, our relatives
are of no use. We die alone. When we enter into the transitional
process, we will proceed alone. To understand these assertions,
take your own dream-state as an analogy. If you're married, even
though you lie in bed and go to sleep together, when you're
dreaming, you're on your own. When you're dreaming, whatever
happens—whether it is a good dream or a bad dream—it is your
own experience. Is your wife of any benefit when you have a
nightmare while you're dreaming? Are your parents or your husband of any benefit while you're dreaming? It seems not. Just as
that is the case while dreaming, so it is during the transitional

process. It is a lonely venture, and our relatives of this life cannot be of benefit to us at that time.

> When the empty reflections of self-appearances arise,
> May the might of compassion of the buddhas arise,
> And may I not experience the fear and terror of the transitional process.

The issue here is one of freedom. When we die under normal circumstances without training in the Dharma, we die without freedom. That is, we do not choose freely where we go, but rather we are propelled by the storm of our previously accumulated karma. To evaluate the degree of freedom that we might have at death, we can look at the degree of freedom we have right now. In terms of your daily life, how much freedom do you have? At nighttime while you're dreaming, how much freedom or control do you have during the dream-state? Just look at the degree of compulsive ideation or thoughts churning in the mind. If we don't have control over these, we can question the degree of control we will have when we enter into the transitional process. The point is to practice now in order to gain greater control during the daytime, and during the nighttime to prepare for a liberating experience in the transitional process after death.

> When the five lights of clear primordial wisdom arise,
> Without fear or terror, may I know my own nature.
> When the peaceful and wrathful forms appear,
> Without fear, may I attain confidence and recognize the transitional process.

The aim of this prayer is to be totally free of doubt at the time of death and to have confidence to gain complete recognition of the events during the transitional process. This is like recognizing the rope to be truly a rope, totally dispelling any notion that it is a snake.

When suffering is experienced due to misdeeds,
May this suffering be dispelled by the Great Compassionate
   One.
When the empty thunder of the natural sound of reality-
   itself roars,
May it be transformed into the sound of Mahāyāna
   Dharma.
When I am helplessly following after karma,
May suffering be dispelled by my chosen deity.
When suffering is experienced due to latent predisposi-
   tions and karma,
May the blissful samādhi of the clear light arise.

The reason we experience suffering at all, whether in this lifetime
or in the transitional process, is due to our own nonvirtuous
actions committed in the past. If we practice now and prepare
ourselves for the dying process, we can be ready for the transitional process. However, if we don't apply ourselves even to the
basic virtues and to avoiding nonvirtues in this lifetime, when we
enter into the transitional process it will be difficult for us to be
able to receive protection from the Great Compassionate One,
Avalokiteśvara, or any other manifestation of the Buddha. What
we experience at that time is the consequence of our own actions.

When we hear such sounds as thunder in the transitional
process, it is crucial to recognize this sound as our own nature,
thereby achieving liberation. If we grasp onto that sound as ordinary and as being something other than our own nature, fear will
arise; and we will not be liberated during that transitional
process. When it goes well, that sound is transmuted into the
sound of Mahāyāna Dharma. Likewise, if we can recognize
sounds now as being the natural sounds of reality-itself and not
grasp onto them as ordinary, with that pure vision, attachment,
aversion, and delusion would not arise.

When you are being propelled along by karma, recall your chosen deity, and take refuge in this being. When suffering arises, be
aware that you are not being punished by someone or something

else; rather, suffering is simply a consequence of your own latent predispositions and actions committed in the past.

> May the five elements not arise as enemies,
> And may I see the realms of the five buddha families.
> When I am miraculously born in the transitional process
>   of becoming,
> May there be no demonic prophecy of my falling back.

Birth into the transitional process of becoming is not actual birth from the womb. Rather, it has a purely visionary nature, so it's called a miraculous birth. People with detrimental latent predispositions may have visions or hear sounds that lead them astray. As they're going toward a pure realm some interference may arise that causes them to go back to one of the three miserable states of existence or to one of the other realms in saṃsāra. This prayer is made to avert that possibility, so that any prophecy of our falling back would be false.

> When I arrive where I intended,
> May there be no fear from confusing misdeeds.
> When vicious growls of carnivorous animals are emitted,
> May they turn into the Dharma sounds of the six syllables.

In the transitional process you may hear sounds as if you're being chased by ferocious animals. This prayer is aimed at transmuting them into the Dharma sounds of the six syllables, namely OM MAṆI PADME HŪṂ.

> When I am driven by snow, rain, wind, and darkness,
> May I attain the divine eyes of clear primordial wisdom.
> May all the comparable sentient beings[57] within the
>   transitional process
> Be without jealousy and be born in fortunate states of
>   existence.
> When I am severely afflicted, hungry, and thirsty,

May the miseries of hunger, thirst, heat, and cold be dispelled.
In the future when I see my father and mother coupling,
May I see the Great Compassionate One with consort.
May I achieve the freedom to be born where I will,
And for the sake of others, may I obtain a supreme body
  adorned with the signs and symbols of enlightenment.[58]
Once I have obtained a supreme body through rebirth,
May everyone who sees or hears me be swiftly liberated.
May I not pursue any misdeeds,
And may the merit that I desire increase, and may I pur-
  sue this.
Wherever I am born,
In each life may I meet my chosen deity.
As soon as I am born, may I know how to speak and walk,
Remember my rebirths, and attain perfect recall.
Simply by hearing, thinking, or seeing,
May I know the variations of great, small, and middling
  excellent qualities.[59]
May there be prosperity wherever I am born,
And may all sentient beings be happy.
O peaceful and wrathful Victors, may we become exactly
Like your form, with your retinue, life span, pure realm,
And with your supreme, excellent signs.
By the compassion of the myriad sublime peaceful and
  wrathful deities,
By the power of the truth of pristine reality-itself,
And by the blessings of the single-pointed practice of the
  Mantradharas,
May these prayers be accomplished.

Colophon

This completes the "Natural Liberation of All
Attainments: A Prayer Concerning the Transitional
Process," which was composed by Padmasambhava, the
Master of Orgyen. Samaya.

Sealed, sealed, sealed.

This was brought from Gampo Dar Mountain by the siddha Karma Lingpa.

Sarva mangalam!

PRAYER OF CALLING FOR HELP TO THE BUDDHAS AND BODHISATTVAS

Homage to the victorious peaceful and wrathful deities!

At the time of death, the following is the call for help to the buddhas and bodhisattvas. Make offerings, both actually prepared and mentally emanated, to the Three Jewels. Hold a stick of fragrant incense in your hands, and earnestly speak these words: "Buddhas and bodhisattvas of the ten directions, endowed with compassion, knowledge, divine vision, mercy, and who are the refuge of the world, please come to this place out of the power of your compassion. Accept these actually prepared and mentally emanated offerings. You compassionate ones are endowed with the primordial wisdom of knowledge, merciful compassion, enlightened activity, and inconceivable power of protection. O you compassionate ones, this person known as [such and such] is proceeding from this life to the next. This world is being left behind. Great beings, take care of me. I have no companions, my suffering is great, I have no refuge, no protector, and no friend. The appearances of this life are fading, and I am going elsewhere. I am entering a dense darkness. I am falling over a great precipice. I am driven by the power of karma. I am going into a great wilderness.[60] I am being carried away by a great ocean. I am driven by the winds of karma. I am going on an endless journey. I am going into a great battle. I have been captured by a great demon. I am afraid and terrified of the messengers of the Lord of the Dead. Due to karma I go from one state of becoming to another. I have no autonomy. The time has come when I must go alone, with no companion. O compassionate ones, provide refuge to this person who has no refuge! Provide protection to the one who has no protector! Provide friendship to one who has no friend! Protect me from the great darkness of the transitional process! Turn back the great whirlwind of karma. Protect me from the great terror of the lord of the dead! Liberate me from the great, long, narrow passage of the transitional process! You compassionate ones, do not be meager in your compassion! Help me! Do not let me go to the three miserable states of existence! Do not deviate from your previous commitment, and let the power of your compassion swiftly arise! O buddhas and bodhisattvas, for this one do not be meager in your compassion, your methods, or your power! Hold me with your compassion! Do not let sentient beings fall under the power of evil karma! May the Three Jewels protect me from the suffering of the transitional process following this life."

That should be recited three times by everyone, including yourself and others. May "The Prayer of Calling for Help to the Buddhas and Bodhisattvas" not vanish until the cycle of existence is empty. Samaya.

Sealed, sealed, sealed.

Sarvam mangalam!

10

The Natural Liberation of the Vast Expanse of the Three Embodiments: A Prayer of the Natural Liberation through Contemplating the Peaceful and Wrathful

OM ĀḤ HŪM

From the vast expanse of the pristine, omnipresent absolute nature of reality,

To Samantabhadra, the Dharmakāya of the Dharmakāya,

I pray from the sphere of the uncontrived vast expanse:[61]

May there be blessings from the sphere of spontaneous original purity.

From the vast expanse of the uncontrived, spontaneous absolute nature of reality,

To the great Vajradhara, the Sambhogakāya of the Dharmakāya,

I pray from the sphere of indivisible birth and cessation:

May there be blessings from the sphere of spontaneous great bliss.

From the vast expanse of the unceasing, clear, pure bindu,

To Vajrasattva, the Nirmāṇakāya of the Dharmakāya,

I pray from the sphere of indivisible awareness and emptiness:

May there be blessings from the sphere of spontaneous appearances and emptiness.

From the vast expanse of spontaneous displays of self-appearances,

To Gangchen Vairocana, the Dharmakāya of the Sambhogakāya,

I pray from the sphere of indivisible appearances and

emptiness:

May there be blessings from the sphere of spontaneous pure appearances.

From the vast expanse of the great bliss of spontaneous clarity and purity,

To the buddhas of the five families, the Sambhogakāyas of the Sambhogakāya,

I pray from the sphere of indivisible clarity and emptiness:

May there be blessings from the sphere of spontaneous great bliss.

From the vast expanse of authentic, self-appearing, primordial wisdom,

To Vajrapāṇi, the Nirmāṇakāya of the Sambhogakāya,

I pray from the sphere of indivisible sound and emptiness:

May there be blessings from the sphere of the vast expanse of primordial freedom.

From the vast expanse of the clear light of self-appearing, primordial wisdom,

To Vajrasattva, the Dharmakāya of the Nirmāṇakāya,

I pray from the sphere of indivisible thoughts and emptiness:

May there be blessings from the sphere of the vast expanse of appearances and liberation.

From the vast expanse of spontaneous self-appearances, free of conceptual elaborations,

To the lords of the three families,[62] the Sambhogakāyas of the Nirmāṇakāya,

I pray from the sphere of spontaneous, natural liberation:

May there be blessings from the sphere of spontaneous knowledge and mercy.

From the vast expanse of myriad unceasing self-appearances,

To the Six Great Sages,[63] the Nirmāṇakāyas of the Nirmāṇakāya,

I pray from the sphere of the natural liberation of masses of thoughts:

May there be blessings from the sphere of manifold natural liberation.

From the vast expanse of stainless lotus light,

To Padmasambhava, the miraculously born Nirmāṇakāya,

I pray from the sphere of the great bliss of union:

May there be blessings from the sphere of spontaneous deeds.

From the vast expanse of spontaneous primordial wisdom of great bliss,

To Yeshe Tsogyal, the sole mother,

I pray from the sphere of indivisible method and wisdom:

May there be blessings from the sphere of spontaneous pure appearances.

From the vast expanse of mind treasures of the primordial wisdom of self-awareness,

To the lineage spiritual mentors, treasure-revealing Nirmāṇakāyas,

I pray from the sphere of heartfelt reverence and devotion:

May there be blessings from the sphere of unceasing compassion.

From the vast expanse of the absolute nature of reality, pure like space,

To "The Profound Dharma of the Natural Liberation of Contemplating the Peaceful and Wrathful,"

I pray from the sphere of nonobjective pervasiveness:

May there be blessings from the sphere of the natural liberation of self-awareness.

From the vast expanse of the pure self-appearances of the foundation,

To my primary spiritual mentor whose kindness is uninterrupted,

I pray from the sphere of powerful faith and reverence:

May there be blessings from the expanse of the Dharmakāya of my own mind.

There are essentially two types of foundation. One is the mirror-like foundation of myriad latent propensities that we've accumulated and that manifest in our experience. When the nature of that foundation is recognized, it is seen as the foundation of primordial reality, which is equivalent to the Dharmakāya. The Sambhogakāya is emanated from the Dharmakāya, and the Nirmāṇakāya is emanated from the Sambhogakāya. When this foundation is not recognized, it's simply the foundation of myriad latent propensities.

> I pray to the Mahāyoga, Anuyoga, and Atiyoga,
> The three supreme teachings of the Dharmakāya:
> May there be blessings from the sphere of the omnipresent vast expanse.
> I pray to the kriya, upaya, and yoga,
> The three supreme teachings of the Sambhogakāya:
> May there be blessings from the sphere of the indivisible stages of generation and completion.
> I pray to the collections of the vinaya, sūtras, and abhidharma,
> The three supreme teachings of the Nirmāṇakāya:
> May there be blessings from the sphere of the spontaneously accomplished welfare of the world.
> Hold us with your compassion so that we may realize the meanings of the nine yānas.
> I pray to the buddhas as many as the atoms in the universe, who are all present in a single atom,
> The retinue of the Dharmakāya:
> Bless us that we may become like you.
> I pray to the innumerable bodhisattvas on the ten grounds,
> The retinue of the Sambhogakāya:
> Bless us that we may become like you.
> I pray to the bodhisattvas, the four classes of śrāvakas and so forth,
> The retinue of the Nirmāṇakāya:

The retinue of the Nirmāṇakāya:
Bless us that we may become like you.
Abandoning nothing, utterly perfect, unborn, and free of
conceptual elaborations—
Bless us that we may realize the contemplation of the
Dharmakāya.
Manifold, nondual, clear and empty, and without an
inherent nature—
Bless us that we may realize the contemplation of the
Sambhogakāya.
Stainless, and proceeding with the courage of a lion and
so forth—
Bless us that we may realize the contemplation of the
Nirmāṇakāya.
In the pervasive space of the pure realms of the uni-
verse—
May I become a disciple of the Dharmakāya.
In the basis and essence of the realm adorned with flowers,
May I become a disciple of the Sambhogakāya.
In the billions of enduring galaxies,
May I become a disciple of the Nirmāṇakāyas,
Who emanate and serve in whatever way is needed.

Colophon

May this sublime Dharma of "The Natural Liberation of
the Vast Expanse of the Three Embodiments: A Prayer
of the Natural Liberation through Contemplating the
Peaceful and Wrathful" not vanish until the world of the
cycle of existence is empty. This is a treasure of Karma
Lingpa. May there be good fortune!

11

The Natural Liberation of the Three Poisons without Rejecting Them: A Guru Yoga Prayer to the Three Embodiments

THIS PRAYER PERTAINS to the three embodiments and refers to all of the nine yānas. The natural liberation of the three poisons refers to the three poisons of delusion, anger, and attachment. When you recognize the actual nature of delusion, you see it to be the Dharmakāya. When you recognize the nature of anger, you see it as the Sambhogakāya. When you recognize the nature of attachment, you see it as the Nirmāṇakāya.

OM ĀḤ HŪM
To the spiritual mentor of the unborn Dharmakāya, free
   of conceptual elaborations,
In the omnipresent palace of the pristine absolute nature
   of reality
I pray with heartfelt reverence and devotion:
May ignorance and delusion be naturally liberated without
   rejecting them,
And may I receive the self-empowerment of the originally
   pure blessings of the Dharmakāya
For spontaneously accomplishing uncontrived, self-arisen,
   primordial wisdom.
To the spiritual mentor of the unceasing Sambhogakāya of
   great bliss,
In the palace of clear, pure primordial wisdom and great
   bliss
I pray with heartfelt reverence and devotion:
May attachment and clinging be naturally liberated with-
   out rejecting them,

And may I receive the self-empowerment of the spontaneous blessings of the Sambhogakāya

For the natural liberation of self-knowing, primordial wisdom and great bliss.

To the spiritual mentor of the indeterminate,[64] self-
appearing Nirmāṇakāya,

In Padma's flawless, pristine palace[65]

I pray with heartfelt reverence and devotion:

May misconceptions and hatred be naturally liberated
without rejecting them,

And may I receive the self-empowerment of the natural
liberation of the blessings of the Nirmāṇakāya

For the natural liberation of self-appearing, primordial
wisdom and self-awareness.

To the spiritual mentor of the three embodiments of
dimensionless great bliss,

In the palace of perfect clear light and self-awareness

I pray with heartfelt reverence and devotion:

May dualistic grasping onto subject and object be naturally liberated without rejecting it,

And may I receive the self-empowerment of the blessings
of the three embodiments of great bliss

For spontaneously accomplishing self-arisen, primordial
wisdom and the three embodiments.

Alas for every one of these miserable sentient beings

Who wander in the cycle of existence out of delusion and
foolishness,

Without realizing their own minds as the Dharmakāya,
free of extremes.

May we all achieve the Dharmakāya!

Alas for every one of these sentient beings with their mistaken desires

Who wander in the cycle of existence out of attachment
and craving,

Without realizing their own awareness as the
Sambhogakāya of great bliss.

May we all achieve the Sambhogakāya!

Alas for every one of these sentient beings with their misconceptions

Who wander in the cycle of existence due to hateful attitudes and dualistic appearances,

Without realizing their own minds as the appearing and liberating Nirmāṇakāya.

May we all achieve the Nirmāṇakāya!

Alas for all beings who have not achieved buddhahood,

Who have not realized their own minds as the indivisible three embodiments,

And thus grasp onto them due to their afflictive and cognitive obscurations.

May we all achieve the three embodiments!

Colophon

"The Natural Liberation of the Three Poisons without Rejecting Them: A Guru Yoga Prayer to the Three Embodiments," in *The Natural Liberation through Contemplating the Peaceful and Wrathful* was composed by Orgyen Padmasambhava. May this Dharma not vanish until the world of the cycle of existence is empty. This is a treasure of Karma Lingpa. May there be good fortune!

Epilogue

THAT COMPLETES THE TEACHINGS on the six transitional processes. I have drawn inspiration for giving these teachings especially from the people here in San Francisco who are ill and who have come to these teachings. They have encouraged me to teach and have supported me. I've been very inspired by these people, because they realize the value of practice. They are like people who have gone many days without receiving any Dharma teaching. Then when they receive it, they focus on their practice day and night, applying themselves to putting these teachings into practice. They have no other thoughts or other concerns. These people are very steady and always come to the teachings. This has given me the inspiration and the ability to teach. These are the circumstances under which these teachings have been given. I have offered these teachings with the hope that they will be of benefit to you. Put them into practice and find benefit from these teachings. Should you wish to receive more extensive teachings, you can go to other lamas, and they can give more extensive explanations of these same topics.

What is it about sick people that makes them especially inspiring? These people are like paper upon which you pour oil, and the oil sinks right in. For these people who are ill, when they receive teachings, the teachings just sink right in. In contrast, among many older students, giving teachings is like throwing a soft ball against the wall. It doesn't do anything to the soft ball, and it doesn't do anything to the wall either. Whatever type of virtue you can follow and whatever nonvirtue you can avoid, it will be to your benefit. I have commented on those who are ill, but what about the rest of us who are not presently ill? We're going to die too. We're right on the tracks to death, so it is simply a conceit to think we are somehow immune to death. If you think you're invulnerable to suffering, more power to you. Or if you've gotten some inside track from Yāma, the lord of death, that you won't have to suffer during the process of dying or thereafter, that's fine; then you have no problem. But, if you don't have the power to avoid death or any of the sufferings of death, then all of the preceding comments pertain to you. Please dedicate the merit of receiving these teachings.

Notes

1. *Zab chos zhi khro dgongs pa rang grol gyi rdzogs rim bar do drug gi khrid yig*, a *gter ma* of Padmasambhava revealed by Karma Lingpa (Kar ma gling pa). Volume 3 of the edition of the *Kar gling zhi khro* cycle from the library of Dudjom Rinpoche (I-Tib-1440, 75-903780). An alternative translation of the first part of the title is *The Natural Emergence of the Peaceful and Wrathful from Enlightened Awareness*. In this second translation, the term *zhi khro* refers to the sādhana, *dgongs pa* to the enlightened awareness of the author, and *rang drol* to the spontaneous emergence of the text from that enlightened awareness.

2. For a full account of Padmasambhava's life and deeds, see *The Lotus-Born: The Life Story of Padmasambhava by Yeshe Tsogyal*, trans. Erik Pema Kunsang (Boston: Shambhala, 1993).

3. For more information on the tradition of hiding and revealing treasures, see Tulku Thondup, *Hidden Teachings of Tibet: An Explanation of the Terma Tradition of the Nyingma School of Buddhism* (Boston: Wisdom Publications, 1997).

4. *Bar do thos sgrol*, or literally *Liberation Through Hearing in the Intermediate State*. This significant work has been translated several times, most recently by Robert A. F. Thurman, *The Tibetan Book of the Dead*, (New York: Bantam Books, 1994).

5. When the Tibetan term *bardo* (literally, the "inbetween") refers specifically to the phase following death and prior to rebirth, one can usefully translate the term as "intermediate state." But in the context of the *six bardos*, which include all of saṃsāra and nirvāṇa, the term "intermediate state" no longer makes sense as a translation for the word *bardo*. In this context, the significance of the term *bardo* is in indicating

that all phases of living, meditating, dreaming, and so on without exception are transitional. All these phases of life and death occur *between* other states. All of them are in process. To reflect this aspect of the term, the term *bardo* has been translated as transitional process in these contexts.

6. *Bar do'i nyams khrid dgongs pa rang grol gyi sngon 'gro rang rgyud 'dul byed lhan thabs.*

7. *gSangs sngags rdo rje theg pa'i chos spyod thun bzhi'i rnal 'byor sems nyid rang grol.*

8. *Zab chos zhi khro dgongs pa rang grol las bar do'i smon lam gsum.*

9. *Bar do'i smon lam thob tshad rang grol.*

10. *Bar do 'phra sgrol gyi smon lam.*

11. *Bar do 'jigs skyob pa'i smon lam.*

12. *Sangs rgyas and byang chub sems dpa' la ra mda' sbran pa'i smon lam.*

13. *Zab chos zhi khro dgongs pa rang grol gyhi gsol 'debs sku gsum klong yangs rang grol.*

14. *sKu gsum bla ma'i rnal 'byor gyi gsol 'debs dug gsum ma spangs rang grol.*

15. The eight mundane concerns are attachment to material gain, transient pleasure, praise, and reputation; and aversion to material loss, transient displeasure, abuse, and disrepute.

16. Although three embodiments of the Buddha were mentioned above, there is no contradiction, since the Nirmāṇakāya and the Sambhogakāya are just two subdivisions of the Rūpakāya; the Dharmakāya is the same in both classificatory schemes.

17. Attachment, hatred, delusion, jealousy, and pride.

18. The meditations on the precious human life of leisure and endowment, on impermanence and death, on the sufferings

of the cycle of existence, and on the nature of actions and their ethical consequences.

19. The word perseverance is relatively weak in English. In Tibetan, the term refers to delight in Dharma and virtue. It's often translated as enthusiasm or enthusiastic perserverance, but it's really a joy and enthusiasm for Dharma practice.

20. "Good breeding" refers to having the great potential and opportunity for practicing Dharma.

21. These are the six states of cyclic existence.

22. Ontological knowledge consists of knowing things "as they really are" (*ji ltar*) and phenomenological knowledge consists of knowing things "as many as they are" (*ji snyed*).

23. "The Victor" (Sanskrit *jina*, Tibetan *rgyal ba*) is an epithet of the Buddha that signifies the Buddha's utter vanquishing of negative mental states, including ignorance.

24. The three realms are the desire, form, and formless realms.

25. The Sanskrit term *sugata* is an alternative word for a fully enlightened buddha.

26. The Sanskrit term *ārya* (Tib. *'phags pa*) refers those practitioners who have unmediated realization of ultimate truth.

27. According to the *Bod rgya tshig mdzod chen mo* (Tse tan zhab drung, Dung dkar blo bzang phrin las, and Dmu dge bsam gtan. Mi rigs dpe skrun khang, 1984), Vol III, p. 2783, the Tibetan term *lu gu rgyud* literally means a rope tying lambs together in a row. This would seem to be used here as a metaphor for a strand or series of interconnected components. This meaning reflects the etymology of the term, for *lu gu* is a variant spelling of *lug gu*, meaning "lamb." [Ibid., pp. 2781 & 2782]; and *rgyud* means *continuum*. To simplify things, I translate *lu gu rgyud* here simply as *strand*.

28. Samaya-preservers are a class of protectors or guardians who help perserve the samayas.

29. One source where the interested reader might begin is Dudjom Rinpoche's *The Nyingma School of Tibetan Buddhism: Its Fundamentals and History* (Boston: Wisdom Publications, 1991).

30. The four continua are the four streams of mental afflictions purified by means of the four empowerments.

31. Fundamental practice consists of hearing, thinking, and meditating on the Dharma.

32. A special physical posture or exercise known in Tibetan as *trül khor* (*'phrul 'khor*).

33. Literally an inflated placenta.

34. When visualizing the syllable in Sanskrit of Tibetan letters, the *visarga* is visualized as two dots, one above the other, to the right side of the syllable. When visualizing the sylable in English letters, the *visarga* is represented by the letter *h* with a dot under it (i.e., ḥ).

35. This is a synonym for buddha nature and tathāgatagarbha.

36. This "stainless, sole eye of primordial wisdom" is a phrase drawn from the text, *Uttering the Names of Manjushri.*

37. "Flat emptiness" is a nihilistic emptiness, a sheer nothingness.

38. The word "signs" refers to something close to our Western notion of conceptual construct. The Dharmakāya is not grounded in any conceptual framework or conceptual construct.

39. This statement implies that with primordial wisdom one perceives all aspects of reality equally.

40. The five bodies of signs are the five elements of earth, water, and so on.

41. "Superimposition" is the imputation upon reality of something that is not there, while denial is the refutation of the existence of something that is there.

42. This assertion is not to be confused with theistic notions of

an external creator, or lord, of the universe, for this awareness is of the nature of the whole of saṃsāra and nirvāṇa.

43. This is a problem of overexertion, practicing so forcefully that the very recognition of the dream-state bolts one out of sleep.

44. This refers to both the pure and impure illusory bodies.

45. That is, astrological calculations are irrelevant to this practice; it is to be followed at all times.

46. The imaginary nature is projected, and yet its own nature is primordial.

47. The aperature of becoming is the aperture for the male and female regenerative fluids.

48. In the practice as it is taught here, you say "HIG-KA" for the whole process of drawing up the bindu and letting it descend, but according to some other traditions, you say "HIG-HIG-HIG-HIG" as you draw it up; and then you say "KA" as you let it descend.

49. "Gathering in life" implies bringing your life to a close once the proximate signs of death are evident and you have determined that death cannot be averted.

50. The "special objects for accumulating merit," are the fields of merit such as your chosen deity and all objects of refuge and devotion.

51. The term *yakṣa* includes a variety of sentient beings, but here it probably refers to asuras, or titans, who may either help or hinder other sentient beings. Yakṣa is also a name for a type of being associated with wealth, and the corresponding Tibetan term also refers to a special type of animal.

52. This refers to Avalokiteśvara or any of object of faith of the dying person.

53. "Apertures" refers to the eyes.

54. *Citta* here means heart.

55. That is, generally speaking, if you reach this phase of practice, you will not experience the transitional process after death. Or even if you do experience this transitional process, you will recognize its nature and attain immediate awakening.

56. This refers to people who are well trained in the stages of generation and completion.

57. Comparable sentient beings are those having something in common with oneself in the transitional process.

58. These are the thirty-two signs and the eighty symbols which are sometimes called the major and minor marks of a buddha.

59. This refers to the ability to recognize Hīnayāna, Māhayāna, and Vajrayāna teachings.

60. In this context, wilderness is a place where you are totally alone, without friends, companions, or support.

61. The sphere of the uncontrived vast expanse refers to the nonexistence of an object of this prayer, of an agent of the prayer, and of the action of praying. It is not that these don't exist at all; rather they are all of the nature of awareness.

62. The lords of the three families are Vajrapāṇi, Avalokiteśvara and Mañjuśrī.

63. The Six Great Sages are six enlightened beings, each one appearing in one of the six states of cyclic existence. For example, Buddha Śākyamuni is the Great Sage of the realm of human beings, and there are others for the asuras, the devas, and so forth.

64. This term means unpredictable, in other words, it doesn't follow some predetermined order or pattern.

65. This palace is located in Amitābha's pure land of Sukhāvatī.

Glossary

abhidharma. Systematic Buddhist phenomenology and soteriology, including descriptions and analyses of the human body and mind, classes of sentient beings, the nature and formation of the universe, and the path to liberation.

adhisāra (Tib. *'phrul 'khor*). Physical postures and exercises used to enhance one's meditative practice.

Anuyoga. A Nyingma category of tantric practice, corresponding to the stage of completion. The Anuyoga practice follows Mahāyoga and precedes Atiyoga.

aperture of hell. The anus, so called because when consciousness leaves the human body at death by way of the anus, it indicates that one is about to be reborn in a hell realm.

ārya. An individual who has gained a nondual, conceptually unmediated realization of ultimate reality, or emptiness.

Atiyoga. A synonym of the Great Perfection (Tib. *rdzogs chen*), a system of theory and practice followed princially by the Nyingma order of Tibetan Buddhism, aimed at the liberating, direct ascertainment of the essential nature of awareness.

Avīci hell. According to the sūtra tradition, the most excruciating of the eighteen classes of hell realms.

bardo (Skt. *antarābhava*). The intermediate state that follows death and is prior to one's next rebirth. More broadly speaking, the term *bardo* can refer to any of the six transitional processes of living, dreaming, meditative stabilization, dying, reality-itself, and becoming.

bindu (Tib. *thig le*). The essential fluids, or "drops," that move through the central channel within the subtle human body; a small orb, usually visualized as being of the nature of light.

bodhicitta. The Spirit of Awakening, or the altuistic aspiration to attain perfect Spiritual Awakening for the benefit of all beings. In tantra, the red and white bodhicittas are the two types of bindus normally located in the central channel at the level of the navel and the crown, which converge at the heart during the dying process and in deep forms of meditation.

bodhisattva. An individual in whom the Spirit of Awakening effortlessly arises as his or her primary motivation, brought forth by great loving-kindness and compassion.

Brahmā aperture. The opening in the central channel at the crown of the head, so called because when consciousness leaves the human body at death by way of the crown of the head, it indicates that one is about to be reborn in a heavenly, or Brahmā, realm.

Breakthrough (Tib. *khregs chod*). The first of the two major phases in the practice of the Great Perfection, aimed at gaining direct, sustained realization of the essential nature of the mind.

buddha nature. The essential nature of the mind, which, according to the Great Perfection, is none other than the mind of the Buddha.

citta. This Sanskrit term normally refers to the mind, but in the higher teachings of the Great Perfection, it sometimes refers to the heart.

clear light. The essential nature of the mind, which is ineffable, yet metaphorically characterized as being of the nature of emptiness and luminosity.

ḍāka. A male counterpart of a *ḍākinī; ḍākas* often manifest as deities who protect and serve the Buddhist teachings and practitioners.

ḍākinī. Female spiritual beings who engage in enlightened activities for the benefit of the world.

ḍamaru. A small hand-drum used in tantric rituals.

deva. A celestial being or "god"; members of the highest of the six classes of sentient beings within the cycle of existence, who experience heightened awareness, bliss, and power, all of which vanish when they perish from that state of existence.

Dharmakāya. The mind of a Buddha, which is said to be unbounded in terms of the extent of its wisdom, compassion, and power.

element of vital energy. The energy, or "wind," that courses through the body; there are five major and five minor types of vital energy, each of which has a specific physiological function. The "life-sustaining energy" is particularly closely associated with the functioning of the mind.

four blisses (Tib. *dga' ba bzhi*). Bliss, supreme bliss, extraordinary bliss, and inborn bliss, which arise in the course of advanced tantric practice.

four empowerments. The vase, secret, wisdom-gnosis, and word empowerments, which authorize an individual to engage in advanced tantric practice.

four immeasurables. Immeasurable loving-kindness, compassion, empathetic joy, and equanimity, which provide the basis for the cultivation of the Spirit of Awakening.

Four Noble Truths. The truths of suffering, its source, its cessation, and the path to that cessation, which provide the structure of Buddhist theory and practice as a whole.

Four Thoughts that Turn the Mind. The contemplations of the value and rarity of a human life of leisure and endowment, death and impermanence, the unsatisfactory nature of the cycle of existence, and the law of karma as it pertains to actions and their moral consequences.

five buddha families. The families of Vajrasattva, Ratnasambhava, Amitābha, Amoghasiddhi, and Vairocana, corresponding to the five psychophysical aggregates of consciousness, recognition, feeling, mental formations, and form in their purified aspects.

fulfillment and confession (Tib. *bskang bshags*). A ritual practice in which one makes offerings to a deity (fulfillment), with the request for protection as one confesses one's ethical infractions (confession).

gaṇacakra offering. A tantric ritual offering.

gandharvas. Celestial fairies or music-makers.

garuḍa. A mythical bird, which is fully developed when hatched and capable of extraordinary powers.

Great Perfection (Tib. *rDzogs chen*). The highest teachings of the Nyingma order of Tibetan Buddhism, consisting of three classes of instruction known as the Mind Class, Expanse Class, and Practical Instruction Class.

guru yoga. Meditative practice in which one devotes oneself to the spiritual mentor as being of the same nature as all the buddhas.

hearing, thinking, and meditation. The three general phases of Buddhist practice, each of which successively gives rise to a deeper level of understanding and wisdom.

Hīnayāna. The "lesser," or "individual," vehicle of Buddhist theory and practice, principally aimed at one's own final liberation from the cycle of existence.

hollow crystal kati channel. The channel of primordial wisdom located in the hearts of all sentient beings.

identitylessness. The absence of an inherent self-nature, or substance. This is of two kinds, personal identitylessness and phenomenal identitylessness, which refer to the lack of a self-existent essence of persons and of other phenomena respectively.

Jñāyakāya. Also known as the Svabhāvakāya, which, according to a common Nyingma interpretation, refers to the indivisibility of the Nirmāṇkaya, Sambhogakāya, and Dharmakāya.

Kriya. The most basic of the three classes of outer tantras, according to the Nyingma classification, the other two being the Upaya and Yoga classes.

lama (Skt. *guru*). A spiritual mentor or any revered spiritual adept.

Leap-over phase (Tib. *thod rgal ba*). The second of the two phases in the practice of the Great Perfection, aimed at rapidly bringing forth the full, spontaneous presence of one's own buddha nature.

māra. A demon or demonic influence that creates obstacles to spiritual maturation. The actual nature of such "demons" is one's own mental afflictions, such as attachment, hatred, and bewilderment, though they may manifest outwardly as well.

Mahāyāna. The "great," or "universal" vehicle of Buddhist theory and practice, aimed at the attainment of perfect Spiritual Awakening for the sake of all sentient beings.

maṇḍala. 1) A symbolic, graphic representation of a chosen deity with its palatial abode and surrounding environment, imagined by meditators in order to sublimate their own sense of personal identity and their experience of their bodies, minds, and surroundings. 2) A symbolic, graphic representation of the world, together with all the bounties of a world monarch, offered to one's objects of refuge.

Mantradharas (Tib. *sngags 'chang*). Literally, "mantra preservers," who have become thoroughly adept in the practice of Buddhist tantra.

Mount Meru. The mythical mountain towering in the center of the idealized representation of our world, surrounded on four sides by four world-sectors, or continents.

mind-itself (Tib. *sems nyid*). Literally, "mindness," this is the essential nature of the mind, which is identical to one's buddha nature.

mind-stream (Tib. *rgyud*). The mental continuum of an individual, which emerges as an ongoing, ever-fluctuating stream throughout the course of one lifetime and from one life to the next.

mudrā. 1) Literally, a "seal," which is a symbolic position or movement, usually of the hands, practiced in meditation and in ritual practice. 2) A consort with whom one practices in advanced stages of tantric meditation.

nine yānas. The nine "vehicles" of spiritual practice, according to the Nyingma classification, including the Śrvakayna, Pratyekabuddhayāna, Bodhisattvayāna, Kriya, Upaya, Yoga, Mahāyoga, Anuyoga, and Atiyoga.

Nirmāṇakāya. The more accessible of the two Rūpakāyas, or "Form Embodiments," of a Buddha (the other being the Sambhogakāya), which manifests in all ways to lead sentient beings to liberation and spiritual awakening.

non-objective. Not arising as an object within the habitual, reified subject/object structuring of perceptual and conceptual awareness; having no inherent existence as an object.

Pāramitāyāna. Literally, the "Vehicle of the Perfections," referring to the Six Perfections of generosity, ethical discipline, patience, zeal, meditative stabilization, and wisdom, which form the structure of the bodhisattva way of life and path to Spiritual Awakening; identical to the Bodhisattvayāna.

parinirvāṇa. The ultimate liberation of a buddha, which is said to take place at death.

prāṇāyāma. A system of meditative techniques for controlling the breath as a means of modulating the vital energies within the body, which, in turn, influence the state of one's consciousness.

pratyekabuddha. A person who finally attains liberation from the cycle of existence alone, without directly relying upon a teacher.

preta. A spirit, being one of the six classes of sentient beings within the cycle of existence, characterized by intense, unsatiated hunger, thirst, and craving.

preta aperture. The aperture in the region of the genitals through which one's consciousness departs from the body at death if one is about to take rebirth as a preta.

ṛṣi. A highly accomplished adept in the practice of meditation.

rakta. The red essential fluid, received from one's mother, which is normally located at the level of the navel, but which rises to the heart when one dies and in deep stages of tantric meditation.

red and white bodhicitta. The two types of essential fluids, or "drops," normally located at the level of the navel and the crown of the head respectively, which converge at the heart during the dying process and in deep meditation.

Rūpakāya. The "form embodiments" of a buddha, including the Sambhogakāya and Nirmāṇakāya, which are the counterpart of the Dharmakāya.

samādhi. Meditative concentration entailing exceptional degrees of attentional stability and clarity.

samaya. Tantric pledges taken when receiving tantric

empowerment, which form the ethical basis for the practice of Vajrayāna.

Sambhogakāya. The subtler of the two types of Rūpakāya, or "form embodiments" of a Buddha, which appear only to higher advanced practitioners.

sangha. Broadly speaking, the community of Dharma practitioners, or more specifically, the community of ordained Buddhist monks and nuns, or the community of bodhisattvas.

siddha. A person who has accomplished one or more of the common or uncommon siddhis.

siddhi. A paranormal ability, of which there are some that are mundane, including the abilities to walk on water, fly through the sky, and so forth, and one that is supramundane, which is the siddhi of perfect Spiritual Awakening.

Six Perfections. The perfections of generosity, ethical discipline, patience, zeal, meditative stabilization, and wisdom, which provide the structure of the bodhisattva's path to Awakening.

Spirit of Awakening. In terms of relative truth, the aspiration to attain perfect Spiritual Awakening for the sake of all sentient beings; and in terms of ultimate truth, the realization of the ultimate nature of reality.

śrāvaka. Literally, a "listener," referring to the direct and indirect disciples of a Buddha who engage in Buddhist practice in order to achieve personal liberation from the cycle of existence.

stūpa. A reliquary containing sacred objects such as the remains of a highly realized being; such a reliquary is also regarded as a symbolic representation of the Buddha's mind.

tantra. The esoteric path of Buddhism entailing "taking the fruition as the path," meaning that one imaginatively enacts the bodily, verbal, and mental behavior of a Buddha as a means to attaining Spiritual Awakening; a treatise that presents the theory and practice of the Vajrayāna.

tathāgata. An epithet of the Buddha, literally meaning "the Thus-Gone One," who has realized ultimate truth.

terma. A treasure of spiritual instructions, of which there are two major types: earth treasures, which are concealed in the earth, and mind treasures, which are concealed in the minds of adepts and are discovered at the appropriate time and revealed to humanity.

thangka. A Tibetan painted scroll, ususually depicting one or more deities or maṇḍalas.

three embodiments. The Dharmakāya, Sambhogakāya, and Nirmāṇakāya.

three poisons. Attachment, hatred, and bewilderment, which are the three fundamental afflictions of the mind.

three yānas. Hīnayāna, Mahāyāna, and Vajrayāna.

three-cornered Dharma-source. A tetrahedron of light visualized at the level of the navel in certain tantric meditations.

torma. A ritual offering, often composed of parched barley meal in the shape of a cone, that is offered in tantric rituals.

tulku. An incarnation of a being who in the preceding life or lives has already gained a high degree of spiritual maturation.

Upaya. The middling class of outer tantras according to the Nyingma categorization.

vajra. A scepter used in tantric rituals, symbolizing skillful means, compassion, and immutable bliss.

Vajrayāna. The highest of the three yānas, or spiritual vehicles, which has come to dominate Tibetan Buddhism.

vajra brothers and sisters. Men and women together with whom one has received tantric empowerment, who therefore comprise one's tantric "family."

victor. An epithet of the Buddhas, indicating their victory over all kinds of mental afflictions and obscurations

Vidyādhara. Literally, a "holder of knowledge," referring to a highly accomplished tantric adept.

vinaya. Ethical discipline, especially of Buddhist monks and nuns.

yakṣa. A class of demigods, or demons, thought to commonly haunt mountain passes and to occasionally inflict harm on people living in their area if they are not appeased.

yāna. A spiritual vehicle in Buddhism, which "carries" one to the farther shore of liberation and Spiritual Awakening.

Bibliography

Note: Works are cited by English titles rather than by author. All works mentioned in *The Profound Dharma of The Natural Liberation* as well as those mentioned by Gyatrul Rinpoche in his commentary are listed. Each entry contains the English title, followed by the Tibetan, and finally the Sanskrit when applicable and known. Authors other than Śākyamuni Buddha or Padmasambhava are also given. Only complete translations in English are noted.

The Account of the Monk's Three Conflagrations
dGe slong 'bar ba gsum gyi gtam rgyud

All-Accomplishing Sovereign
Chos tham cad rdzogs pa chen po byang chub kyi sems kun byed rgyal po

Ancient Wisdom: Nyingma Teachings of Dream Yoga, Meditation and Transformation
by Gyatrul Rinpoche
trans. by B. Alan Wallace and Sangye Khandro
Ithaca: Snow Lion Publications, 1993.

The Blazing Lamp
sGron ma 'bar ba

Crown Jewels Sūtra
mDo rin chen rtog

Descent into Laṅkā Sūtra
mDo lang kar gshegs pa

Laṅkāvatārasūtra
trans. by D.T. Suzuki
London: Routledge, Kegen and Paul, 1932.

The Fifty Verses of Guru Devotion
Bla ma lnga bcu pa
by Aśvaghoṣa
trans. by Geshe Ngawang Dhargyey, et. al.
Dharamsala: Library of Tibetan Works and Archives, 1975.

Great Bliss Instructions on the Lower Orifice
'Og sgo bde chen po'i kid

A Guide to the Bodhisattva Way of Life
Byang chub sems dpa'i spyod pa la 'jug pa
Bodhisattvacaryāvatāra
by Śāntideva
trans. by Vesna A. Wallace and B. Alan Wallace
Ithaca: Snow Lion Publications, 1997.

The Jewel-Studded Gem
Nor bu phra bkod

The King of Samādhi Sūtra
Ting nge 'dzin rgyal po'i mdo
Samādhirājasūtra

Liberation Through Hearing in the Transitional Process
Bar do'i thos grol
trans. as *The Tibetan Book of the Dead*
trans. Robert A. F. Thurman
New York: Bantam Books, 1994.

Liberation Through a Narrow Passage
'Phrang grol

The Lion's Perfect Strength
Seng ge rtsal rdzogs

The Mound of Jewels
Rin chen spungs pa

Natural Liberation of Fear: Cheating Death
'Chi bslu 'jigs pa rang grol

Natural Liberation of Signs: Signs of Death
'Chi ltas mtshan ma rang grol

Natural Liberation through Contemplating the Peaceful and Wrathful
Zhi khro gongs pa rang grol

Nirvāṇa Traces
'Das rje

No Letters
Yi ge med pa

Pearl Rosary
Mu tig phreng ba

Perfection of Wisdom
Phar phyin
Prajñāpāramitā
A combination of the 18,000 line, the 25,000 line, and the 100,000 line sūtra was made by E. Conze and published as *The Large Sūtra on Perfect Wisdom*.
Berkeley: University of California Press, 1975.

Prayer Calling for Help
Ram mda' sbran pa'i smon lam

Primary Tantra on the Penetration of Sound
sGra thal 'gyur chen po rtsa ba'i rgyud

Primary Words of the Transitional Process
Bar do rtsa tshig

Self-arisen, Unborn, Natural Clarity
Rang byung skye med rang gsal

Self-Arising Awareness
Rig pa rang shar

The Set of Aphorisms
Ched du brjod pa'i tshom
Udānavarga
trans. as *The Tibetan Dhammapada: Sayings of the Buddha*
by Gareth Sparham
London: Wisdom Publications, 1986.

The Seven Treasures of Longchen Rabjampa
mDzod bdun
by Klong chen rab 'byams pa

Sūtra of Basket Weaving
Za ma tog bkod pa'i mdo
Karaṇḍavyūhasūtra

Sūtra Synthesizing the Contemplations of the Buddha
Sangs rgyas dgongs pa 'dus pai mdo

Tantra Equal to Space, Which Synthesizes the Definitive Meaning of the Great Perfection
rDzogs pa chen po nges don du 'dus pa nam mkha dang mnyam pa'i rgyud

Tantra of the Lamp of Primordial Wisdom
Ye she mar me'i rgyud

Tantra of the Sun of the Clear Expanse of the Great Perfection
rDzogs pa chen po klong gsal nyi ma'i rgyud

Tantra of the Three Phrases of Liberation by Observation
blTas pas grol ba tshig gsum pa'i rgyud

Tantra of the Union of the Sun and Moon
Nyi zla kha sbyor gyi rgyud

Transforming Compassion into the Path
sNying rje lam khyer

Transforming Felicity and Adversity into the Spiritual Path
bDe sdug lam khyer
by 'Jigs med bstan pa'i nyi ma
trans. by B. Alan Wallace in *Ancient Wisdom: Nyingma Teachings of Dream Yoga, Meditation and Transformation*

Uttering the Names of Mañjuśrī
'Jam dpal mtshan brjod
Manjuśrīnāmasaṃgīti

The Vajra Array Compendium Sūtra of Knowledge
rDo rje bkod pa kun 'dus rig pa'i mdo

Words of My Perfect Teacher
Kun bzang bla ma'i zhal lung
by Ögyen Jigme Chökyi Wangpo (Patrul Rinpoche)
trans. by the Padmakara Translation Group
San Francisco, CA: HarperCollins Publishers, 1994.

Index

About the Contributors

THE VENERABLE GYATRUL RINPOCHE, also referred to as Payul Gyatrul, was born in Tibet in 1925. He was recognized by Jamyang Khyentse Lodrö Thaye to be the incarnation of Tsampa Kunkyap, a Payul lineage meditator who spent his life in retreat. The young Gyatrul was educated by his tutor Sangye Gön at the Payul Dhomang Monastery.

Gyatrul Rinpoche has been teaching in North America since 1972 and has founded several Dharma centers in the US, principally Tashi Choeling near Ashland, Oregon.

B. ALAN WALLACE, who trained for ten years in Indian and Swiss monasteries, has taught Buddhist theory and practice in Europe and America since 1976. He has served as interpreter for numerous Tibetan scholars including H.H. the Dalai Lama. After earning a doctorate in religious studies at Stanford University, he has gone on to edit, translate, and write twenty books on Tibetan Buddhism, medicine, language, and culture. He is presently a professor in the Department of Religion, University of California, Santa Barbara.

Dr. Wallace is the author of *The Bridge of Quiescence: Experiencing Buddhist Meditation*, *Choosing Reality: A Buddhist View of Physics and the Mind*, and *Tibetan Buddhism From the Ground Up*.

Wisdom Publications

Wisdom Publications, a not-for-profit publisher, is dedicated to making available authentic Buddhist works for the benefit of all. We publish translations of the sutras and tantras, commentaries and teachings of past and contemporary Buddhist masters, and original works by the world's leading Buddhist scholars. We publish our titles with the appreciation of Buddhism as a living philosophy and with the special commitment to preserve and transmit important works from all the major Buddhist traditions.

If you would like more information or a copy of our mail-order catalogue, please contact us at:

Wisdom Publications
199 Elm Street
Somerville, Massachusetts 02144-3195 USA
Telephone: (617) 776-7416
Fax: (617) 776-7841
E-mail: info@wisdompubs.org
Web Site: http://www.wisdompubs.org

THE WISDOM TRUST

As a not-for-profit publisher, Wisdom Publications is dedicated to the publication of fine Dharma books for the benefit of all sentient beings and dependent upon the kindness and generosity of sponsors in order to do so. If you would like to make a donation to Wisdom, please contact our Somerville office.

Thank you.

Wisdom Publications is a non-profit, charitable 501(c)(3) organization and a part of the Foundation for the Preservation of the Mahayana Tradition (FPMT).